Bloom's Modern Critical Views

African-American
  Poets: Volume 1
African-American
  Poets: Volume 2
Aldous Huxley
Alfred, Lord
  Tennyson
Alice Munro
Alice Walker
American Women
  Poets: 1650–1950
Amy Tan
Anton Chekhov
Arthur Miller
Asian-American
  Writers
August Wilson
The Bible
The Brontës
Carson McCullers
Charles Dickens
Christopher Marlowe
Contemporary Poets
Cormac McCarthy
C.S. Lewis
Dante Aligheri
David Mamet
Derek Walcott
Don DeLillo
Doris Lessing
Edgar Allan Poe
Émile Zola
Emily Dickinson
Ernest Hemingway
Eudora Welty
Eugene O'Neill
F. Scott Fitzgerald
Flannery O'Connor
Franz Kafka
Gabriel García
  Márquez
Geoffrey Chaucer
George Orwell

G.K. Chesterton
Gwendolyn Brooks
Hans Christian
  Andersen
Henry David Thoreau
Herman Melville
Hermann Hesse
H.G. Wells
Hispanic-American
  Writers
Homer
Honoré de Balzac
Jamaica Kincaid
James Joyce
Jane Austen
Jay Wright
J.D. Salinger
Jean-Paul Sartre
John Donne and the
  Metaphysical Poets
John Irving
John Keats
John Milton
John Steinbeck
José Saramago
Joseph Conrad
J.R.R. Tolkien
Julio Cortázar
Kate Chopin
Kurt Vonnegut
Langston Hughes
Leo Tolstoy
Marcel Proust
Margaret Atwood
Mark Twain
Mary Wollstonecraft
  Shelley
Maya Angelou
Miguel de Cervantes
Milan Kundera
Nathaniel Hawthorne
Native American
  Writers

Norman Mailer
Octavio Paz
Paul Auster
Philip Roth
Ralph Ellison
Ralph Waldo
  Emerson
Ray Bradbury
Richard Wright
Robert Browning
Robert Frost
Robert Hayden
Robert Louis
  Stevenson
The Romantic Poets
Salman Rushdie
Samuel Taylor
  Coleridge
Stephen Crane
Stephen King
Sylvia Plath
Tennessee Williams
Thomas Hardy
Thomas Pynchon
Tom Wolfe
Toni Morrison
Tony Kushner
Truman Capote
Walt Whitman
W.E.B. Du Bois
William Blake
William Faulkner
William Gaddis
William Shakespeare:
  Comedies
William Shakespeare:
  Histories
William Shakespeare:
  Romances
William Shakespeare:
  Tragedies
William Wordsworth
Zora Neale Hurston

Bloom's Modern Critical Views

RAY BRADBURY
New Edition

Edited and with an introduction by
Harold Bloom
Sterling Professor of the Humanities
Yale University

BLOOM'S
LITERARY CRITICISM
An imprint of Infobase Publishing

Bloom's Modern Critical Views: Ray Bradbury—New Edition

Copyright © 2010 by Infobase Publishing
Introduction © 2010 by Harold Bloom

Bloom's Literary Criticism
An imprint of Infobase Publishing
132 West 31st Street
New York NY 10001

Library of Congress Cataloging-in-Publication Data
Ray Bradbury / edited and with an introduction by Harold Bloom. — New ed.
    p. cm. — (Bloom's modern critical views)
    Includes bibliographical references and index.
    ISBN 978-1-60413-805-4 (hardcover)
    1. Bradbury, Ray, 1920– —Criticism and interpretation. 2. Science fiction, American—History and criticism. I. Bloom, Harold. II. Title. III. Series.
    PS3503.R167Z853 2010
    813'.54—dc22

                                        2009030891

Bloom's Literary Criticism books are available at special discounts when purchased in bulk quantities for businesses, associations, institutions, or sales promotions. Please call our Special Sales Department in New York at (212) 967-8800 or (800) 322-8755.

You can find Bloom's Literary Criticism on the World Wide Web at
http://www.chelseahouse.com.

Contributing editor: Pamela Loos
Cover design by Alicia Post
Composition by IBT Global, Troy NY
Cover printed by IBT Global, Troy NY
Book printed and bound by IBT Global, Troy NY
Date printed: January 2010
Printed in the United States of America

10 9 8 7 6 5 4 3 2 1

This book is printed on acid-free paper.

All links and Web addresses were checked and verified to be correct at the time of publication. Because of the dynamic nature of the Web, some addresses and links may have changed since publication and may no longer be valid.

Contents

Editor's Note

My brief introduction respects Bradbury as a benign moral fabulist while sadly noting how slender are his characterizations.

Wayne L. Johnson surveys Bradbury's short stories, while Lahna Diskin regards his portrayals of children as a race apart from his adults.

The Martin Chronicles are interpreted by Robert Plank as case histories of their characters, after which George R. Guffey also broods on unconscious mental processes in the same work.

William F. Touponce invokes Gaston Bachelard's *The Poetics of Reverie* to study Bradbury, while Ben P. Indick considers drama to be the relevant literary context.

The survival of books in a world after catastrophe is contrasted by Susan Spencer in regard to *Fahrenheit 451* and Walter Miller's *A Canticle for Leibowitz*.

Diverse sources for *The Martian Chronicles* are gathered together by Jonathan Eller, after which Jacqueline Foertsch finds common features in some apocalyptic narratives of Paul Auster, Margaret Atwood, Bradbury, and George Orwell.

To conclude the volume, elements of time and space in *The Martian Chronicles* are detailed by Walter J. Mucher.

HAROLD BLOOM

Introduction

Science fiction, despite its vast, worldwide audience still exists on the borderlands of imaginative literature. I am being sadly accurate and hardly haughty. William F. Touponce, in his essay on Ray Bradbury's "The Golden Apples of the Sun," cites the eminent critic Geoffrey H. Hartman as sharing in the French appreciation for Bradbury's achievement. One remembers that the French have exalted Jerry Lewis and Mickey Rourke as masters of cinema. Perhaps Hartman read Bradbury in French translation, since Bradbury, like Poe, improves in translation.

Bradbury, indeed, is one of the masters of science fiction and fantasy, and he is highly inventive and humane. His palpable failure is in his style: His language is thin, and his characters are names on the page. *Fahrenheit 451* and *The Martian Chronicles* lack the literary distinction of Ursula Le Guin's *The Left Hand of Darkness,* David Lindsay's *A Voyage to Arcturus,* and John Crowley's *Little, Big,* and *Aegypt* series. But I enjoy reading Bradbury, once each, and have no case to urge against him. He writes popular fiction, like John Grisham and Michael Crichton, though his mode differs from theirs. At a time when all literary and aesthetic standards are collapsing, one urges a little perspective on readers. Bradbury is an admirable entertainer and deserves appreciation precisely as such.

Like many other readers, I judge Bradbury's best story to be "The Golden Apples of the Sun," a simplistic but winning allegory of Promethean quest. The rocket ship *Capa de Oro* (Cup of Gold) heads straight for the sun, in order to scoop up a chunk of that divine heat. Its captain is only barely characterized, but clearly he is the most benign of Prometheans. He is no

1

Ahab, and the sun is not Moby Dick. Ahab cried out that he would strike the sun if it insulted him, but Bradbury's captain regards the sun as an energy field not as an antagonist. This amiable thief of fire wishes only to bring home something that will burn endlessly, to human benefit.

To call "The Golden Apples of the Sun" a short story is to endanger it. You cannot read it side by side with Chekhov, Flannery O'Connor, Hemingway, or Borges. It is a parable, and probably Bradbury is best thought of as a fabulist, a teller of moral tales. His morals tend to extrude, but doubtless he has done his audience much good, here and abroad. Like many other science fantasists, he is a belated apostle of the Enlightenment.

WAYNE L. JOHNSON

Medicines for Melancholy

Magic is a pervasive theme in Bradbury's work. This might have been foreordained the day in 1931 when, during a performance in Waukegan, the great magician Blackstone presented eleven-year-old Bradbury with a live rabbit. In any case, that incident reflects the type of magic usually found in Bradbury's work, that is: theatrical magic, legerdemain, as opposed to anything genuinely supernatural. For Bradbury, the magical power certain people and things seem to have lies in their capacity to stimulate, expand, or sustain the imagination. They accomplish this by altering our perception and challenging our view of reality, so that we are led to view things in a fresh, new way. This process is more interesting, Bradbury seems to say, than anything truly miraculous. Should a sorcerer literally create a rabbit out of thin air, little would be accomplished outside of our being intimidated by his power. But when the theatrical magician pulls his rabbit out of a hat, we know it is a trick, and because we know it is a trick we are amused, intrigued, and our curiosity is aroused.

Bradbury is, of course, a self-styled story-telling magician, and though within a particular story his brand of magic may be thwarted, misused, or may backfire, still the story itself will like as not lead us to, and sharpen our awareness of, that point where reality and imagination meet, where imagination may restructure reality and create a new order.

From *Ray Bradbury*, pp. 13–32, 152–54, 161–66. © 1980 by Frederick Ungar.

3

Magic People

Lacking supernatural powers, Bradbury's magicians use in-born talents and acquired skills to perform their wonders. The old man in "To the Chicago Abyss" is blessed—or in his case, perhaps, cursed—with a vivid memory and an eloquent tongue. He wanders about in a world devastated by atomic war, recalling for whoever will listen what it was like before the holocaust. The man cannot stop himself, even though he is constantly being hunted by the special police who regard him as a source of unrest. The old man's magic is his ability to recall the details of the past so vividly that his listeners are transported there. For some, the experience is too painful, and hence, terrifying, as when the old man takes a woman by surprise:

> "Coffee."
> The woman gasped and stiffened.
> The old man's gnarled fingers tumbled in pantomime on his unseen lap.
> "Twist the key! Bright-red, yellow-letter can! Compressed air. Hisss! Vacuum pack, Ssst! Like a snake! . . . The scent, the odor, the smell. Rich, dark, wondrous Brazilian beans, fresh-ground!"
> Leaping up, reeling as if gun-shot, the woman tottered.

Though his behavior is a bit bizarre, the man is still a professional. He recognizes his talent and employs it in what he regards as a socially useful way:

> What did I have to offer a world that was forgetting? My memory! . . . I found the more I remembered, the more I *could* remember! Depending on who I sat down with, I remembered imitation flowers, dial telephones, refrigerators, kazoos (you ever play a kazoo?), thimbles, bicycle clips, not bicycles, no, bicycle *clips*! isn't that wild and strange?

This old man is the quintessential Bradbury magician. He embodies characteristics of people and objects found throughout Bradbury's work in this ability to conjure up the past, to evoke nostalgia through the *experience* of another time.

If the old man's talent is a bit dangerous in view of the society in which he finds himself, a similar talent is fatal to Leonard Mark in "The Visitor." Leonard arrives on Mars and is greeted by a number of homesick exiles from Earth. One of them, Saul, asks Leonard what New York is like now.

"Like this," said Leonard Mark. And he looked at Saul.

New York grew up out of the desert, made of stone and filled with March winds. Neons exploded in electric color. Yellow taxis glided in a still night. Bridges rose and tugs chanted in the midnight harbor. Curtains rose on spangled musicals.

Saul put his hands to his head, violently.

"Hold on, hold on!" he cried. "what's happening to me?"

Though Mark is telepathic, and able to impress his vision directly upon another's mind, his effect is similar to that produced by the old man. But where the old man's talent was appreciated by only a few of his fellows, Mark's ability puts him very much in demand. In a short time, greed and exploitation take their toll—the exiles begin to fight over exclusive rights to Mark, and in the struggle, he is killed.

There is a modest echo of this exploitation of another person's talent in "The Great Wide World Over There." The story explores the relativity of power by showing how a perfectly modest talent may seem great, even magical, to someone with no power at all. Cora and Tom live in isolation in the mountains and are illiterate. When they are visited by their nephew Benjy, who can read and write, it is as though a guest from another world has arrived.

A simple object like Benjy's pencil is almost a magic wand to Cora's eyes: "She wanted to touch the pencil, but hadn't touched one in years because it made her feel foolish and then angry and then sad." Benjy writes letters all over the world for Cora, mostly to companies, asking for free booklets. Though she cannot read any of these, Cora feels in touch with the world beyond the horizon as the junk mail pours in. But she is dependent on Benjy to sustain this miracle, and the door to it closes forever when Benjy leaves.

"The Man in the Rorschach Shirt" is a more active magician. Once a world-renowned psychiatrist, Immanuel Brokaw has taken his practice underground. Wearing a shirt with crazy patterns on it, he strolls about the beaches of California, and when he meets someone who is troubled, he attempts to cure them in his own unusual way.

> I walk along in my own time and way and come on people and let the wind flap my great sailcloth shirt now veering north, south, or south-by-west and watch their eyes pop, glide, leer, squint, wonder. And when a certain person says a certain word about my ink-slashed cotton colors I give pause. I chat. I walk with them awhile. We peer into the great glass of the sea. I sidewise peer

into their soul. Sometimes we stroll for hours, a longish session with the weather. Usually it takes but that one day and, not knowing with whom they walked, scot-free, they are discharged all unwitting patients.

Bradbury suggests that the storyteller, the psychic, the literate relative, the psychiatrist can all seem like magicians, given the right contexts. They alter our reality and we don't know how they do it. The musician can also have this power, and Bradbury explores this idea twice in "Getting Through Sunday Somehow" and "The Day It Rained Forever." Interestingly enough, both musicians are women, and both are harpists. The first story concerns a man wandering the streets of Dublin in a depressed mood. Suddenly he hears a tune being played by an old woman with a harp, and "as if a cork had been pulled, all the heavy gray sea waters vanished down a hole in my shoe; I felt my sadness go." When the man tries to tell the old woman of the effect she has had on him, he sounds as if he is recovering from a magic spell:

Imagine you're an American writer, looking for material, far from home, wife, children, friends, in a hard winter, in a cheerless hotel, on a bad gray day with naught but broken glass, chewed tobacco, and sooty snow in your soul. Imagine you're walking in the damned winter streets and turn a corner, and there's this little woman with a golden harp and everything she plays is another season, autumn, spring, summer, coming, going in a free-for-all. And the ice melts, the fog lifts, the wind burns with June, and ten years shuck off your life.

A different change of climate is called for in "The Day It Rained Forever," which takes place in a seedy hotel that "stood like a hollowed dry bone under the very center of the desert sky where the sun burned the roof all day." What the sweltering clients need is a miracle, and a miracle worker arrives in the form of Miss Hillgood. Like the old lady in Dublin, Miss Hillgood uses her music to produce a much-appreciated change of climate:

Each time her fingers moved, the rain fell pattering through the dark hotel. The rain fell cool at the open windows and the rain rinsed down the baked floor boards of the porch. . . . But more than anything the soft touch and coolness of it fell on Mr. Smith and Mr. Terle. . . . Seated there, they felt their heads tilt slowly back to let the rain fall where it would.

So it is that Bradbury's artist-magicians operate on three levels: changing the apparent climate, the emotional state of their audience, and ultimately the feelings of the reader.

"The Drummer Boy of Shiloh," also a musician of sorts, is not aware of the power his skill holds until his General tells him that his drumming is the heartbeat of the army. The tempo the drummer sets during battle may spell the difference between victory and defeat, because, the General says, "blood moving fast in them does indeed make men feel as they'd put on steel."

Bradbury sees the technician too as a kind of magician, insofar as he changes the way in which reality is viewed. In "Tyrannosaurus Rex" we meet a Hollywood special effects expert. John Terwilliger is a specialist in three-dimensional animation. He is apparently patterned after Willis O'Brien, creator of King Kong, or Ray Harryhausen, Bradbury's friend and creator of the monster in "The Beast from 20,000 Fathoms." Terwilliger performs his magic in his studio, photographing miniature jungles and foot-high dinosaurs so that they appear to be full size on the movie screen. "Rubber, steel, clay, reptilian latex sheath, glass eye, porcelain fang, all ambles, trundles, strides in terrible prides through continents as yet unmanned, by seas as yet unsalted, a billion years lost away. They *do* breathe. They *do* smite the air with thunders. Oh, uncanny!"

Bradbury's magician does not always seek to affect the world at large. Sometimes his skills may be used to promote his own domestic tranquillity, as in the case of Fiorello Bodoni. Bodoni, a poor junk dealer, cannot afford to send his family on an actual rocket trip, so he buys a scrap, mock-up rocket and rigs it electronically for a facsimile trip around Mars. Bodoni's wife knows, but the children do not, that "The Rocket" is not real, still the joyful artifice of it appeals to her: "Perhaps . . . perhaps, some night, you might take me on just a little trip, do you think?"

In "The Best of All Possible Worlds" it is the husband who profits from his wife's skills. Mr. "Smith's" wife is an accomplished actress, who keeps her husband from seeking other women by frequently altering her appearance and becoming any sort of woman he might desire. Both Mr. Smith and Mrs. Bodoni enjoy their partners' artifices, and become for them an audience—something that is essential to the magician and the fiction writer as well. An audience prepared to employ what Coleridge calls "that willing suspension of disbelief for the moment, which constitutes poetic faith." Viewed this way, magic can be regarded as a kind of conspiracy wherein artist and audience agree to experience the joy of magic by playing their respective parts. This can backfire occasionally, as Bradbury suggests in "Invisible Boy." Old Lady, living a lonely life in the Ozark Mountains, tries to trick her visiting relative Charlie into prolonging his stay with her by promising to teach him how to make himself invisible. The trick is accomplished simply by Old Lady pretending she can't see Charlie any more. This soon becomes quite a strain as Charlie takes advantage of his invisibility to dash about stark naked. Old Lady must then trick Charlie into becoming "visible" again.

The theme of a boy trying to exercise his personal magic power takes on poignant overtones in "The Miracles of Jamie." Here we find magician and audience combined in one person as Jamie tries to convince himself that he has magical power and that through it he can make his dying mother well. But, though it is not always clear, there is a dividing line between a "willing suspension of disbelief" and simple self-deception. Jamie crosses that line with tragic consequences.

> Inside the walls of Jericho that was Jamie's mind, a thought went screaming about in one last drive of power: Yes, she's dead, all right, so she is dead, so what if she is dead? Bring her back to life again, yes, make her live again, Lazarus, come forth, Lazarus, Lazarus, come forth from the tomb, Lazarus come forth.
>
> He must have been babbling aloud, for Dad turned and glared at him in old, ancient horror and struck him bluntly across the mouth to shut him up.
>
> Jamie sank against the bed, mouthing into the cold blankets, and the walls of Jericho crumbled and fell down about him.

Magic Things

Human beings are not the only sources of magic for Bradbury. Animals and physical objects may also affect our reality in mysterious ways. Certainly Martin's dog in "The Emissary" has a certain magical effect, aside from the dreadful supernatural powers it seems to exercise at the end of the story. The dog does not change reality for Martin, but rather deepens and broadens it. The boy cannot venture into the world outside his bedroom but the dog can, and brings back touches of it that enrich the invalid's life.

The bird in "The Parrot Who Met Papa" is another magical animal with a fabulous memory that the characters in the story suspect might include Hemingway's last, unwritten novel. Another magic fowl is the namesake of "The Inspired Chicken Motel," a bird whose eggs seem to have the gift of prophesy. Inanimate things can be magical too. This is not a surprising suggestion from a writer such as Bradbury, for whom nostalgia is so important. The ability of an object to recall the past from which it came, and so to generate a whole complex of emotional responses, can certainly transcend whatever practical function the object might have had. Other objects may possess qualities that allow them to transform the present, and in so doing, alter the shape of the future. Of course, such power often does not lie within the object itself, but rather within the mind of the beholder. In this case, the magical effect an object has may depend upon the state of the mind perceiving it.

We find an unhealthy mind in "And So Died Riabouchinska," a classic story of a schizophrenic ventriloquist who loses control over what his dummy says. Fabian's dummy, Riabouchinska, was modeled after a woman Fabian once loved. Since the dummy represents the better half of Fabian's mind, Fabian can no longer control it after he has committed murder.

Many minds contemplate the contents of "The Jar" which Charlie buys at a carnival and brings home to show off to his neighbors. Everyone is curious about what the jar holds, and Gramps finds himself lying awake nights to "think about that jar settin' here in the long dark. Think about it hangin' in liquid, peaceful and pale like an animal oyster. Sometimes I wake Maw and we both think on it . . ." Juke, recalling how he once drowned a kitten, sees his own guilt in the jar: "I know to this day the way that kitten floated after it was all over, driftin' aroun', slow and not worryin', lookin' out at me, not condemnin' me for what I done. But not likin' me, neither. Ahhhh. . . ." Jahdoo has a more mystical explanation: "That be the center of Life, sure 'nuff! . . . That am Middibamboo Mama, from which we all come ten thousand years ago. Believe it!" And Mrs. Tridden, whose child was lost in the swamp years ago, sees through eyes burdened with loss: "My baby . . . my baby. My Foley, Foley! Foley, is that you?"

In "The Jar," Bradbury suggests that magic can be a function of need. Given an ambiguous situation or object, an imaginative viewer may fantasize a new reality based on his personal need to enrich, repair, complete or transcend his life. This theme is explored again in "A Miracle of Rare Device." Two drifters travelling through the Arizona desert stumble across a spot on the roadside from which an unusual mirage may be seen. As the two men watch, a wonderful city seems to rise up against the distant mountains. The two men set up a sign and charge twenty-five cents for passing motorists to stop and see the view. Soon they discover that everyone who stops sees a different city in the mirage. One man sees Paris, another Rome, still another sees fabled Xanadu with its "sunny pleasure-dome with caves of ice!" The spot is magic because it nurtures imagination. It is interesting that the villain of the piece, Ned Hopper, sees no mirage at all. And when Hopper files a claim on the roadside spot, evicts his rivals, and takes over their business, the magic in the spot vanishes. None of the people who stop when Hopper is present see anything at all. The drifter Robert understands: "Right now I'm feeling sorry for Ned Hopper. . . . He never saw what we saw. He never saw what anybody saw. He never believed for one second. And you know what? Disbelief is catching. It rubs off on people."

As important to Bradbury as magic which manifests itself in a public way, is magic which operates on a more intimate level affecting one or more individuals. It is not surprising, given Bradbury's passion for nostalgia, that most of these items of intimate magic are connected in some way with the past. There is the wonderful brass bed in "The Marriage Mender." The bed has been in Antonio's family since "before Garibaldi!" It is one of the few valuable possessions belonging to the Italian immigrant and his wife, Maria. But so far it has failed to cooperate with Antonio and Maria's attempts to conceive a child. Fortunately, the bed is imbued with enough trappings of Bradbury magic—a "shimmering harp," a "fabulous dream machine"—to fulfill its function before Antonio is foolish enough to replace it.

Then there is "The Pumpernickel," a common loaf of bread that sets Mr. Welles off on a lengthy reminiscence about his old gang. Mr. Welles eventually learns to let the past go, but this is not so easy for some lonely settlers on Mars in "The Strawberry Window."

Bob and Carrie live in a tin shack in a frontier town on Mars. Both are terribly homesick. Carrie wants to return home, but Bob wants to stick it out anyway. In a desperate move, Bob spends all of the family's savings on artifacts from their old home on earth—a piano, a bed, some parlor furniture, and the entire front porch. Most important in terms of its magical effect, and its symbolic relation to all the other objects, is the front door with its stained glass window. The window alters the color of things viewed beyond it. It changes perception in a comforting way because of the associations it conjures up. When viewed through the panels of colored glass, the alien planet seems more like home:

> There was Mars, with its cold sky warmed and its dead seas fired with color, with its hills like mounds of strawberry ice, and its sand like burning charcoals sifted by the wind. The strawberry window, the strawberry window, breathed soft rose colors on the land and filled the mind and the eye with the light of a never-ending dawn.

This putting on, in effect, of rose-colored glasses is not the escape from reality the gesture ordinarily implies. For Bradbury, this deliberate alteration of perception forms a bridge between old reality and new. In looking through the glass, Bob and Carrie are reminded of the underlying similarities between their old home and their new one, and hence of the continuity of their lives. This artifact from the past gives them the strength to face the future. Bradbury seems most happy with illusions of this sort, which bring about recognition rather than mystification.

Of course, an object suffused with the magic of nostalgia can be a springboard to escape, and Bradbury treats this idea handsomely in "A Scent of Sarsaparilla." The object in question is a whole room, appropriately an attic. Mr. Finch retires to his attic to escape the cold of winter and his nagging wife, Cora. The attic is the ideal room for Bradbury, jammed as it is with nostalgia-laden objects from the past. If a single one such as the strawberry window can have a wonderful effect, then the potential of a whole roomful of such objects can be awesome. In this case, the cumulative power of the furnishings of Mr. Finch's attic is so great that it accomplishes a real feat of magic and literally transports Finch back in time. It may seem to be cheating a bit, in the context of these other stories, for Bradbury to introduce genuine magic in this way. But the story profits from the irony of the attic being a real time machine, and in any case, Finch's surrender to the emotional spell of the attic is complete even before he steps out of the window into the past.

Perhaps Bradbury's most famous and beautifully drawn magical device is "The Wonderful Ice Cream Suit." In this tale, science fiction and fantastic elements are combined in an essentially straight story, replete with humor and sharp characterization. The centerpiece of the story is, of course, the suit itself. For the six Mexican Americans who individually lack sufficient money to buy it, the white suit represents a technology almost beyond their com-prehension. Each is convinced that if he could possess the suit his entire life would be changed for the better. The connection with science fiction is subtle, yet here is a manufactured object which can change the shape of the future. But the suit is possessed of magical qualities, too, for it can fulfill wishes. The only problem is: how to possess it? It is Gomez who hits upon the idea of rounding up six men of about the same size, each with ten dollars in his pocket: "Are we not fine? . . . All the same size, all the same dream—the suit. So each of us will look beautiful at least one night each week, eh?"

The suit is a vehicle too for Bradbury's pet themes of metamorphosis and point-of-view altering reality. The suit changes each man who wears it, allowing him to fulfill his personal dreams of power, sexual attractiveness, or economic well being. At the same time, each man acknowledges the appeal the suit has for the others, and in so doing, invests the suit with a kind of objective power. It may be said that the suit wears the man just as much as the man wears the suit. The ice cream suit is probably Bradbury's most well-rounded magical device. It is more than just the vehicle for an individual's escape into fantasy or nostalgia. It forms a bond of understanding and affec-tion among the men, allowing them, however briefly, to transcend their indi-vidual poverty and loneliness. At the same time, the men realize that their humble circumstances are just the setting the suit requires to perform its magic. As Martinez notes, "If we ever get rich . . . it'll be kind of sad. Then we'll all have suits. And there won't be no more nights like tonight. It'll break up the old gang. It'll never be the same after that."

Horror

The horror story is not just a story in which something frightening happens. In the tradition of such masters as Poe and Lovecraft before him, Bradbury's horror stories touch upon some of the deepest human fears and superstitions.

The emotional and visceral effect that a well written horror story has on the reader is usually produced by a rigorous, almost mathematical structure. There is an underlying formula that the reader follows, at least subconsciously. This may be a simple face-the-consequence formula, in which the main character makes a pact with the devil or performs a similar rash act. Or a situation may be set up which, if repeated with certain variations, could precipitate dire results. For example, a child is characterized with the habit of opening a particular drawer to locate a toy pistol hidden there. Should the toy pistol be replaced with a real one, the child's innocent action creates a situation fraught with terror. The underlying structure of a good horror story educates the reader to the ground rules of the tale, maintains a sense of unity through the emotional turmoil, and provides a sense of inevitability at the ending. To appreciate Bradbury's use of structure in his horror stories, we will look at two of them in some detail.

"The Emissary" is a fine example of the effective use of structure. Little Martin is an invalid whose main contact with the outside world is through his Dog. The story consists primarily of three visits which the dog makes to Martin's bedroom. The first visit establishes the pattern of all of the dog's visits. We learn that Dog dashes out of doors to play for a while, then bounds back indoors, upstairs, and into Martin's bed. By inhaling the odor of the dog's coat and examining the fragments of leaf and twig clinging to it, Martin is able to reconstruct the season, the weather, and the path that Dog has followed: " . . . Dog had rattled down hills where autumn lay in cereal crispness, where children lay in funeral pyres, in rustling heaps, the leaf-buried but watchful dead, as Dog and the world blew by." In the opening pages of the story, we are also introduced to the fact that Dog has a bad habit of digging holes where he is not supposed to. Dog's second visit to the bedroom reveals his function of bringing guests to Martin's bedside. On this occasion, it is Martin's favorite visitor, Miss Haight, his school teacher. After this second visit, Miss Haight is killed in an automobile accident. Some weeks later, Dog runs off and disappears. It is then contrived for Martin to be left alone in the house late one night, thus setting the stage for Dog's third visit. Dog's third visit follows the pattern of those already established. Because of this, the reader is able to notice ominous little variations in the pattern which suggest that something may be amiss. The dog is heard barking a long way off, drawing nearer, then farther away again. Martin wonders at this, but we see the implication that the dog is guiding someone along the way—someone who cannot move as fast as he can. Finally Dog is right outside the house. The downstairs door opens—"Someone was kind enough to have opened the door for Dog." The dog dashes upstairs and jumps onto the bed as usual, and as usual, Martin begins his detective work to see where the dog has been. The sensory picture here is as vivid as ever, but this time quite disturbing:

> It was a smell of strange earth. It was a smell of night within night, the smell of digging down deep in shadow through earth that had lain cheek by jowl with things that were long hidden and decayed . . .
>
> What kind of message was this from Dog? What could such a message mean? The stench—the ripe and awful cemetery earth.

There are only nine sentences left in the story by this time, but no more are needed. We cannot escape the conclusion even if we stop reading. Bradbury does not even have to use much description, for our imaginations are already at work constructing the horror which Martin finally hears climbing the stairs "one foot dragged after the other, painfully, slowly . . ." Bradbury has the excellent good taste to end the story with the words—"Martin had company."—the same words which preceded Miss Haight's first visit to the room. "The Emissary" is a classic tribute to the sort of Halloween story told around campfires. Its emotional effect almost buries the meticulous precision of its structure. Looking back over the story, it is possible to find many subtle touches contributing to the pervasive sense of death at the conclusion. For instance, even in the passage quoted above regarding Dog's first visit, a passage intended to convey the crisp high spirits of an autumn afternoon, we find references to "funeral pyres," and "leaf-buried but watchful dead."

"The October Game" also uses a repeated event to involve the reader in the story, but in a different way. We are introduced at the outset to Mich Wilder's intention to do violence to his wife, but the means by which he is to achieve this is withheld for some time. Instead the story sets up the atmosphere of a Halloween party, and suggests that Wilder may try to get at his wife through their child. Suddenly we are in the darkened basement with the Wilders and some neighborhood children as the game called "the witch is dead" begins. As the supposed "parts" of a chopped-up witch are passed around the room, the explanation of what the parts actually are is suggested by the children: "He gets some old chicken innards from the icebox and hands them around and says, 'These are her innards!' And he makes a clay head and passes it for her head, and passes a soup bone for her arm . . ." Meanwhile Mrs. Wilder notices that her daughter is missing. Suddenly, the reader joins Mrs. Wilder in mentally replaying the game so far, this time with a macabre possibility very evident. Our discoveries accompany Mrs. Wilder's second by second, and the suspense, though sustained for only a short time, attains a high pitch. The ending is something of a throwaway, and the story is marred somewhat by its repellent theme, still the tale remains one of Bradbury's most memorable.

"The Emissary" and "The October Game" are organized to set the reader up for the shock of a surprise ending. In these cases it works because the surprise has been well organized. But stories with surprise endings are frequently unsatisfying since they leave the reader with a sense of having been tricked. Most exciting horror tales, Bradbury's included, are stories of suspense in which the lay of the plot is revealed very early, and the reader is kept on edge awaiting the outcome. Alfred Hitchcock has very effectively distinguished between surprise and suspense. Surprise, according to Hitchcock, is when we watch two men having a conversation and suddenly a bomb located under their table goes off. There has been no preparation, so the effect is brief. If however, we know beforehand that the bomb is under the table, and we know what time it is going to go off, and we can see a clock on the wall behind the men, then the entire scene becomes charged with suspense. In this case, says Hitchcock, " . . . The public is participating in the scene. The audience is longing to warn the characters . . . 'You shouldn't be talking about such trivial matters. There's a bomb beneath you and it's about to explode!'"

Most of Bradbury's horror stories follow Hitchcock's principles of suspense and clue the reader in to what is going on quite early. The mother of "The Small Assassin" knows her baby is trying to kill her from the first line of the story. Young Charles in "Fever Dream" senses that his body is being taken over by some alien force on the first page. An invasion of Earth by creatures from another world is foreshadowed during the first few sentences of "Zero Hour" and "Boys! Raise Giant Mushrooms in *Your* Cellar!" Suspense leads to horror in these stories as the characters involved meet tragic fates.

Bradbury's horror stories, then, are primarily technical pieces aimed at achieving a narrow, specific effect. The stories demand a strict attention to form, and are not generally noted for subtlety of plot or characterization. An exception is "The Next in Line," a horror tale mixed with a skillful study of a deteriorating relationship. The story has all of the formal characteristics of the horror and suspense tale discussed so far. The crucial event of the tale, a visit to the cavern of the mummies of Guanajuato, is introduced on the first page, and the funeral of a child on the second page reaffirms the atmosphere of lurking death that builds toward the story's climax.

But the development of "The Next in Line" is much more extended and subtle than the average horror tale. The story examines in detail the shambles

Marie and Joseph's marriage has become, primarily through Marie's eyes. The horrific element in the story, Marie's fear of dying and being hung among the mummies, does not represent an outside force intruding upon Marie's life, but a morbid development within her own mind. On the third page of the story, as she watches the child's funeral, Marie automatically refers to the child as female:

> She did not think it unusual, her choice of the feminine pronoun. Already she had identified herself with that tiny fragment parceled like an unripe variety of fruit. Now, in this moment, she was being carried up the hill within compressing darkness, a stone in a peach, silent and terrified, the touch of the father against the coffin material outside; gentle and noiseless and firm inside.

The rest of the story traces Marie's gradual surrender of life into an embrace of death. The mummies, horrible as they are, become merely symbolic of her obsession. In the end, we are not so much shocked by Marie's fate as by her husband's complicity in it.

Death

Bradbury does not like Marie's attitude of surrender. This is not surprising from a man who in recent years has vigorously espoused the conquest of space as the surest way of guaranteeing humankind's immortality. One senses Bradbury is more sympathetic with Aunt Tildy in "There Was an Old Woman," who, when Death calls upon her in the guise of a handsome gentleman, is quite rebellious: "You just skit out of here; don't bother me, I got my tattin' and knittin' to do, and no never minds about tall, dark gentlemen with fangled ideas." When Death succeeds in lulling Tildy to sleep long enough for him to separate her body from her soul, the irascible old lady's spirit counters by marching to the mortuary and reclaiming her body.

Bradbury was profoundly affected by his visit to Mexico, shortly after the end of World War II, during the festival of *El Dia de Muerte*—the day of death. There is more about this visit in Chapter 8, but the important thing to be noted here is the extent to which Bradbury was struck by Death as an overwhelming tangible reality. Stories such as "The Next in Line" and "*El Dia de Muerte*" directly reflect the vividness of this experience. Death as involved in these stories is crushingly final; once it has entered and taken effect, there is nowhere for either character or writer to go. "*El Dia de Muerte*" concerns itself with three deaths—that of a boy named Raimundo (Bradbury's first name in Spanish), that of a bull in the ring, and that of another boy playing Christ on the cross at the top of a church steeple. The deaths are set against the celebrations throughout Mexico on the Day of the Dead. As part of the celebrations, candy skulls with different names on them are sold everywhere. Raimundo has one with his name on it which is shattered when he is hit by a car. At the story's conclusion, " . . . The sugar skull with the letters R and A and I and M and U and N and D and O was snatched up and eaten by children who fought over the name."

As if to liberate himself from the crushing finality of Death as an emotional force and as a subject in writing, Bradbury has occasionally taken a cue from the Mexicans and their candy skulls. He often, in effect, reduces Death to a palatable symbol, a somewhat theatrical figure in a Halloween costume whose mask, if somewhat frightening, is still only a mask. This is the case in "There Was an Old Woman," where Death, as a handsome young man, is seen as no match for her vitality. It is the case again in "Death and the Maiden," in which another old lady, Old Mam, attempts to elude death by barricading herself inside the house. Death tries out various disguises, but none are successful until he appears as Old Mam's long-dead love, Willy. Death is no longer implacable, but subtle, and his summons is open to negotiation. Old Mam does not give in until she has been promised the return of a day of her youth, and the favor of sleeping next to her lover for eternity.

An interesting variation on the above story, in which an old woman confronts the lover of her youth, is found in "The Tombling Day." While helping to move coffins from an old graveyard to a new one, Grandma Loblilly opens the box containing the body of her lover of sixty years before. The body has been perfectly preserved, and at first Grandma is dismayed at the comparison between his youth and her age. But when the body suddenly disintegrates, Grandma's eyes are cleared. Wisest of the three old ladies, she doesn't bother to reject death, but instead reaffirms her embrace on life: "I'm young! I'm eighty, but I'm younger'n *him*! . . . I'm younger'n all the dead ones in the whole world!"

This high-spirited attitude in the face of death is an important one to Bradbury. It figures significantly in the novel *Something Wicked This Way Comes* as exemplified by one of the epigraphs chosen for that book, a quote from *Moby-Dick* in which Stubb says, "I know not all that be coming, but be it what it will, I'll go to it laughing."

One of the traditional Halloween representations of Death is as the Grim Reaper. Bradbury takes this personification literally in the fantasy "The Scythe." This story of a poor man and his family who take over a farm from a dying man, could easily descend into allegory, but never does. Drew discovers slowly, and in a matter-of-fact way that he has taken over Death's job, and that every stalk of wheat he cuts marks the end of a human life. Drew struggles with his role several times, but eventually reconciles himself to making his living being Death.

Juan Diaz also uses death to support his family in "The Lifework of Juan Diaz," save that he supports his family by *being* dead. Juan's wife steals his mummified remains from the graveyard and sets them up in her home as a tourist attraction. As a result, Juan is able to support his family better in death than he did in life.

We encounter death as a kind of life-style in "The Dead Man." Here, Odd Martin, the town lunatic, insists that he is dead, finally finds a woman to share his conviction, marries her, and is last seen traveling with his bride toward the cemetery. This image of death as a state of mind is explored in a less macabre way in two stories. "Jack-in-the-Box" ends with young Edwin gladly embracing the "death" of the outside world his mother had been shielding him from. In "The Wonderful Death of Dudley Stone," a famous writer is confronted by a jealous rival who intends to kill him. Stone agrees to "die" by simply not writing any more books. The rival is satisfied, and Stone, through his "death" is able to relax and enjoy life for the first time.

In these lighter stories, we may get the feeling that death is being bandied about a bit. Bradbury seems to be holding death at arm's length, reducing it to an abstraction, a concept, a delusion, a fantasy. In so doing, he provides an out for himself, a means of transcending death in stories in which there is no implied hope of immortality among the stars.

NOTES

p. 4 "Coffee . . ." Bradbury, "To the Chicago Abyss," from *Machineries of Joy*, p. 193.

p. 4 "What did I have . . ." Ibid., p. 199.

p. 5 "Like this . . ." Bradbury, "The Visitor," from *The Illustrated Man*, p. 130.

p. 5 "She wanted to touch . . ." Bradbury, "The Great Wide World Over There" from *Golden Apples*, p. 103.

p. 5–6 "I walk along . . ." Bradbury, "The Man in the Rorschach Shirt," from *I Sing the Body Electric*, p. 252.

p. 6 "as if a cork . . ." Bradbury, "Getting Through Sunday Somehow," from *Long After Midnight*, p. 103.

p. 6 "Imagine you're an American . . ." Ibid., p. 106.

p. 6 "stood like a hollowed . . ." Bradbury, "The Day it Rained Forever," from *Medicine for Melancholy*, p. 173.

p. 7 "blood moving fast . . ." Bradbury, "The Drummer Boy of Shiloh," from *Machineries of Joy*, p. 45.

p. 7 "Rubber, steel, clay . . ." Bradbury, "Tyrannosaurus Rex," from *Machineries of Joy*, p. 22.

p. 7 "Perhaps . . . perhaps . . ." Bradbury, "The Rocket," from *Illustrated Man*, p. 185.

p. 8 "willing suspension . . ." Samuel Taylor Coleridge, *Biographia Literaria*, chap. XIV. Quoted here from *English Poetry and Prose of the Romantic Movement*, George Benjamin Woods, ed. (Chicago: Scott Foresman and Company, 1950), p. 398.

p. 8 "Inside the walls . . ." Bradbury, "The Miracles of Jamie," from *After Midnight*, p. 236.

p. 9 "think about that jar . . ." Bradbury, "The Jar," from *The October Country*, p. 88.

p. 9 "sunny pleasure-dome . . ." Bradbury (quoting "Kubla Khan" by Coleridge), "A Miracle of Rare Device," from *Machineries of Joy*, p. 121. For the complete text of "Kubla Khan," see *The New Oxford Book of English Verse*, Sir Arthur Quiller-Couch, ed. (New York: Oxford University Press, 1939), pp. 668–670.

p. 9 "Right now, I'm feeling . . ." Bradbury, "A Miracle of Rare Device," from *Machineries of Joy*, p. 126.

p. 10 "before Garibaldi!" Bradbury, "The Marriage Mender," from *Medicine for Melancholy*, p. 60.

p. 10 "There was Mars . . ." Bradbury, "The Strawberry Window," from *Medicine for Melancholy*, pp. 171–172.

p. 11 "Are we not fine . . ." Bradbury, "The Wonderful Ice Cream Suit," from *Medicine for Melancholy*, p. 31.

p. 12 "Dog had rattled . . ." Bradbury, "The Emissary," from *October Country*, p. 105.

p. 13 "He gets some . . ." Bradbury, "The October Game," from *After Midnight*, p. 244.

p. 14 "The public is . . ." François Truffaut (quoting Alfred Hitchcock), *Hitchcock*, p. 52.

p. 15 "She did not think it . . ." Bradbury, "The Next in Line," from *October Country*, p. 18.

p. 15 "You just skit out . . ." Bradbury, "There Was an Old Woman," from *October Country*, p. 225.

p. 16 "the sugar skull . . ." Bradbury, "*El Dia de Muerte*," from *Machineries of Joy*, p. 92.

p. 16 "I'm young! . . ." Bradbury, "The Tombling Day," from *Body Electric*, p. 199.

p. 16 "I know not all . . ." Herman Melville, *Moby-Dick*, chap. XXXIX (New York: Grosset & Dunlap, n.d.), p. 191.

ANNOTATED BIBLIOGRAPHY

No complete bibliography of Ray Bradbury's work exists at this writing, and since it is beyond the scope of this book to include one, the listing below is confined to sources quoted from or consulted for this book. Until a complete bibliography does appear, those produced by Indick, Nolan, and Slusser (as listed below) may be helpful. Except for the most recent collections, which were widely distributed in hardcover, I worked primarily from the paperback editions of Bradbury's books, since they are the most readily available. The dates shown are, of course, from the specific edition used, but note that in many of the earlier or later paperback editions of the same title—especially among the Bantam editions—the page references remain valid.

Works by Ray Bradbury

"The Ardent Blasphemers." Introduction to *20,000 Leagues Under the Sea* by Jules Verne. New York: Bantam Books, 1964.

"Beyond 1984." *Playboy*, January 1979, p. 170.

Dandelion Wine. New York: Bantam Books, 1976. Contains Bradbury's autobiographical introduction "Just This Side of Byzantium."

Fahrenheit 451. New York: Ballantine Books, 1953.

The Golden Apples of the Sun. New York: Bantam Books, 1961.

"Gotcha!" *Redbook*, August 1978, p. 95.

The Halloween Tree. New York: Alfred A. Knopf, 1972.

The Illustrated Man. New York: Bantam Books, 1952.

I Sing the Body Electric! New York: Alfred A. Knopf, 1969.

Long after Midnight. New York: Alfred A. Knopf, 1976.

The Machineries of Joy. New York: Bantam Books, 1965.

Mars and the Mind of Man. (with Arthur C. Clarke, Bruce Murray, Carl Sagan, and Walter Sullivan). New York: Harper & Row, 1973. Contains discussions and photographs on some of the most recent discoveries about Mars, which may be compared with the theories of Lowell.

The Martian Chronicles. New York: Bantam Books, 1972. This edition does not have the prefatory note by Clifton Fadiman found in the 1954 edition.

A Medicine for Melancholy. New York: Bantam Books, 1960.

The October Country. New York: Ballantine Books, 1956.

Pillar of Fire and Other Plays. New York: Bantam Books, 1975.

R is for Rocket. New York: Bantam Books, 1976.

S is for Space. New York: Bantam Books, 1976.

The Small Assassin. Frogmore, St. Albans, England: Panther Books, 1976. This British paperback contains several stories from *Dark Carnival* not subsequently reprinted in *October Country*. It is available in some of the larger U.S. bookstores.

Something Wicked This Way Comes. New York: Bantam Books, 1963.

"Steiner out of Kong by Cooper." Album notes to the original motion picture score of "King Kong," composed by Max Steiner. Los Angeles: United Artists Records, UA-LA373-G. 1975.

"A Summer Day." *Redbook*, August 1979, p. 51.

Switch on the Night. New York: Pantheon Books, 1955.

Timeless Stories for Today and Tomorrow. New York: Bantam Books, 1961. 26 stories of fantasy by various authors, edited and with an introduction by Bradbury.

The Vintage Bradbury. New York: Vintage Books, 1965. Introduction by Gilbert Highet.

When Elephants Last in the Dooryard Bloomed. New York: Alfred A. Knopf, 1977.

The Wonderful Ice Cream Suit and Other Plays. New York: Bantam Books, 1972.

Zen and the Art of Writing and The Joy of Writing: Two Essays. Santa Barbara, CA.: Capra Press, 1973.

Other Sources

Brackett, Leigh. *The Sword of Rhiannon.* New York: Ace Books, 1953.

Burroughs, Edgar Rice. *A Princess of Mars*. New York: Ballantine Books, 1963.

Čapek, Karel. *R. U. R.* from *R. U. R. and The Insect Play* by the Brothers Capek. Translated by P. Selver. New York: Oxford University Press, 1961.

Elliot, Jeff. "The Bradbury Chronicles." Interview. *Future*, October 1978, p. 22.

Ellison, Harlan, ed. *Again Dangerous Visions*. New York: New American Library, 1972.

Goldstone, Tony, ed. *The Pulps: Fifty Years of American Pop Culture*. New York: Chelsea House, 1976. A good popular history of the sort of magazine in which Bradbury published many of his early stories. Contains the otherwise uncollected story "Wake for the Living," first published in 1947 in *Dime Mystery Magazine*.

Gunn, James. *Alternate Worlds: The Illustrated History of Science Fiction*. Englewood Cliffs, NJ.: Prentice-Hall, 1975. Another good popular history, well-illustrated. Includes many details about writers and editors with whom Bradbury has been associated.

Hamilton, Edith. *Mythology*. New York: New American Library, n.d. A very readable reference work summarizing many of the Greek, Roman and Norse myths that influenced Bradbury's writing.

Herrigel, Eugen. *Zen in the Art of Archery*. New York: Vintage Books, 1971. The direct inspiration for Bradbury's essay "Zen and the Art of Writing."

Hoyt, William Graves. *Lowell and Mars*. Tucson: University of Arizona Press, 1976.

Indick, Ben P. "The Drama of Ray Bradbury." N.p.: T-K Graphics, 1977. A critical essay in pamphlet form. Treats Bradbury's radio, stage and screen plays. Includes a list of published plays. The pamphlet may be located in some science fiction book stores.

Johnson, Wayne L. "The Invasion Stories of Ray Bradbury." In *Critical Encounters: Writers and Themes in Science Fiction*, edited by Dick Riley. New York: Frederick Ungar Publishing Co., 1978.

———. Unpublished interview with Ray Bradbury on October 5, 1978.

Kraus, Maggie, comp. "Tour of the North Branch of the Waukegan River: The Streets that Border the Ravine." Mimeographed. Waukegan, Ill.: Waukegan Historical Society—Heritage Committee Waukegan Bicentennial Commission, n. d.

Lewis, Barbara. "Ray Bradbury, the Martian Chronicler." Interview. *Starlog*, August 1979, p. 28.

Ley, Willy. *Watchers of the Skies: An Informal History of Astronomy from Babylon to the Space Age*. New York: Viking Press, 1963.

Lieberman, Archie. *The Mummies of Guanajuato*. New York: Harry N. Abrams, 1978. A photographic tour of Guanajuato and of the famous mummies. Bradbury's story "The Next in Line" is included as an introduction.

Lowell, Percival. *Mars As the Abode of Life*. New York: Macmillan Co., 1909.

———. *Mars and Its Canals*. New York: Macmillan Co., 1907.

Madsen, Axel. *John Huston*. Garden City, N.Y.: Doubleday & Company, 1978. Contains details of Bradbury's stay in Ireland while working on the screenplay for "Moby Dick."

Meredith, Burgess. "Burgess Meredith Reads Ray Bradbury." Phonograph record. Bergen Field, N.J.: Lively Arts Recording Corp. Lively Arts 30004, n.d. Dramatic readings by Meredith of "There Will Come Soft Rains" and "Marionettes, Inc."

Mitchell, Lisa. "Ray Bradbury: He Sees the Future—and it Works." *Family Weekly*, 16 July 1978, p. 4.

Naha, Ed. "The Martian Chronicles." *Future Life*, November 1979, p. 18. Magazine article detailing the filming of Bradbury's book for television.

Nolan, William F. "The Published Books and Stories of Ray Bradbury." Appendix to *The Martian Chronicles* by Ray Bradbury. Garden City, N. Y.: Doubleday & Company,

1973. A chronological listing of Bradbury's books and short stories published through 1972.

———. "Ray Bradbury: A Biographical Sketch." Preface to *The Martian Chronicles* by Ray Bradbury. Garden City, N. Y.: Doubleday & Company, 1973.

———. *The Ray Bradbury Companion.* Detroit: Bruccoli Clark Books, 1975. Introduction by Bradbury. Contains biographical information, many photographs of Bradbury's family and friends, reproduction of some of Bradbury's manuscripts, information on foreign editions of various works, and other details of Bradbury's work and career.

Rovin, Jeff. *From the Land Beyond Beyond.* New York: Berkeley Windhover Books, 1977. Contains details of Ray Harryhausen's films, including his work on "The Beast from 20,000 Fathoms."

Slusser, George Edgar. *The Ray Bradbury Chronicles.* San Bernardino, CA: Borgo Press, 1977. Critical essay in booklet form. Concludes with a list of Bradbury's published books.

Truffaut, François. *Hitchcock.* New York: Simon and Schuster, 1967.

Wells, H. G. *The Complete Science Fiction Treasury of H. G. Wells.* New York: Avenel Books, 1978.

LAHNA DISKIN

Bradbury on Children

"*The reason why grownups and kids fight is because they belong to separate races. Look at them, different from us. Look at us, different from them*" (*Dandelion Wine*, 27). So writes twelve-year-old Douglas Spaulding in his first journal. It is a truth central not only to the summer of 1928 in *Dandelion Wine* but to Ray Bradbury's general view of children. To trace the unfolding of this truth in his fiction, I will focus on two novels, *Dandelion Wine* and *Something Wicked This Way Comes*, as well as several short stories.

Early in *Dandelion Wine* Tom Spaulding wonders why his older brother wants to record "new crazy stuff" in a "yellow nickel tablet." Succinctly, Douglas explains his reason for preserving his special observations:

> "I'm alive."
> "Heck, that's old!"
> "*Thinking* about it, *noticing* it, is new. You do things and don't watch. Then all of a sudden you look and see what you're doing and it's the first time, really. . . ." (*Wine*, 26)

He goes on to say that his record is in two parts. The first is called "RITES AND CEREMONIES" and the second "DISCOVERIES AND REVELATIONS or maybe ILLUMINATIONS, that's a swell word, or INTUITIONS, okay?" (*Wine*,

From *Ray Bradbury*, edited by Martin Harry Greenberg and Joseph D. Olander, pp. 127–55, 224 © 1980 by Martin Harry Greenberg and Joseph D. Olander.

27). These headings are more than felicitous keynotes for what will happen to and around the boys during the summer; they suggest conditions of existence and signify operations in the ethos of children—children as a different species. For example, the boys in Bradbury's two novels consecrate their friendship with diversions, often secret, which grow into private systems of symbols. Often in the form of ceremonies, these systems insulate them from the restrictions and machinations of adults. The rituals and discoveries, together with the revelations and illuminations, enable Bradbury's children to cross boundaries that separate reality and fantasy. They come and go from one domain to the other, and often unite the two. If we grant that reality and fantasy are cultures, then children have the idiopathic ability to cross cultures. While this kind of traffic may be second nature to some adults, it is first nature to children. In their passage between dimensions, the children in Bradbury's fiction, not always benignly and often intentionally, overstep society's norms. They sanction certain actions and behavior which they know to be outlawed by society. Sometimes murder is the kind of freedom practiced by members of Bradbury's separate race.

With libidinous joy, Bradbury's boys share the events of human life with the adults in their families and communities. But their sharing differs in quality from that of their parents and townspeople. Their fix on the phenomena comprising day-to-day existence is charged with meanings which they construe from lore and legend, from myth and imagination. Re-creation, in its most inventive sense, is their daily enterprise. At times, the very air they breathe is compounded of wonder and magic, a potent elixir that transforms even the seasons of the year—summer in the case of *Dandelion Wine* and autumn in *Something Wicked This Way Comes*. For them, being alive means perceiving phenomena with an openness and acceptance by which natural processes are transmuted and turn miraculous or portentous. They rambunctiously perpetuate the freedom of childhood. Even when they behave maliciously, they are obeying their own credo, their own laws, which decree that they resist the inexorable transformation they will undergo when they migrate to adulthood. Their most outrageous actions are instinctive ploys against the inevitable doomsday of exile from childhood. Thus, in both books, the boys live at the quick of life, marauding each moment. They are afire with ecstatic temporality, resplendent immediacy.

Douglas and Tom Spaulding—along with their friends, John Huff and Charlie Woodman, in *Dandelion Wine*—live in a different zone, or season, of boyhood from that inhabited by James Nightshade and William Halloway in *Something Wicked This Way Comes*. Nevertheless, they share their origins as members of a separate race. In the truest sense of their attributes, they are creatures of a world, a secondary state, both within and beyond the planet they cohabit with their parents and other grownups. The significance of being *within* and *beyond* is that they are attuned to the higher and lower ranges of the phenomena of nature and the mysteries of the supernatural. The innocence of Bradbury's children is also part of their secondary state, for it is an estate of sanctuary and sometimes unholy sanctity. To be innocent in the context of Bradbury's fiction is to be uninhibited in imaginative daring, regardless of the consequences. When they participate in the activities of home and town, his young characters abide within a wholesome worldliness. When they venture outside those circles, they cross over into a beyond that is often sinister, a forbidding but still enticing supra-worldliness. As commuters between the two dimensions, they try to relate the different conditions of life in each, "make sense of the interchange." In *Dandelion Wine* their coordinate worlds are symbolized by the town and the ravine, each struggling at some "indefinable place" to "possess a certain avenue, a dell, a glen, a tree, a bush."

Invariably, Bradbury's boys are full of urgent emotions and are generally conscience-free. They are alternately generous and greedy, benevolent and cruel. Withal, they represent integrated, untrammeled, unpremeditated self-expression. They excel at magnifying people, places and events. Their mental extravagance can be viewed as their peculiar racial talent for enhancement.

Bradbury's principle of enhancement makes his boys kin to the spirit that pervades much of e. e. cummings' poetry. Indeed, there is an affinity between the poet's view of life and his license with language and syntax, and Bradbury's children and their license with time. In affirming that he is alive and often alone, cummings manipulates temporal relationships and diminishes fixity in form. Similarly, Bradbury's boys are devout libertarians, because their "spirit's ignorance"—hence innocence—eclipses "every wisdom knowledge fears to dare."[1] They dare whatever must be ventured to play out their fantasies. Never halfhearted, they are creatures "whose vision can create the whole," who are "free into the beauty of the truth."[2] Significantly, the truths they sometimes find have beauty which only they can behold. As members of a separate race, they are "citizens of ecstasies more steep than climb can time with all his years."[3] The idea in this line of poetry applies to Bradbury's concept of children, while cummings' technique applies to their way of stalling time. The inversion of subject and verb, with *can* intervening, is an arrangement suggesting almost incessant movement or activity accompanied by equilibrium. In exchanging places, *climb* and *time* exchange functions to suggest restless equation. There is a sense of alternation and reciprocity in the tempo of a romp, to forestall the irreversible course of linear time. Like cummings' citizen, Bradbury's boys buck the tyranny of the clock. They turn with the sun and moon, plundering the days of summer in *Dandelion Wine* and the nights of autumn in *Something Wicked This Way Comes*. Too busy to capitulate, the boys in both books chase life and death and celebrate the mystique of both. For all the children in Bradbury's fiction, "everything happens that can't be done."[4] True to cummings' sense of life, the ears of their ears awake, the eyes of their eyes are opened. They are continually poised to find "treasures of reeking innocence" and move among "such mysteries as men do not conceive."[5]

In *Dandelion Wine* Douglas and Tom Spaulding celebrate the arrival of summer with certain simple family ceremonies. On his first excursion of the season with Tom and his father for fox grapes and wild strawberries, Douglas is seized by an overwhelming and inexplicable force: "the terrible prowler, the magnificent runner, the leaper, the shaker of souls . . ." (*Wine*, 6). His startled awareness is an epiphany, a connection, a communion with the natural world. Through every inch and fiber of his body, he knows that he is a creature of Earth, a vibrant strand in what Shelley saw as the great "web of being."

Still reminiscent of Shelley, this time his skylark, Douglas is like an "unbodied joy whose race has just begun."[6] The experience is tumultuous, dizzying, and it cannot be shared with his father. Douglas has what Shelley described in his essay, "On Life," as a "distinct and intense apprehension" of the natural world in relation to himself. He feels (to pursue Shelley's theory) as though his nature "were dissolved into the surrounding universe or as if the surrounding universe were absorbed into his being."[7] Suddenly he is privy to a spirit world in which his embodied but seemingly personified emotions are manifested psychologically. The scene suggests the way in which the boy's emotions and the processes of nature become symbolic entities unto themselves, spirits and demi-spirits. Douglas's great burst of psychic energy has the power to become an almost visible presence projecting itself into the outside world. This dramatic presence is both noumenal and extra-noumenal, in that Douglas both conceives of and perceives the phenomena that possess him. The connection between the boy and animate nature gives him the sense of potent and splendid interrelatedness, as well as autonomy. Finding his identity in the woodland sense world, he extols his self-affirmation with utter abandon. In the passage on pages 9–10 of *Dandelion Wine*, Bradbury evokes the notion of Douglas's emotional and spiritual immersion in a green molecular music within the multitudes of sunlit leaves and blades of grass. The almost audible and felt hum of slow sap inside everything that grows pulses invisibly and harmonizes with Douglas' lyric blood. As he counts "the twin hearts beating in each ear, the third heart beating in his throat, the two hearts throbbing his wrists, the real heart pounding his chest," his internal manifesto catches the mystic integration between himself and planet Earth. It is the private rhapsody of his soul's sacrament in nature with its power to intensify or raise his consciousness of life. The importance of Douglas's summer baptism is that, for Bradbury, it is an experience reserved for children. All of Bradbury's boy characters have the potential for the ordeal and the initiation because, as a race, children live in a state of readiness for the verities and illuminations of their manifest sensations.

The parents in Bradbury's stories are another breed. As such, they have lost the capacity to attend to and follow their sensations. Habit and workaday concerns have dulled them to the imaginative dimensions they once frequented as children. The impedimenta of adulthood change one's outlook and impair his capacity to apprehend the world openly with keen, clear senses. Age can clog or even close the channels between man and nature. Bradbury hints that Mr. Spaulding was once like his son. In *Something Wicked This Way Comes*, Mr. Halloway is a somewhat forlorn character, gently envious of his son's singular endowments as a member of a race he can only dimly, if at all, remember as his own.

In Bradbury's canon, children are, by contrast, agents who can transfigure and sometimes metamorphose persons, things, and events. They are, in other words, apostles of enhancement. In *Dandelion Wine*, dandelions, snowflakes, shoes, and rugs are some of the elements they use. For the Spaulding boys, gathering the dandelions for wine is no ordinary chore. The essence of summer is the dandelion wine, crocked and bottled and sequestered in "cellar gloom." It is a precious potion that perpetuates the season long after it would have otherwise passed into oblivion. As summertime reincarnated and resurrected, it is a sovereign remedy for winter miseries. The boys believe that it is as life-giving as the season from which it comes. They plunge into the sea of dandelions, awash in the golden splendor. To Douglas's mind, all the ingredients of the brew are consecrated, even rain-barrel water, like "faintly blue silk" that "softened the lips and throat and heart."

Tom shares his brother's capacity for enhancement. In the midst of Douglas's contact with "the Thing," and in contrast to his secret silent communion, Tom proclaims his own right to glory for having preserved a February snowflake in a matchbox: "I'm the only guy in all Illinois who's got a snowflake in summer.... Precious as diamonds, by gosh" (*Wine*, 8). Tom's broadcast is like a badge of honor in full view. Douglas fears that Tom's excitement will scare off the Thing. Then he realizes that the presence was not only unafraid of Tom but that "Tom drew it with his breath . . . was part of it!"

The notion of enhancement also applies to Douglas's determination to have new sneakers. Bradbury's boys are adventure-bound in feet bared to summer's textures and tempos or shod in "Cream Sponge Para Litefoot Shoes." Douglas knows that for the exploits of Summer 1928, last year's lifeless, threadbare sneakers will never do. After all, a knight is not a knight without his jambeaus and sollerets, just as the boys of summer in Green Town, Illinois, are not ready for "June and the earth full of raw power and everything everywhere in motion" without new sneakers. Douglas believes that the Para Litefoot brand can be an antigravity device for jumping over fences, sidewalks, dogs—even rivers, trees, and houses. "The magic was always in the new pair of shoes," ready to transform him into antelope or gazelle.

Rug-cleaning is an annual family event which undergoes enhancement. It sounds like an authentic ritual complete with coven, when Bradbury says: "These great wire wands were handed around so they stood, Douglas, Tom, Grandma, Great-grandma, and Mother poised like a collection of witches and familiars over the dusty patterns of old Armenia" (*Wine*, 64). Amid the "intricate scrolls and loops, the flowers, the mysterious figures, the shuttling patterns," Tom sees not only a parade of fifteen years of family life but pictures of the future as well. All he needs to do, especially at night under the lamplight, is adjust his eyes and peer around at the warp and woof and even the underskin.

The encounters of several children, including Tom and old lonely Helen Bentley, are the best evidence in *Dandelion Wine* of the time gulf between two different races, children and adults. Mrs. Bentley is dislocated in time; thus she is a displaced person. Isolated by choice in her widowhood, she has never accepted the fact that time is irredeemable. Instead she is caught in the backwater of carefree, loving years as a child, a young woman, and a wife. Consigning life to yesterday, she has sacrificed both the present and the future, which have little substance or reality for her. Little Jane and Alice, Tom Spaulding's playmates, find her ensconced, even engulfed, among the mementos of a lifetime. Denying that she was ever their age, they accuse her of stealing the treasures she shows them. The comb she wore when she was nine, the ring she wore when she was eight, her picture at seven—all are discredited and then confiscated by the heartless children. When she is frustrated in her attempts to authenticate a past which means everything to her, she accepts a bittersweet truth: "Oh, God, children are children, old women are old women, and nothing in between. They can't imagine a change they can't see" (*Wine*, 74). She summons her husband's spirit to save her from despair. Consoled, she realizes that he would have agreed with the girls: "Those children are right. . . . They stole nothing from you, my dear. Those things don't belong to you *here,* you *now.* They belonged to her, that other you, so long ago" (*Wine*, 75). Long years after her husband's wisdom and death, she discovers that time is a trickster. It gulls the young with delusions of permanence. To the children who frolic about her and taunt her, change is a hoax; they will not allow it to intrude on their eternal Now. The people who inhabit their present are immanent. Understanding the children's fix on time, Helen Bentley acquiesces by disposing of her pictures, affidavits, and trinkets—the superfluity of a lifetime. Thereby, the erstwhile sentimentalist divests herself of the stultifying past. She resigns herself to the present and submits to the unrelenting ridicule of the intransigent children. With no trace of moral solicitude, they persist. In the closing dialogue of the chapter, Bradbury shows Jane and Alice as adamant persecutors:

> "How old are you, Mrs. Bentley"
> "Seventy-two."
> "How old were you fifty years ago?"
> "Seventy-two."
> "You weren't ever young, were you, and never wore ribbons or dresses like these?"
> "No."
> "Have you got a first name?"
> "My name is Mrs. Bentley."
> "And you always lived in this one house?"
> "Always."
> "And never were pretty?"
> "Never."
> "Never in a million trillion years?"
>
> . . . . .
>
> "Never," said Mrs. Bentley, "in a million trillion years."
> (*Wine*, 77)

Equally unenlightened, Douglas and Tom conclude that "old people never *were* children!" Saddened by their unreasonable doubt, they decide that "there's nothing we can do to help them."

In the case of Helen Bentley, the children are skeptics of anything that contradicts the reality of their immediate perceptions. No matter what she claims and has to back up her claims, they discount it as belying appearances. In the case of Colonel Freeleigh, however, they are willing to suspend disbelief. A relic like Helen Bentley, he is sick and dying. But it isn't his declining health that accounts for the difference in the way Douglas and his friends respond to him. They compromise or extend their credulity for him because they associate him with far-off places and high adventure. Naive and eager for vicarious exploits, the boys enter Colonel Freeleigh's house and his presence to sit at his feet and hear him recount the bizarre events of his life. His vivid extrapolations from American history beguile them as he holds his small audience captive with stagey accounts of oriental magic, Pawnee Bill and the bison, and the Civil War. Capricious and egocentric, the boys dismiss Helen Bentley as a fraud while at the same time mythologizing Colonel Freeleigh. In fact, he becomes their human time machine. Douglas even decides that their discovery, the "Colonel Freeleigh Express," belongs in his journal. His entry shows an inconsistency and an ingenuous lack of logic which typify his "race":

> " … 'Maybe old people were never children, like we claim with Mrs. Bentley but big or little some of them were standing around at Appomattox the summer of 1865.' They got Indian vision and can sight back further than you and me will ever sight ahead." (*Wine*, 88)

Jane and Alice reject the chance to travel back into Helen Bentley's romantic past, but Douglas and his friends become regular time travelers with Colonel Freeleigh. Bradbury may be suggesting that the girls are too young for the vicarious excursions in which the boys indulge. Three or four years in age may explain Douglas's capacity to appreciate the colonel. Still, he underestimates Helen Bentley as yet another vehicle for adventure. The girls and boys alike exhibit a form of casual opportunism inherent in members of their race.

Some of Bradbury's boys possess exemplary talents. Generally, these are a variety of strenuous physical arts performed outdoors. The children he depicts are in their glory when, unconfined, they challenge any terrain with their arms and legs and voices. Joe Pipkin in *The Halloween Tree* is the newest model of his separate race. One of nine boys in the story, he is impresario of the band's escapades. Fleet, irrepressible, and altogether earthspun, he is a joyous "assemblage of speeds, smells, textures; a cross section of all the boys who ever ran, fell, got up, and ran again" (*Halloween*, 9). He becomes the symbolic and elusive victim in a series of travels in time and space when his friends seek the origins of All Saints' Day. In the literal story line, Joe is hospitalized with acute appendicitis; but on the figurative level, he is surrealistically embroiled in the rituals which his friends witness under the auspices of the magical Mr. Moundshroud. Although Joe is always precariously reincarnated in different countries across different ages, he is a free spirit who, though melodramatically endangered, is ultimately invincible. Bradbury makes him central to the story through recurring appearances by means of supernatural projection. The description of Joe is pertinent, since Pipkin typifies Bradbury's exceptional boys, whose prowess and gallantry distinguish them among their peers:

> Joe Pipkin was the greatest boy who ever lived. The grandest boy who ever fell out of a tree and laughed at the joke. The finest boy who ever raced around the track, winning, and then, seeing his friends a mile back somewhere, stumbled and fell, waited for them

to catch up, and joined, breast and breast, breaking the winner's tape. The jolliest boy who ever hunted out the haunted houses in town, which are hard to find, and came back to report on them and take all the kids to ramble through the basements and scramble up the ivy outside-bricks and shout down the chimneys and make water off the roofs, hooting and chimpanzee-dancing and ape-bellowing. The day Joe Pipkin was born all the Orange Crush and Nehi soda bottles in the world fizzed over; and joyful bees swarmed countrysides to sting maiden ladies. On his birthdays, the lake pulled out from the shore in midsummer and ran back with a tidal wave of boys, a big leap of bodies and a downcrash of laughs. (*Halloween*, 9)

What is interesting here is how Bradbury interlaces his account of Joe's classic boyhood skills and charms with fanciful parallels. His method of idealizing Joe is consistent with the way the characters themselves romanticize their lives.

Joe Pipkin's prototype is John Huff in *Dandelion Wine*. Like his later counterpart, John excels at a variety of things. To his friend, Douglas Spaulding, he is a prince graced with goodness and generosity. At the beginning of the chapter in which Douglas learns that John will move away, Bradbury catalogs John's versatility—the arts and accomplishments that the other boys his age admire and envy. He makes it clear that boys like Huff and Pipkin are true worthies, deserving of awe and emulation. They are blithe spirits who rejoice in their openheartedness, vitality, and youth. Their overt alliance with others of their race and nature is their *joie de vivre*. Generically elite by virtue of their boyhood, they defy temporal and terrestrial realities in their play. They sport on the threshold where fabulous fictions burst into psychic wonderworks. John Huff and his kind fictions in the very hub of time, spending their energy without reservation. The following passage is like a paean in which Bradbury exalts John as champion stock and makes him legendary:

He could pathfind more trails than any Choctaw or Cherokee since time began, could leap from the sky like a chimpanzee from a vine, could live underwater two minutes and slide fifty yards downstream from where you last saw him. The baseballs you pitched him he hit in the apple trees, knocking down harvests. He could jump six-foot orchard walls, swing up branches faster and come down, fat with peaches, quicker than anyone else in the gang. He ran laughing. He sat easy. He was not a bully. He was kind. His hair was dark and curly and his teeth were white as cream. He remembered the words to all the cowboy songs and would teach you if you asked. He knew the names of all the wild flowers and when the moon would rise and set and when the tides came in and out. He was, in fact, the only god living in the whole of Green Town, Illinois, during the twentieth century that Douglas Spaulding knew of. (*Wine*, 102)

John's imminent departure makes him notice things he missed during all the years he lived in Green Town. For instance, the first time he really pays attention to the stained-glass window in the Terle house he is frightened. The thought of all the other things he may have missed makes him panicky and sad, afraid he will forget everything he ever knew in his hometown after he has left. The point of noticing reiterates the attitude of awareness that serves as the keynote of the novel when Douglas begins his notebook. Thus Douglas learns the color of John's eyes on the brink of separation.

There is precious little time left for the two friends to share. Believing he can outwit time, Douglas wants to defer the inevitable farewells. He persuades himself that the best way to stop time is to stand still, for time, he knows instinctively, moves in and with him. He and John can stay together if they will only linger, stop moving, stretch the minutes in shared silence. Run and romp, and time is squandered; tarry, and the clock can be controlled. Later, when Douglas and his friends play statues, John is immobilized for a few minutes and becomes the object of Douglas's close scrutiny. Bradbury turns his last long look into another hymn of praise. Not even the rules of the game can stop the course of time, though. When the sound of John's running mingles with the sound of Douglas's pounding heart, they are lost to each other. Feeling abandoned and betrayed, Douglas, "cold stone and very heavy," knows only anger and hurt. Because he cannot accept the loss, he repudiates John for his desertion. By having Douglas disown John for his involuntary departure, Bradbury shows again how immanence prevails for members of his separate race.

A few, singular townspeople—such as Clara Goodwater who uses spells, wax dolls, and elixirs, and dreamer Leo Auffmann who wants to invent a "Happiness Machine"—mixed liberally with the imaginations of Douglas and Tom Spaulding, equals the elements of bizarre and memorable events. If the events are ongoing and inexplicable, the boys are all the more delighted. The evil Lonely One is their favorite until, to their dismay, Lavinia Nebbs dispels the mystery. On the same night that yet another woman becomes the victim of someone the townspeople have named the Lonely One, Lavinia stabs an intruder in her home. Everyone except the boys believe he is the killer. When the police pronounce the case closed, the delicious terror of a murderer at large ends for the boys. At first they feel bereft of their villain.

The thrill of the spooky, unseen night stalker has been destroyed. As long as he was alive and lurking about town in the deep of night, danger and doom in the wake of his appearance were their perverse delight. He gave them something scary to talk about. With fear and sudden death in their midst, Green Town had an element of excitement. Since Lavinia's desperate act of self-preservation, however, the town has turned dreary, like "vanilla junket," according to Charlie Woodman. This unwelcome change evokes the boys' special powers of enhancement. It is Tom Spaulding who retaliates and persuades the other boys that the intruder was a case of mistaken identity. Reality merges with illusion, fact with fancy, when he refuses to believe that the nondescript man dead in Lavinia's house is the dreaded Lonely One. After all, the stranger waiting for Lavinia "looked like a *man*"—to be exact, "like the candy butcher down front the Elite Theater nights." As Tom conjures up the scoundrel he chooses to perpetuate as the Lonely One, we find the influence of the classic horror story. In conversation with his brother and Charlie Woodman, he insists that the real Lonely One is tall, gaunt, and pale with "big eyes bulging out, green eyes, like a cat." Anyone "little and red-faced and kind of fat" with sparse sandy hair, like the intruder, will never do. Thus when the glamour of the Lonely One is threatened, the boys are reduced, though only temporarily, to the commonplace. Natural sensationalists, they must spice the otherwise bland social scene. Morality, then, isn't an issue. Justice and personal safety are inconsequential when they find their fantasy lives in jeopardy.

Douglas and his friends are inhabitants of two separate milieus, each with distinct geographic features, each the stage for different pursuits. One is the community of Green Town with its homes, stores, churches, and schools, a safe and conventional domain of people engaged in predictable public and private lives. The other is the sequestered ravine abounding in secret possibilities for adventures, for rites and ceremonies observed only by children. Each area, a discrete and organic network of life, is the adversary of the other; each is jealous of its territory and dominion: For Douglas, each domain represents a different set of values, each with a powerful sanction allying him to its laws and conditions of existence. In town he participates in rites and ceremonies of the kind already discussed but which are ordained by adults. There he is a subject bound by the restraints of civilization, by an order he had nothing to do with creating. Bradbury makes us privy to his activities in the fellowship of parents and townspeople. We watch him gather fruits and dandelions, help Grandpa hang the porch swing, and help the women clean the rugs. But when he disappears into the ravine, we do not follow. Neither Bradbury nor we as readers penetrate the sanctity of the ravine where Douglas and the other boys go in defiance of parental authority and general community taboos.

We can only guess at the games and escapades played out in the seclusion of the ravine. There the boys abandon themselves to the Marvellian ideal of green thoughts in a green shade—the greenness of invention and the greenness of nature untouched by humanity. The ravine is the uncontaminated wilderness unchanged by people with their penchant for taming, landscaping, and redesigning nature. Unassailable, it is no-man's-land to the people of Green Town. They have persuaded themselves that it is a dimension within their midst, as untampered with as it is undocile, that should remain untrespassed by anything not native to it.

It may well be that Douglas and the other children are native to the ravine. They enter devil-may-care to pursue their devilment. Within its range, adults have been murdered. The children, nonetheless, come and go in charmed safety. We are left outside where, on the borders of its heavy presence, we can sense its plants and animals. Bradbury denies us the exact details of shapes and shades and deals instead in densities. Obscurity is his dramatic mode for enhancing a dimension reserved for his race of children. The ravine has outlived its colors, colors which Bradbury does not name or show as such, instead enveloping them with invisibility and anonymity. The vegetation, animals, and insects are beyond us, too recessed to see. We are confronted with an intense statis—a vast, deep, above all impenetrable, aliveness that is both alluring and forbidding. This receding intensity and mystery bestow on Bradbury's ravine an aura of agelessness and venerability. Embedded within its depths are secret processes and life forces with the gargantuan capacity for renascence.

One evening Douglas is in the ravine later than usual. Besieged by fear, his mother takes Tom to hunt for him. For the first time in his life Tom experiences the helplessness and isolation, the utter terror, at the prospect of death encroaching on their lives. He is riddled with all the fears his fertile imagination can produce. Still, they head for the ravine:

> He could smell it. It had a dark-sewer, rotten-foliage, thick-green odor. It was a wide ravine that cut and twisted across town—a jungle by day, a place to let alone at night, Mother often declared. (*Wine*, 41)

The awesome nighttime power of the ravine coalesces into an almost animate thing, an entity that concentrates its jungle spirit toward a climax, "tensing, bunching together its black fibers, drawing in power from sleeping countrysides all about, for miles and miles." Tom knows that in the menacing darkness and thick silence they are poised on the brink of either Douglas's annihilation or his salvation. Suddenly, as in defiance of what seem to Tom to be demonic elements of possession, a trinity of laughing innocents appears. Douglas, John Huff, and Charlie Woodman emerge as scapegraces, for clinging to their bodies and clothes are the nameless rank odors as well as magic aromas of the ravine. Many days and nights will pass before soap, water, and other civilized hygienic measures wash away and annul the interlude in the ravine where the boys were creatures of the wild.

Besides the ravine, Summer's Ice House and the arcade are favorites of the boys. The arcade in particular can ward off Douglas's unusual morbid thoughts of his own mortality. It is a fantasy world "completely set in place, predictable, certain, sure." Best of all, its various attractions—the robot, the gorilla, the Keystone Kops, the Wright brothers, Teddy Roosevelt, Madame Tarot—are everlasting, deathless. For this reason, the arcade becomes Douglas's sanctuary from the losses of the summer—the deaths of Great-grandma and Colonel Freeleigh and the departure of John Huff. Before the season took its toll in human life, Douglas was a cocky little navigator in the stream of time. Afterward, he turns to the arcade for solace and escape as, at summer's end, his confidence in his alliance with time has been undermined. He philosophizes that everything there is to do in the arcade pays off. For every coin deposited in a slot there is fiction or reaction. Something always happens. The effect of this insight is like coming "forth in peace as from a church unknown before." Douglas's exuberant response to the mechanical amusements in the arcade is another example of enhancement at work. It is here that he discovers "Mme. Floristan Mariani Tarot, the Chiromancer, Soul Healer, and Deep-Down Diviner of Fates and Furies." If there is anything he consciously wants, it's someone who can heal his bereaved soul and read his uncertain fate. In the spirit of revelation, he believes that beneath Mme. Tarot's metal exterior and inside her machinery there is a captivating Italian girl, a princess under a spell, imprisoned in wax. When he deciphers the word *Secours* written, as he believes, in lemon juice under her "regular" message, he is sure she is a prisoner of Mr. Black, the proprietor.

With the help of Tom and his father, who can recall his own fascination with the circus, Douglas steals the Tarot Witch. He vows to master the arts of black magic and to free her from captivity. Then in gratitude she will foretell his future, save him from accidents, insure his immortality—in short, empower him to sing and dance in defiance of death. This episode is another example of how, for Bradbury's boys, belief is not a matter of appearances belying facts; rather, appearances do, indeed, betoken truth, albeit a truth different from that perceived by adults. For Douglas and others of his race, the key is the arcana they construe from their natural psychic awareness and from bits and pieces of occult lore combined with an ingenuous faith in supernatural agencies.

The large and small daily dramas of life revolve around Douglas, each one involving him differently, each touching him and leaving its illumination. The summer's changes and losses engender a written recitative in his journal, his personal "history of a dying world." He transcribes his testament by the wan and fitful light of the fireflies he has collected in a Mason jar for just this momentous entry in his record of revelations and discoveries. The eerie green glow or halflight emitted by the insects befits his grim denunciation:

YOU CAN'T DEPEND ON *THINGS* BECAUSE ...

*... like machines, for instance, they fall apart
or rust or rot, or maybe never get finished at all ...
or wind up in garages ...*

*... like tennis shoes, you can only run so far,
so fast, and then the earth's got you again ...*

*... like trolleys. Trolleys, big as they are,
always come to the end of the line ...*

YOU CAN'T DEPEND ON *PEOPLE* BECAUSE ...

*... they go away.
... strangers die.
... people you know fairly well die.
... friends die.
... people murder people, like in books.
... your own folks can die. (Wine, 186)*

In addition to revealing dejection over the end of human relationships, Douglas's statement reveals his disappointment when rare contraptions fail: Leo Auffmann's Happiness Machine, the Green Machine (the only electric car in town), and the retired trolley.

Until the summer's toll, Douglas typified the members of his race in believing that he was immortal. Now, unexpectedly, time and death have come to collect, and they must be reckoned with. The scene containing the foregoing passage shows Douglas an unresolved mixture of defiance and resignation. It also foreshadows his own near-fatal encounter with death. Abed in his room, he is swept into unconsciousness by a fever as "killing hot" as the August month. Powerless to cure him, his family can only pray for the languishing boy now lost in a limbo fraught with hallucinations and spectres.

In desperation, Tom appeals to someone he knows will have the special cure for his brother: Mr. Jonas, the junkman. Mr. Jonas has a hoard of treasures in the guise of junk to swap or give away. As an all-round good Samaritan, he is also known to have remedies for affliction, to give people rides in his wagon, to deliver babies, to keep sleepless souls company till dawn. Bradbury suggests that he is unworldly, wise, and benevolent.

In response to Tom's appeal, the local sage diagnoses Douglas's ailment. Douglas, he claims, was born to suffer emotionally. He is one of those special people who "bruise easier, tire faster, cry quicker, remember longer." Without hesitation, Mr. Jonas concocts a miracle in the form of aromatic spirits of rare and wholesome air, vintage winds and breezes like "green dusk for dreaming," blended with assorted fruits and herbs, the various sweet plants of earth. Then without witnesses or fanfare and in the secrecy of deep night, he leaves his brew for Douglas to inhale, literally to inspire. Revived, restored, and returned to the land of the living, Douglas exhales the spellbinding breath of his redemption, a blend of "cool night and cool water and cool white snow and cool green moss, and moonlight on silver pebbles lying at the bottom of a quiet river and cool clear water at the bottom of a small white stone wall" (*Wine*, 221). Appropriately, both the solution that enables Douglas to survive the crisis of mortality and the person who administers it are extraordinary. The elixir and Mr. Jonas belong to a dimension where enchantment is the norm.

In "The Man Upstairs," a short story not part of the collection in *Dandelion Wine*, 11-year-old Douglas Spaulding single-handedly uncovers the incredible identity of "something not-human" that comes in the guise of a boarder to live with him in his grandparents' house. Immediately he instinctively dislikes the grim, black-garbed Mr. Koberman whose forbidding presence changes the very character of his room. Sensing something "alien and brittle," Douglas wonders about the stranger who works at night and sleeps by day, who uses his own wooden cutlery at meals, and who carries only new copper pennies in his pockets. One of Bradbury's most original devices becomes the means by which Douglas, with uncanny detection, reveals the "vampire" or "monster" presumably responsible for the "peculiar" deaths in town. On the landing between the first and second floors there is an "enchanted" stained-glass window where in the early mornings, Douglas stands "entranced," "peering at the world through multicolored windows." One morning he happens to see Mr. Koberman on his way home and Douglas is shocked by what he sees:

> The glass *did* things to Mr. Koberman. His face, his suit, his hands. The clothes seemed to melt away. Douglas almost believed, for one terrible instant, that he could see *inside* Mr. Koberman. And what

he saw made him lean wildly against the small red pane, blinking. (*October Country*, 216)

After Koberman deliberately breaks the magic window, Douglas turns the panes into instruments of revelation with a dexterity worthy of his grandmother's expertise with chickens. Watching grandmother, "a kindly, gentle-faced, white-haired old witch," clean and dress chickens is one of Douglas's "prime thrills" in life. His delight and curiosity during her regular preparation of the birds partly explains the inspiration for his imaginative, intrepid, and resourceful method of destroying the unnatural Koberman. Douglas's fascination is significant. There, amid "twenty knives in the various squeaking drawers of the magic kitchen table," he is absorbed as grandmother performs her art.

In this story, young Douglas, like his older version in *Dandelion Wine*, takes life head-on, fearing nothing. Like his grandmother, he calmly and adroitly vivisects Koberman. Inside the creature he discovers an assortment of strange objects of all shapes and sizes: a smelly bright orange elastic square with four blue tubes and a "bright pink linked chain with a purple triangle at one end." Everything he finds is pliable and resilient with the consistency of gelatin. When he sees that the monster is still alive after the operation, Douglas uses "six dollars and seventy cents worth of silver dimes," the total amount in his bank, to kill him. Without hysteria or commotion—indeed, as though destroying something unnatural was the most natural act in the world—Douglas merely tells his grandfather that he has something to show him. "It's not nice, but it's interesting." To the adults, the Koberman episode is heinous—a "ghastly affair," according to Grandfather. Douglas, in contrast, is the willful innocent whose attraction to the inscrutable and aversion to the sinister stranger ordained his action. He can only wonder why it should be "bad" because he does not see or feel anything bad.

The authorities agree that Douglas's act was not murder but rather a "mercy." When Douglas speculates on the matter, he proudly appraises his handiwork and compares it to his grandmother's skill: "All in all, Mr. Koberman was as neat a job as any chicken ever popped into hell by Grandma." His complete lack of shock or terror recalls how his grandfather had teased him about being a "cold-blooded little pepper" and a "queer duck." Ironically, his composure is as unnatural from an adult point of view as his victim was to adults and children alike. Throughout the story Bradbury shows that Douglas is indisposed by Koberman's presence and habits, as well as intrigued and repelled by his strangeness. These factors, combined with his fascination with the ritual carnage in his grandmother's kitchen, prompt his self-styled liberties with life and death. In *Dandelion Wine* Douglas celebrates with radiant subjectivity the sanctity of life in nature and humanity; in "The Man Upstairs" he exhibits an unabashed objective preoccupation with living organisms and their vital processes, from the lowly chicken to a lowly subhuman grotesque. Any means justify his ends. That Koberman is a menace does not seem to be as imperative to him as the irrefutable fact of Koberman's difference, his essential alienness. Douglas's audacity and imperturbability are a strain of the ruthlessness we find full-blown in the children Bradbury creates in "The Veldt," "The Small Assassin," and "Let's Play 'Poison'." The children of these three stories destroy adults who threaten their autonomy. In "The Man Upstairs" Douglas plays judge and executioner only secondarily, or incidentally, to satisfy his curiosity, eliminate a nuisance, and practice, as his grandmother's disciple, his version of fowl butchery.

If the Green Town that Douglas and Tom Spaulding inhabit is a latter-day Arcady—a summer idyll, even with the changes and losses of 1928—then the Green Town that James Nightshade and William Halloway inhabit is "October Country." The town of *Something Wicked This Way Comes* is singled out for a visit by a pair of underworlders who run a sinister circus out of season. Will's father recalls an old religious tract which explains the origins of Cooger and Dark and sets the tone for the events of the novel:

> "For these beings, fall is the ever normal season, the only weather, there be no choice beyond. Where do they come from? The dust. Where do they go? The grave. Does blood stir in their veins? No: the night wind. What ticks in their head? The worm. What speaks from their mouth? The toad. What sees from their eye? The snake. What hears with their ear? The abyss between the stars. They sift the human storm for souls, eat flesh of reason, fill tombs with sinners. They frenzy forth. In gusts they beetle-scurry, creep, thread, filter, motion, make all moons sullen, and surely cloud all clear-run waters. The spider-web hears them, trembles—breaks. Such are the autumn people. Beware of them." (*Wicked*, 142)

To underscore this motif, Bradbury has created as his principal characters two boys who are native to the season, born two minutes apart on Halloween. Their names—Halloway and especially Nightshade—are thematically meaningful. Close by nativity, next-door neighbors, and best friends, they are, nevertheless, a study in contrasts. Will is "one human all good," the offspring of a "man half-bad and a woman half-bad" who "put their good halves together." His surname serves as a characternym: Halloway. He goes a *hallowed* way. Will is trusting and sunny. The elder Halloway ponders the difference between his son and Jim, and marks Will's innocence:

... he's the last peach, high on a summer tree. Some boys walk by and you cry, seeing them. They feel food, they are good ... you know, seeing them pass, that's how they'll be all their life; they'll get hit, hurt, cut, bruised, and always wonder why, why does it happen? how can it happen to *them*? (*Wicked*, 14)

Jim Nightshade, in contrast, is intense, enigmatic, and high-powered. A natural scamp, he is always ready for adventure, particularly under cover of darkness. Bradbury declares that "no one else in the world had a name came so well off the tongue." Indeed, an intensity and quality of darkness consonant with his surname pervade his visage and temperament. Charles Halloway wonders:

Why are some people grasshopper fiddlings, scrapings, all antennae shivering, one big ganglion eternally knotting, slip-knotting, square-knotting themselves? They stoke a furnace all their lives, sweat their lips, shine their eyes and start it all in the crib. Caesar's lean and hungry friends. They eat the dark, who only stand and breathe.

That's Jim, all bramblehair and itchweed. (*Wicked*, 14)

Jim is the perpetual and spirited seeker who, around his widowed mother, is absent-spirited and reserved. Everywhere he gives off a steely resolve to outrace time. Similar to Joe Pipkin in *The Halloween Tree* and John Huff in *Dandelion Wine*, Jim is descended from Mercury. His feet are winged, and running is his natural means of locomotion. Enchantment is his psychic milieu. Compelled by a smoldering passion for experience, he is reminiscent of Hermann Hesse's Demian: "as primeval, animal, marble, beautiful and cold ... secretly filled with fabulous life."[8] In his isolation and independence, Jim ranges the town like a demon—not exactly supernatural but elusive and a shade more than human; he is intermediate between the extra-human and the human. "Marbled with dark," Jim is "the kite, the wild twine cut ... as high and dark and suddenly strange." Better than anyone else, Will understands their differences:

And running, Will thought, Boy, it's the same old thing. I talk. Jim runs. I tilt stones, Jim grabs the cold junk under the stones and—lickety-split! I climb hills, Jim yells off church steeples. I got a bank account, Jim's got the hair on his head, the yell in his mouth, the shirt on his back and the tennis shoes on his feet. How come I think he's richer? Because, Will thought, I sit on a rock in the sun and old Jim, he prickles his arm-hairs by moonlight and dances with hoptoads. I tend cows. Jim tames Gila monsters. Fool! I yell at Jim. Coward! he yells back. (*Wicked*, 35)

Although they are as different as night and day, together Will and Jim form an invincible yet vulnerable brotherhood. They combine bright simplicity and dark complexity. Living within the sanctioned circle of home and the larger sphere of the town, they conspire to venture beyond the narrow world of adults. To resist enslavement to an orderly, predictable existence, they cavort on the outskirts of Green Town where Rolfe's Moon Meadow becomes the wilderness equivalent of the ravine in *Dandelion Wine*. In contrast to the group in *Dandelion Wine* and the larger tribe of nine in *The Halloween Tree*, there are only two representatives of Bradbury's separate race in *Something Wicked This Way Comes*. The curious cult formed by the two boys in *Something Wicked* is all the more dramatic for its polarities, which heighten the efficacy of their bond. Will and Jim join the tender and the firm, the bold and the gentle.

The pursuits and pastimes of this doughty pair usually occur under the protection of the moon, when they "softly printed the night with treads," like creatures liberated and afoot when most human beings sleep. Brothers of nocturnal creatures similar to the wind, "they felt wings on their fingers" and "plunged in new sweeps of air" to fly to their destination. All of Bradbury's boys are glorious runners; in spirit they are a cross between bird and man.

To observe their rites and ceremonies, Will and Jim use private signals and symbols. They "prefer to chunk dirt at clapboards, hurl acorns down roof shingles, or leave mysterious notes flapping from kites stranded on attic window sills." Their most elaborate strategy derives from a relic pine-plank boardwalk that Will's grandfather preserved in the alley between the houses. The boys have contrived to make it into a transmitter, a crude but ingenious and serviceable apparatus on which one or the other summons his partner to leave his bedroom and descend the iron rungs embedded in the house and hidden by the ivy. "Ulmers" and "goffs" are examples of another way Will and Jim communicate. These are code words for the ugly, evil creatures that invade their sleep, souring dreams into nightmares.

The only place in Green Town that can match their double-duty imagination is the library where Charles Halloway works. For the boys it is "a factory of spices from far countries," fabulous with accounts of both real and fictitious events to transport them from the ordinary to the extraordinary. Yet nothing heroic or cataclysmic recorded in books can match the dreadful events that befall Will and Jim when Cooger and Dark's Pandemonium Shadow Show comes like a plague to town. Well named, the carnival of devastation is operated by two immortal hellhounds who have been wreaking their horrors every twenty to forty years for at least a hundred years.

On an ominous night in October the theater of evil arrives, heralded by a poster-hanger plaintively singing a Christmas carol. The "terrified elation" of Charles Halloway portends the doom bearing down on him, his son, Jim, Miss Foley the teacher, Mr. Crosetti the barber, and other unwary residents. Bradbury chooses the "special hour" of 3:00 A.M. when "the soul is out" and it is "a long way back to sunset, a far way on to dawn" for the coming of the circus train. It pulls into Rolfe's Moon Meadow to the infernal wail of a play-erless calliope which sounds like church music unnervingly changed.

Will and Jim respond to the train whistle, summoning thoughts of the "grieving sounds" that all trains make in the deep of night. Accompanied by fluttering black pennants and black confetti, the carnival's whistle is more poignant than any the boys had ever heard. Bradbury uses enchantment to catch the boys' attitude toward the whistle that sounds like "the wails of a life-time," "the howl of moon-dreamed dogs," "a thousand fire sirens weeping, or worse." The calamitous sound is so excruciating that Will and Jim shriek and scream, lurch and writhe in involuntary concert with the lament, like "groans of a billion people dead or dying."

Pursuing the sound, they watch as Mr. Dark, another of Bradbury's illus-trated characters, emerges "all dark suit, shadow-faced" and gestures the train to life. The awed witnesses hardly dare to believe their eyes, but at the same time they are too engrossed to doubt what they behold. From its unnatural beginnings, Will and Jim know that what has come to town is no ordinary circus. When the tents materialize from fragments of the night sky and not canvas, they know the circus is worse than strange; it is wrong.

The hell on wheels that passes for a circus will test the boys' innocence, their "patterns of grace," with diabolical amusements and attractions. One is the fatal Mirror Maze, "like winter standing tall, waiting to kill you with a glance." Another is the "lunatic carousel" that runs backwards, unwinding the years, or forward, whirling them ahead, to leave the rider changed in size but unchanged inside, either too young or too old in body for a brain that stood still. To their horror, Will and Jim find that the seller of lightning rods, who at the beginning of the story sells Jim an elaborate model, has been transformed by Cooger and Dark into a dwarf, "his eyes like broken splinters of brown marble now bright-on-the-surface, now deeply mournfully forever-lost-and-gone-buried-away mad."

The carnival thrives on human sensuality, vanities, cravings, fantasies, and nightmares. Bradbury intimates that the boys' salvation derives from their attributes as members of his separate race. The ordeal they undergo in resisting the perverse attractions of the Shadow Show proves their fortuity as innocents. Unlike the adults who succumb, they withstand the atrocious marvels of the carnival and survive the vengeance of Mr. Dark. The depraved Cooger and Dark are dealers in phantasms. As agents of Satan, they range the world to ensnare and afflict the souls of the weak and gullible. With Charles Halloway as his spokesman, Bradbury explains that Cooger and Dark are monsters who have "learned to live off souls." People, he conjectures, "jump at the chance to give up everything for nothing." Souls are, above all, free for the taking, because most people do not understand or appreciate what they give away "slapstick" until it is lost.

The side-show freaks were all "sinners who've taken on the shape of their original sins." They have been damned to live as physical representatives of the sins they practiced before encountering Cooger and Dark. Tortured by guilty consciences, they are "madmen waiting to be released from bondage, meantime servicing the carnival, giving it coke for its ovens." The cast of grotesques and list of their transgressions outnumber the Seven Deadly Sins. In contrast to these poor wretches, Will and Jim possess certain natural virtues, chiefly justice and fortitude, as well as three theological virtues—faith, hope, and charity. Even so, everyone has it in him or her, Halloway cautions, to be an autumn person. Children like Will and Jim are still summer people, "rare" and "fine."

Here, as in *Dandelion Wine*, Bradbury delineates children's relationship with time. In *Something Wicked This Way Comes* he enlarges and distorts the symbols that stand for the preoccupations of adults. One is the mirror with which they worship appearances, while another is chance, or fortune, which they court as Lady Luck. Allegorically, the carnival shows how such instruments and behavior can warp their lives and lead them to perdition. In the story adults who rely on appearances and who gamble with destiny are lured by the Mirror Maze, the Dust Witch, and the wayward carousel. All are distorted expressions of human superficiality and frivolity. As members of the race of children, Will and Jim are neither victims of vanity nor fatalists. Gamboling apace of time, they are not slowed by dependence on the past nor driven by pursuit of the future. Unlike the acts and amusements of the carnival, their games and escapades are harmless. They escape from Cooger and Dark because they are integral personalities. They are innocent because they are free of sin, and this is their ultimate protection.

In Bradbury's modern variation on a morality play, Cooger and Dark perpetrate a studiously false fantasy world, grotesque and lethal. Timeless villains, they represent time deranged. But their ministry of evil is challenged by two boys whose spontaneous whim-wham and sportive spirits overcome their machinations. As Charles Halloway says, "sometimes good has weapons and evil none." He can only stand back and marvel at the boys, in loving envy of their characteristics as a breed. He knows very well that while he can advise them, he cannot share their camaraderie and freedom.

Chapters 29 and 30 are a surprising switch. Until then, one senses that Jim is the leader, the one who initiates action, the real daredevil of the two. Indeed, he does hear "ticks from clocks" that tell "another time"; but it is Will whose courage and inventiveness foil the Dust Witch sent by Dark to find out where the boys live. When her balloon approaches, they know that

> She could dip down her hands to feel the bumps of the world, touch house roofs, probe attic bins, reap dust, examine draughts that blew through halls and souls that blew through people, draughts vented from bellows to thump-wrist, to pound-temples, to pulse-throat, and back to bellows again. (*Wicked*, 105)

Although scared, Will plays his hunch and jumps lively. He uses the garden hose to wash away the "silver-slick" ribbon the Dust Witch paints on the roof of Jim's house to mark it for easy detection when Dark comes to capture them. But that is only a partial solution, for Will knows that the witch is still aloft, ready to return to the meadow and report to Dark. Armed with his Boy Scout bow and arrows, he challenges the witch to a kind of match. His plan is to lure her to an empty house and there, atop its roof, shoot her balloon with an arrow and puncture it. But his bow breaks before he can discharge an arrow. Undaunted, he throws the arrowhead at the balloon and slits the surface of the "gigantic pear" as "dungeon air raved out, as dragon breath gushed forth. "Alone, Will defeats the Dust Witch, though he nearly breaks his neck in the process.

The determination and defiance that Will exhibits in this episode pave the way for the desperate antics of he and his father when Jim's life is at stake. Believing Jim dead, Will bursts into tears, only to be urged by his father to vent another kind of hysteria—the madness and hilarity of absolute defiance:

> " . . . Damn it, Willy, all this, all these, Mr. Dark and his sort, they *like* crying, my God, they *love* tears! Jesus God, the more you bawl, the more they drink the salt off your chin. Wail and they suck your breath like cats. Get up! Get off your knees, damn it! Jump around! Whoop and holler! You hear! Shout, Will, sing, but most of all laugh, you got that, laugh!" (*Wicked*, 208)

Will and his father resurrect Jim with levity, not gravity—with mirth, not lamentation. Their rhapsody and bombast—indeed, their grandiosity—is Dionysian: redemption in revelry.

Like Douglas Spaulding's cure, Jim Nightshade's revival is miraculous. Cooger and Dark are destroyed and their captive freaks are liberated. The boys emerge from the meadow unscathed. They are "exultant" as they leave the wilderness behind. Together with Charles Halloway, they bang "a trio of shouts down the wind."

In "Jack-in-the-Box" and "The Veldt," Bradbury has created two technologically advanced houses which are the center of life for several of his young characters. In the first story, Edwin's explorations take place in a vast house designed as a substitute for the natural world. Unlike the wilderness of the ravine in *Dandelion Wine* and the meadow in *Something Wicked This Way Comes*, the interior geography of "Jack-in-the-Box" is precisely circumscribed and carefully controlled. What's more, Edwin's access to the various regions is rigidly prescribed. On each birthday he is allowed to enter another part of the house. The second story has a house equipped with a psychoramic playroom. There Wendy and Peter Hadley can range anywhere in the world. Dominance of one species by another is an important aspect of both stories. In "Jack-in-the-Box," adults are the overlords until the end, whereas, in "The Veldt," the Hadley parents abdicate their authority to the superhouse which, in cahoots with the children, conspires to win complete dominance.

The only world Edwin has ever known is the multi-storied domain built by his late father as a self-sufficient hideaway and bulwark against the world at large. Perhaps more than any other child in Bradbury's fiction, Edwin is an innocent incarcerated by adult neuroses, subjugated by the delusions and defenses erected as compensation by adults in retreat from life. Like his toy, the jack-in-the-box, he is confined, even trapped.

His dying mother (who, unbeknown to him, doubles as his teacher) has nurtured him on the legend of a godlike father destroyed by society, whose legacy is the universe of the house, safely cloistered in a wilderness tract beyond the deadly clutches of the "Beasts." He is taught that a circumscribed existence in the house means life and happiness but that death awaits him beyond the dense circle of trees which make the estate an enclave. His indoctrination makes everything—most of all, himself—fit into place:

> Here, in the Highlands, to the soft sound of Teacher's voice running on, Edwin learned what was expected of him and his body. He was to grow into a Presence, he must fit the odors and the trumpet voice of God. He must some day stand tall and burning with pale fire at this high window to shout dust off the beams of the Worlds; he must be God Himself! Nothing must prevent it. Not the sky or the trees or the Things beyond the trees. (*October Country*, 161)

We learn from his mother's cryptic remarks that Edwin's father was killed (before Edwin's birth)—"struck down by one of those Terrors on the road." Her attitude and admonitions are thinly veiled denunciations of the way human beings have turned their machines, chiefly automobiles, into weapons of destruction.

In describing Edwin, Bradbury creates the image of a lonely, delicate boy. Like his mother, Edwin is otherworldly. Pensive and luminous, he is an *isolato* who wanders among the artificial climates of the house:

> And her child, Edwin, was the thistle that one breath of wind might unpod in a season of thistles. His hair was silken and his eyes were of a constant blue and feverish temperature. He had a haunted look, as if he slept poorly. He might fly apart like a packet of ladyfinger firecrackers if a certain door slammed. (*October Country*, 157)

His isolation from others of his race, however, has not repressed or weakened the attributes he shares with boys like Douglas Spaulding and Jim Nightshade. Shut in though he is, he is a latent leaper and runner whose agitation is a prelude to flight and reason. Not even the persistent legend of his mighty father and the house that will someday be his kingdom can quell his curiosity about the outside. When he longs to see the Beasts, we know that his mother's systematic attempts to inculcate a fear of society have failed. The house, too, has failed, for Edwin's unrest implies that a child's mind and emotions thrive when, unrestrained, he is free to grow where his imagination and feet lead him. Edwin's curiosity also suggests that the seemingly ideal setting created by adults is inadequate. In creating their own playgrounds, children are architects whose imaginary constructs and original renovations do not need to conform to conventions and rules.

On the day when Edwin finds his mother dead, he flees from the house and garden world to run jubilantly among the "Terrors" and "Beasts" of town, touching everything he can reach, filling his eyes and mind with life. In a world wondrously new to him, he is finally free, like the jack-in-the-box he liberates by throwing it out of the house. Joining his counterparts in Bradbury's other stories, Edwin exults in the flux of time, awash in its tides, reborn on its crest.

"The Veldt," "The Small Assassin," and "Let's Play 'Poison'" are a trio of stories with diabolical children. Together, they comprise a fiendish tribe within the separate race. In "The Veldt," Bradbury takes up the theme of the insidious struggle for total power and control that children wage behind the facade of innocence. Though only ten years old, Wendy and Peter Hadley know that their parents are a mortal threat to the real and imaginary geographies which they can project in their electronically cosmic nursery. When George and Lydia Hadley begin to worry about their children's obsession with a particular setting, George insists that they have nothing to fear from a purely mechanical wonder that is "dimensional superreactionary, supersensitive color film and mental tape film behind glass screens." His sophisticated terminology, however, does not explain the children's keen interest in the recurring veldt scene. The children's psychological alienation has produced the reality of Africa. Each time they project their wishes, the veldt materializes with greater intensity, until it is fully animated and empowered to serve their ends.

The Hadley's Happylife Home—the complete home of the future—has usurped their role. Supremely attentive to all the needs of the children and their parents, the house has advanced technological means for disaffecting the children. The playroom, in particular, has succeeded in its takeover by systematically fulfilling their fantasies. In its role as surrogate, it provides a reliable escape to exotic lands for Wendy and Peter. But the African projection stops being child's play when it becomes a daily rehearsal for parental carnage.

The correspondence between the names of James Barrie's memorable characters in *Peter Pan* and those of Bradbury's children cannot be coincidental. In both works of fiction, Wendy and Peter are devotees of never-never land, a dimension that is beyond the constraints and conventions imposed on demanding, if not persecuting, adults, and which is outside the limitations and changes decreed by time. In "The Veldt," Wendy and Peter go beyond the point of no return. The vengeance they wreak on their parents leaves them unaffected and undisturbed. Afterward, when David McClean, a psychologist and family friend, finds them nonchalantly and cheerfully picnicking in the savage setting they have stimulated, they show no signs of remorse or guilt. They are unholy terrors for whom expediency and self-preservation are the sole dictates of behavior. Like the baby in the next story, they are amoral and conscience-free.

The unnamed infant in "The Small Assassin" is the most precocious terror of the lot. Even before his birth his mother has undeniable intimations of his deadly intentions. Vainly, Alice Leiber tries to tell David, his father, how "vulnerable" they are to him, because "it's too young to know love, or a law of love ... so new, so amoral, so conscience-free." With cunning treachery the baby murders Alice and later, David. After Alice's death, David theorizes about the unconscionable cause and effect. He maintains that the infant is motivated by hate for being expelled from his mother's womb into a precarious existence at the mercy of adults. He sees the baby as only one of possibly countless infant aliens—"strange, red little creatures with brains that work in a bloody darkness we can't even guess at." David argues that they have "elemental little brains, aswarm with racial memory, hatred, and raw cruelty, with no more thought than self-preservation." His speculations force him to conclude that his son is a freak, preternaturally "born perfectly aware, able to think, instinctively." Like insects and animals, he was at birth capable of certain functions which normally develop gradually:

> "Wouldn't it be a perfect setup, a perfect blind for anything the baby might want to do? He could pretend to be ordinary, weak, crying, ignorant. With just a *little* expenditure of energy he could crawl about a darkened house, listening. And how easy to place obstacles at the top of stairs. How easy to cry all night and tire a mother into pneumonia. How easy, right at birth, to be so close to the mother that *a few deft maneuvers might cause peritonitis!*" (*October Country*, 141)

The family doctor, who is a staunch advocate of a "thousand years of accepted medical belief," persists in believing that the child is "helpless, not responsible." Not until the infant turns on the gas in his father's room and asphyxiates him does the horrified Dr. Jeffers admit that the Leiber baby is an unnatural, scheming menace who must be stopped. In extrapolating the infant's motivation from reasonable psychological theory, Bradbury conjectures that all children have the potential for Baby Leiber's destructive *élan vital*.

In the last story of this unsettling trio, Bradbury depicts children per se as antagonists. In the opening scene sixteen children maliciously and capriciously send one of their classmates to his death from a third-floor window. Mr. Howard, their teacher, is appalled, and resigns after suffering a nervous breakdown. It is he who most clearly articulates Bradbury's position: "Sometimes, I actually believe that children are invaders from another dimension." The authorities dismiss the event as an accident, contending that the children could not have understood what they did. Howard, made irascible if not paranoid by the tragedy, disputes this. He believes he knows the terrible truth:

> " ... sometimes I believe children are little monsters thrust out of hell, because the devil could no longer cope with them. And I certainly believe that everything should be done to reform their uncivil little minds....
>
> "You are another race entirely, your motives, your beliefs, your disobediences. ... You are not human. You are—children."[9]

To Howard's way of thinking, all children belong to a cult of aliens. Subterfuge and subversion are their natural modus operandi. Their choice of playgrounds is sufficient evidence, for they love "excavations, hiding-places, pipes, and conduits and trenches." If Howard knew the Spaulding brothers and the other boys in *Dandelion Wine*, he would acknowledge with considerable horror but no surprise that their favorite haunt, the ravine, is a no-man's land fit only for subhuman creatures. Certainly he would count Jim Nightshade and Will Halloway among the race of little aliens, because they love to reconnoiter at night. Howard decided that even children's games are fiendish. Hopscotch, for example, is hardly what it seems to adults. The figures drawn on the ground are actually pentagrams. Other sports are accompanied not by innocent rhymes but by incantations disguised by sometimes sweet yet often taunting voices.

The morbid game through which Howard is perversely immortalized is called "Poison." His introduction to this pastime with its dead men, graves, and poison—only confirms his convictions about children. His dread of children inspires dread in the children who know him. The animosity is reciprocal. The mischief they cause in retaliation to his outbursts and attacks is inevitable, and vice versa. The open conflict precipitates Howard's doom when, in pursuit of his tormentors, he falls into an excavation and is buried alive. The cement square that later covers the spot bears the not-so-accidental inscription: "M. Howard—R.I.P." Alive, he was the adversary of a race whose members were his nemesis. Dead, he is profaned whenever they dance on his makeshift grave as they play "Poison."

* * *

As a separate race, Bradbury's children are uninhibited earthly creatures with an unalloyed, undiluted exuberance. Their innocence enables them to transcend the forces that influence and often control the lives of adults. In his fiction, children live and move in a dimension where they are generally exempt from the dilemmas that afflict their elders. Each sphere of activity—home, town, wilderness—has heightened or enhanced elements which, to them, give it a psychological credence that it does not possess for the adults with whom they share it.

Unlike their parents, Bradbury's children are not hounded by time. All things considered, it's as though they course in tune with time in all its seasons. Unthreatened by a sense of mutability and mortality, they have a capacity for unequivocal, immediate action that is neither complicated nor diminished by the second thoughts which lead adults to prudence, apprehension, or indecision. The impulsive spontaneous behavior of Bradbury's boys is seldom spoiled by conscience, for egocentricity is their prime mover.

The adults they treat with disdain are people whose authenticity they doubt. The adults they respect are individuals whose lives they can romanticize and enter with vicarious abandon. For some of Bradbury's children, however, all adults are adversaries simply because they belong to another race—separate and different if only for an age. Engrossed in their own exploits or engaged in a conflict with adults to preserve their ethos, the children who inhabit Bradbury's stories might well exclaim with e. e. cummings: "we're anything brighter than even the sun."[10]

NOTES

1. "how many moments must (amazing each," in *e. e. cummings: A Selection of Poems*, New York: Harcourt, Brace, and World, 1965, p. 187.

2. cummings, "all worlds have halfsight, seeing either with," in *e. e. cummings: A Selection of Poems*, p. 188.

3. Ibid.

4. cummings, "if everything happens that can't be done," in *Poems 1923–1954*, New York: Harcourt, Brace and Company, 1954, p. 161.

5. cummings, "all worlds have halfsight, seeing either with" and "how many moments must (amazing each," in *e. e. cummings: A Selection of Poems*, pp. 187, 188.

6. Percy Bysshe Shelley, "To a Skylark," in *English Romantic Writers*, ed. David Perkins, New York: Harcourt, Brace and World, 1967, p. 1,033.

7. Ibid., p. 1,068.

8. Hermann Hesse, *Demian*, New York: Bantam Books, p. 55.

9. Ray Bradbury, "Let's Play 'Poison,'" in *The Small Assassin*, London: New English Library, 1970, p. 128.

10. e. e. cummings, "if everything happened that can't be done," in *Poems 1923–1954*, p. 161.

ROBERT PLANK

The Expedition to the Planet of Paranoia

Ray Bradbury's most famous book is not a book; *The Martian Chronicles* (1950) are chronicles in outward appearance only. Rather they are individual stories strung on a chronological line, glued together here and there with smudges of connective tissue. They were clearly written independently, and many of them were originally published separately. The book purports to relate events that took place between January 1999 and October 2026, but many of them could have taken place—as far as they could have taken place at all—at different times and in a different sequence. This is particularly true of the first three expeditions from Earth to Mars. All three of them are wiped out, each in an unconventional manner, and each of them quite differently. Each expedition anticipates a certain type of Mars inhabitant, but there is little similarity between them.

None of the survivors, Martian or Terran, learn anything from their experience. None of these expeditions leaves a trace of itself, except that when the fourth expedition arrives fourteen months after the third, its members find a town full of Martians who have been dead ten days from chicken pox (the author's device, perhaps, to make sure they will not repeat their tricks?). It is concluded that the Martians have been infected unintentionally by members of the third expedition—"and as quickly as that it was forgotten."[1] All that Earthmen can know, or care, is that the men of the third expedition landed on

From *Extrapolation* 22, no. 2 (Summer 1981): 171–85. © 1981 by The Kent State University Press.

Mars and were never heard from again. Although some geographical features are named for the more eminent among them (p. 102), these expeditions might as well never have taken place. Or, of course, they could have occurred in a different order. It is justified, therefore, to talk about "April 2000: The Third Expedition" as if it were an independent work,[2] with not more than an occasional glance at the rest of the book.

"The Third Expedition" is a short (sixteen pages in the Bantam edition) and compact story. It observes the three classical unities of place (in and around the landed spaceship), of time (from one morning to the next), and of action. Plucking many chords of emotion, it moves deftly from utter bewilderment to revelation of conflict and swiftly to catastrophe. It is a masterpiece of its type. Later, we shall consider what that type is. The story divides itself naturally into three phases: (1) the idyll—from the landing to nightfall. The pace is leisurely, and this phase takes up the bulk of the tale, about thirteen pages. (2) the murders during the night. (3) the funeral in the morning. The last two are compressed into barely three pages.

Phase One. The spaceship is arriving on Mars. It carries a crew of seventeen, but one person has died en route. We are introduced to three of the survivors: John Black, captain; Samuel Hinkston, archaeologist; Lustig, navigator (perhaps Jews will not have first names in 2000 A.D.? No, it later turns out that it is David). The other men are neither named nor otherwise individualized. Black is eighty years old, but looks like forty—science in the second half of our century has rejuvenated him. Hinkston is forty-five; Lustig fifty. The spaceship has landed on a lawn in the middle of a town that down to the last small detail (a sheet of music entitled "Beautiful Ohio" sits on a piano) looks exactly like Green Bluff, Illinois (where Captain Black was raised), of long ago. They are later informed that the town is Green Bluff, Illinois, that it was founded in 1868, and that the year is 1926 (when Black was six years old).

The minds of the three men, understandably reeling, race through all sorts of theories to comprehend the incomprehensible. Have they, through an unexpected quirk of space travel, landed on Earth instead of Mars and thereby gone back in time? Have members of the first or second expedition survived and built—in an incredibly short time—a replica of an American town? Were space travel and the colonization of Mars secretly initiated before World War I? Has a super-clever and super-powerful psychiatrist then combatted nostalgia among the colonists by "rearranging the civilization" so that it increasingly resembles Earth, until "by some vast crowd hypnosis" he has convinced everyone that it really *is* Earth?

Naturally, none of these hypotheses seems in the least plausible. The men are left in a state of stupefied bewilderment until a shattering experience provides the straw of an explanation—each encounters some aspect from his past. Lustig sees his grandparents. Hinkston espies his old house and runs to it. Black encounters his brother Edward, who conducts him to their parents. The other men, who were left behind in the ship with orders to man the guns, have meanwhile forgotten their duty, abandoned the ship, and mingled with a crowd of Martians who have festively assembled on the lawn. "Then each member of the crew, with a mother on one arm, a father or sister on the other, was spirited off down the street into little cottages or big mansions" (p. 42). And so an "explanation" of the awesome mystery is offered—through the grace of God, these deceased relatives have been given a second life, in a town on Mars that exactly duplicates their environment on Earth. By implication, the space trip has been providentially arranged to grant the sixteen Earthmen a reunion with their loved ones. The men are still confused, but they readily submit to their elders' admonitions not to question the Lord's infinite wisdom and mercy. The festivities come to an end; night falls. Groggy with happiness, the men lie down to sleep.

At this point it is perhaps appropriate to interrupt the narrative for some preliminary remarks on Phase One, be it only to note several features of the story that do not quite fit into its general sweep. No discrepancies appear at first reading, but on closer scrutiny they cannot be ignored. Though they may seem minor, they turn out to have great significance. I do not mean to say that the story as such is incredible. Of course it is. What I want to point out is that even if we accept the author's premises and treat the work as though it were a credible tale, there are still some things in the natural course of events that would have gone differently. It is for this reason that one must wonder why Bradbury placed his emphases in the curious way that he did.

When Lustig meets his grandparents, who have been dead for thirty years (in other words, they died when he was twenty) he "sounded as if at any moment he might go quite insane with happiness." He "sobbed . . . turned . . . kissed . . . hugged . . . held" (p. 40). That the men are overjoyed is natural. But is it natural for that joy to be so all-pervasive? Would anyone, suddenly coming face to face with the dead returned to life, feel nothing else? No admixture of horror, no trace of awe? No fleeting moment of resurgent animosity, no quick pang of guilt? Would a person touch the body that he saw buried years ago, without the least hesitation? Yet, in the story as told, there is not the slightest element of ambivalence. The negative feelings are totally absent. In the events that swiftly follow, however, these pent-up feelings break out with the elemental force of murderous fury.

Though the space travelers are grown, even old, men, they do not meet dead children or wives. Their reunion is with parents, grandparents, siblings—persons who died when the spacemen were young—representing ascending rather than descending relationships. Ed Black, the only sibling whose age is given, was seven years John's senior. When he died at twenty-six, John was nineteen.

They do not even think of others who may have died, or who were left behind on Earth, except for Captain Black, who fleetingly thinks of "Marilyn" (not otherwise identified). After a brief hesitation, Ed tells him that she is out of town, but will be back in the morning. The dead have not aged. They are all exactly as they were at the moment of their deaths. The same motif occurs in an even weirder form in another of the stories, "April 2026: The Long Years."

There is a similar tendency to extend time backward in the description of the town. All that nostalgia would associate with a small American town of 1926 is here: an iron deer on the lawn, popular songs of the period, Victorian architecture, a robin singing in an apple tree, a grandfather clock, a brass band, front porches, and a turkey dinner. There is a "victrola," but no radio, no telephone, no automobile. It is an old-fashioned town remembered from childhood, more quintessentially so than a town ever truly was. Furthermore, we are given to understand that all the astronauts hail from places like Green Bluff, Illinois. Of course, no one knows what the distribution of the population of the United States will be in 2000. These men, however, must have been born in our own time, and we know that now some 80 percent of the population comes from cities or suburbs.

Another motif, mental influence, is only hinted at here and will be revealed in all its devastating import in Phase Two. Seeing the town, Black finds it so similar to Green Bluff that it frightens him. Then he is informed that it *is* Green Bluff. Yet, Hinkston, the archaeologist, makes the professional judgment that no artifact there is older than 1927. Two pages later, a stranger tells them that the year they have come to is 1926. Do the men discover these things because they are sharp enough to recognize the truth, or do they become true because the men think they are true? And it is Hinkston who spins out the fantastic theory about it all being the work of a master psychiatrist who influenced minds sufficiently to create an entire culture. It is the measure of Bradbury's skill that all these motifs are muted, unobtrusive. If the reader notices them at all, he does so subliminally. It also raises a question as to whether the author's skill may have operated more unconsciously than consciously.

Phase Two. Consummate skill characterizes Bradbury's transition from Phase One to Phase Two. Day and night, life and death are not in sharper contrast than these two, but one phrase bridges the abyss between them. Captain Black shares a bed with his brother Ed, the same brass bed they had shared in life, in the same room with the college pennants and such. They lie down, "side by side, as in the days how many decades ago?" They talk a little, then fall silent.

The room was square and quiet except for their breathing.
"Good night, Ed."
A pause. "Good night, John." (p. 45)

It is that phrase, "a pause," that makes the transition. The tumbling from one joyful surprise to the next is over; the time has come to think. The shift is abrupt and complete. Phase Two has begun.

To prepare for the tremendous acceleration of his narrative, Bradbury skillfully narrows the focus. Of the sixteen men, only three are singled out for individual consideration. Then two of the three, Hinkston and Lustig drop away. The last part of Phase One is exclusively concerned with Black and his dead relatives (a residue, perhaps, of the hierarchic-patriarchic orientation so predominant in the science fiction of somewhat earlier days—if you can have the captain, why bother with lesser men?).

Phase Two consists almost entirely of Black's internal monologue. A quite new realization suddenly hits him: what if all he has lived in during this day has been a phantom world called into being by the Martians in order to destroy the invaders? That would mean that after taking all they needed to know from his mind, the Martians had conjured up the image of Green Bluff in 1926 and altered themselves to appear as the dead relatives. With their sixteen enemies safely bedded down, the Martians will spring a trap. In the night they will change back into their real selves and kill their guests.

At first Black naturally shrinks from these thoughts, but as he thinks through them, the theory becomes distressingly convincing. All the pieces fall into place, and the puzzling events assume a new, menacing meaning. He must act at once to rescue himself; for there is not a moment to lose. Unarmed, he cannot hope to subdue his pursuers, so he tries to sneak out. But what seemed to be his brother sleeping peacefully by his side has now become a Martian—wide awake, challenging him: "Captain John Black broke and ran across the room. He screamed. He screamed twice. He never reached the door" (p. 47). The long, leisurely spell of blissful illusion has been broken in one devastating moment. Like lightning, terrible and brief, truth has struck; it has brightly illuminated the scene, making everything clear in a flash, only to be extinguished by the stabs of death. But in what sense can we speak here of truth?

Any interpretation of an imaginative work like "The Third Expedition" is hazardous because it is bound to be subjective. Still, it is hard to see how anybody could read it any other way than to accept Black's last theory as the correct one; the outcome proves it. The various explanations that the men tentatively put together before they met their beloved dead are, of course, to be discarded. But even the theory that Mars is the abode of departed souls, which they dazedly accepted from their relatives, does not stand up. It was only make-believe in the purest sense of the word; the Martians made the Earthmen believe. It cannot explain why Black and his fifteen companions are murdered. Black's theory does.

To say that the theory is "correct" means that it is correct within the framework of the story. It is the premise of the story that the reunion with the dead really happened, and if we accept this, we must also accept the explanation. In other words, if we willingly accept that the astronauts landing on Mars had the experiences described in the story, then we must also accept Black's final theory. Bradbury's art has compelled us to silence the voices of critical judgment within ourselves. However, Black's theory is in fact built on several large assumptions: (1) that the Martians are able, instantaneously and without any resources but their telepathic power, to probe Black's memories, drain his mind, and know everything he has ever known; (2) that the Martians have the power to compel their victims to perceive as real an entire world around them which does not in fact exist, and to blank out most genuine reality (though they still perceive each other, they fail to perceive the bleak Martian soil where they see green lawns, etc.); (3) that though they appear as loving relatives, the Martians are, in truth, malevolent, bent on killing. These are the assumptions that form the typical world picture of the paranoiac.

Phase Three. The story could have ended with John Black never reaching the door, but instead there is a brief coda. The reader's first impression is that the conclusion is simple and fitting. The Martians have murdered the sixteen strangers, and now they bury them with appropriate rites, except that the rites are not appropriate. The only purpose of the whole phantasmagoria was to lure the Earthmen to their deaths. Having achieved this, the Martians are by themselves. There is no discernible reason for them to maintain the macabre masquerade. Yet, to some extent they do. They weep; they pretend to mourn. For what? No one is left alive whom they could want to deceive.

This "effort aimed at a void" has worried science fiction critic Jörg Hienger, who in his book *Literarische Zukunftsphantastik* devotes several pages to Phase Three. If everything on Mars that resembles Earth, he asks, is but illusion—images telepathically extracted from the minds of the astronauts and hypnotically projected back into them—who has the illusion after the men are dead? He finds the question unanswerable. Given this fact and the even weightier observation that the entire ceremony serves no purpose for the Martians—and they, after all, are the ones who have arranged it—he concludes that Bradbury here postulates an end of rationality per se, thus achieving a powerful effect of the uncanny dissolving into the comical.[3]

Hienger's analysis has the redoubtable advantage of that rigorous logic that is the pride of German philosophy, but he applies the criterion of consistency to external events when it would be more fittingly applied to the mental processes of the author (more of that later). Bradbury may simply have felt, as his readers appear to feel, that the burial is a proper and soothing ending, with its comic relief welcome after a night of horror. Phase One offered the fulfillment in fantasy of deep longings, Phase Two of deep fears.

We have come to identify with the hero, to whom these were vouchsafed; now we would want for him what we would want for ourselves should tragic death overtake us—a decent burial. How many people are there who have not drawn satisfaction from imagining their own funeral, with all those who in life offended them among the mourners—"when it's too late, you'll be sorry." This is an infinitely more banal interpretation than Hienger's, but that is no reason to reject it. The reader's first impression may not have been so far off after all.

From here there are two roads to an understanding of what "The Third Expedition" is all about. We can (1) analyze the mental processes in the characters as though these were actual persons, that is, as though Bradbury had written a case history, or a tale of people who could possibly exist and the situations to which they are compelled to react could possibly arise. Or, we can (2) consider the events as projections of the author's mind. We will take route 1 first.

Bradbury deals with three types of deviant mental functioning: illusions, defined as misinterpretations of actual perceptions (trivial optical illusions are the best-known examples); hallucinations, defined as perceptions subjectively experienced without appropriate objective stimulus (such as seeing somebody who is not there); and delusions, defined as false judgments without rational basis (the belief of a psychotic that he is Jesus Christ is a popular example). The hallucinating person may be aware to various degrees that his senses deceive him. The hallucination raises a question, though no answer may be forthcoming. Delusions provide answers, though there may have been no obvious question. The men, faced with the hallucinations that provide the foundation of Phase One, look frantically for an answer. In Phase Two, they find one.

The lines between these three types of malfunctioning are fluid, and there are mixed forms. There is also an infinite variety in degree of firmness and impact, from the hardly noticeable to the overpowering. In fact, illusions, hallucinations, and delusions can only be called deviations or malfunctions in the sense that an ideally operating mental apparatus would be free of them. But nobody's is. They occur fleetingly in normal life. They may be provoked in more substantial form by various kinds of illness, by drugs, or by any stress. Only in their more malignant forms do they become indicative of physical or mental illness.

Phase One is saturated with hallucinations. A web so complete that it covers the entire scene and blots out almost all normal perception does not exist in reality, so it is unavoidable that the men look for an agent beyond human experience to have caused the phenomenon. Two questions arise. Why do the men shift from their original attitude of thinking of the cause as a benevolent agent (Hinkston proclaims at an early stage that "certainly a town like this could not occur without divine intervention") to the assumption of a radically malevolent agent? And why is the "good" agent seen as supernatural ("divine intervention") while the evil one ("incredibly brilliant" Martians) is not?

In deciding that his experiences are the work of a superhuman power, Black follows, though unaware, a hoary tradition. Primitive men attributed all extraordinary events to the action of superhuman beings—spirits, demons, gods. The external appearance of these imagined beings was an unequivocal revelation of their nature; the inimical ones among them were of ghastly ugliness. We have only to look at idols that men did not adore, but rather tried to propitiate to find proof. These idols entered Christianity and the tradition of Western civilization condensed in the form of the Devil. He is still surpassingly ugly. His suspect exterior has rubbed off on literature and the arts. The villain in many popular nineteenth-century novels and plays is invariably recognizable for what he is. The young girl he wants to seduce, exploit, and ruin is incarnate innocence. Modern audiences wonder how she can be so naïve that she is not immediately warned by his black moustache and shifty eyes. But we have not always done much better. The beings that have replaced the Devil are still monsters. J.R.R. Tolkien, who consciously harks back to the Middle Ages, holds a middle line: the good are not necessarily the beautiful, but those on the side of Sauron are, as the saying has it, ugly as Hell.

Growing sophistication has wrought a fundamental change in another respect. Men, now believing that they have a soul that matters more than the body, are no longer annihilated by brute force. The frontal assault is detoured through their minds. The Devil, who in the medieval version wrung Dr. Faustus' neck as though he were killing a chicken, now works by seduction. He is not only the Prince of Darkness but also the Father of Lies. His principal "lie" is his ability to deceive his victims by setting all they desire before their eyes—by making them hallucinate. Legends are full of such instances.

It is a wide jump in time, but not much of a leap in substance from here to "The Third Expedition." What has happened is that the poor Devil has been secularized. In our enlightened age, we find it easier to believe in malignant octopuses on Mars than in him. God has also been secularized (in Arthur C. Clarke's *2001*, for instance, His role has been reassigned to the slabs and their masters), but not as completely. Belief in Him is still widespread and respectable. So, it does not jar that Black believes in God, but not in the Devil; that when he needs to postulate a benign influence he resorts to the idea of divine intervention, and when he needs to postulate an evil one, he turns to the Martians. But why does he have to switch from good to evil at all? Here it is instructive to consider Bradbury's immediate forerunners.

To postulate alien intelligences endowed with the hallucinogenic power that earlier ages reserved for the Devil and his cohorts is commonplace in science fiction; so much so that Hienger goes as far as to think that any alert reader versed in science fiction will have anticipated the solution long before Black proclaims it (which would be a pity, since suspense would be gone). In *Seekers of Tomorrow*, Sam Moskowitz cites two more direct precursors, both strikingly similar to Bradbury's tale: Campbell's *Brain Stealers of Mars* (1936) and especially Stanley G. Weinbaum's "A Martian Odyssey" (1934). Weinbaum's desert octopus (or whatever it is—he refers to it as "the Dream-Beast" or simply "the black horror") has undisputably the same hallucinogenic powers that make Captain Black's adversaries so formidable and uses them to similar sinister ends. It is more enlightening, though, to review the differences in Bradbury's and Weinbaum's treatment of the same motif.

Weinbaum uses it in one of many equally incredible adventures. He does not seem to know what jewel he holds in his hands, giving it away so lightly. The event remains without consequence. The loyal Martian "ostrich" protects the hero from succumbing to the lure, as in effect this intended victim remains indestructible through all his harrowing experiences. With Bradbury, the hallucinogenic power is squarely the core of the plot, and it is victorious. Resistance is impossible. Far from being inconsequential, the stratagem is decisive. The hallucination is less complete in Weinbaum's tale—the baiting apparition stands in an otherwise unaffected Martian landscape—while in Bradbury's the hallucination is all-embracing. Weinbaum has the alien power more or less reveal itself in defeat, but with Bradbury it remains, in victory, beyond perception. Its lack of shape and the absence of hints as to its nature enhance the uncanny atmosphere in "The Third Expedition."

There is a more fundamental difference: the role of the hallucinated person in the life of the victim. Weinbaum's character, Jarvis, thinks of Fancy Long, a New York entertainer on the as yet uninvented television, who is evidently a flirt. He may have had an affair with her, but all he will say is, "I know her pretty well—just friends, get me?" Do we get him? That was published in 1934. In any event, she clearly represents normal, conventional, adult heterosexual attraction. Things are totally different on Bradbury's Mars. Overt sexuality is absent and is kept out by the incest barrier: since all the beloved dead are blood relatives, there are no friends or "just friends." Rather, the relationship is anchored in the victim's childhood, long before adult love relationships could emerge. Moreover, the relatives are all dead, while Fancy Long is very much alive.

The comparison with Weinbaum's story makes the core of Phase One even clearer than the oddities we noted earlier. Phase One is a regression to childhood. The ambivalence of childhood was absent, having been repressed in passage to adolescence. Such ambivalence, however much of it there may have been in actual childhood, has no place in remembered childhood. Time has come to a standstill—as it always does in the unconscious. When we dream of a person we have not seen since childhood, we see him as he was then, not as we know he is now. The mental influencing, too, fits more naturally into the outlook of a child, since so much of his experience is of being manipulated by beings more powerful and of more penetrating intelligence than he is.

We are now in a position to see why the shift from the benign to the malign was unavoidable. It was the reaction to the fling beyond human limits that is embodied in Phase One. The dynamics of human development do not permit going backwards. But in Phase One the men *have* gone back, have indulged in regression. The overwhelming bliss they feel stems from their being allowed to wallow without restraint in regression. E. P. Bernabeu, author of one of the few psychological studies on science fiction stresses this point in a passage devoted to "The Third Expedition": "The reliving of his 'happiest moments' is evidently in the author's plot a form of autistic gratification for which the condign punishment of the 'explorers' is their destruction."[4] This somewhat theoretical formulation is supplemented by observation on actual behavior. People love to "go back to childhood," certainly, but it has to be a prettified childhood. Disneyland and its numberless imitations are huge successes. They reconstruct childhood fantasies. When it comes to a more real reliving of childhood, people hesitate. They shy away from psychoanalysis, but also from more mundane endeavors. The newspapers reported in June, 1977, that the inventor of Kitty Litter had developed Jones, Michigan, into a replica, as faithful as possible, of a typical town of some years ago (Green Bluff, Illinois, circa 1926?). However, the expected tourists did not come. Everything had to be auctioned off. He had invested $1,500,000 and retrieved $190,000.

The punishment for Black and his crew had to be more severe. They had "drunk the milk of paradise." Their "condign punishment" must be death. Therefore, the shift from divine intervention to the infernal machinations of Martians logically follows. It sets the tone for Phase Two. Moreover, it unifies the two very different phases. We can now take a closer look at outstanding problems that run through both phases: the subject of mental influencing and the question of the identity of the "relatives."

That somebody mistakes a person he encounters for a close relative, or sees a relative who is not there, is of course not an everyday occurrence, but it is not particularly rare. It is invariably a relative of deep emotional significance for the viewer. The experience is always surprising and often has a great impact. Many examples from both fiction and nonfiction could be given, but a few will suffice. The interest in extraordinary experiences around the moment of death has brought a spate of testimonials. Several years ago, *McCall's* related the story of a woman who had been given up by her doctors:

> As I lay in my bed I opened my eyes—and there, standing around my bed, were both sets of my grandparents, whom I had loved very much and who had died years before. I saw them as vividly as I am looking at you now ... they looked just as I knew them when I was a girl. ... I wanted to go with them ... I felt such peace and love from their presence ... and I have never again been afraid of death.[5]

Winston Smith, in George Orwell's *1984* (1948), under a stress that approaches or even surpasses that of imminent death, thinks he recognizes his mother in a fellow prisoner. The idea is not as unreasonable as it may seem because his mother had disappeared many years ago, and he has no way of knowing whether she is still alive or what she might be like now. On the other hand, he has no reason to think that she would be in the same prison as he at the same time or that she would look like that other woman.

The use of this motif in literature sometimes approaches the metaphorical. Heinrich Lersch, a German pacifist poet who wrote shortly after World War I, relates in a poem how he saw a dead soldier entangled in the barbed wire in front of his trench and how from day to day he became more convinced that it was his brother (of course, he was not). Similar episodes are found in autobiographical writings of former mental patients. For example, Fritz Peters relates in *The World Next Door* (1949) how he thought, for no manifest reason, that an elderly fellow patient was his father. An encounter that does not involve clear-cut mistaken identity but is relevant to our study because of the abrupt shift of feeling and roles is found in Arthur Schnitzler's *Flight into Darkness*.[6] The protagonist develops paranoia. As his brother, who is trying to lead him back to human companionship, embraces him, the sick man feels attacked by a hostile force and stabs him through the heart.

The idea of being influenced or indeed dominated by powerful enemies who exert a mysterious influence on the mind has, of course, long been recognized as a characteristic symptom of paranoia and related conditions. Especially since Viktor Tausk's pioneering study *On the Origin of the "Influencing*

Machine" in Schizophrenia (1919), the mechanism of this delusion and its role in the development of the disease have been better understood. Psychiatric practice considers it, rightly, a symptom of clear and ominous meaning.

This is not the place to discuss the lamentable phenomenon, with its overtones of credulity combined with surrender of autonomy, that nowadays more people who are not themselves paranoid will accept this special delusion than ever before. We must also forego examining whether the latest technological "progress" has in fact made such an assumption more credible than it was in earlier times. The increased willingness to believe in mental influencing is no doubt part of the general loss of certainty resulting from the fact that so much that used to be impossible has become possible, and so it is easy to fall into the trap of thinking that everything is possible. It is also partly due to the increased empathy with the mentally ill, praiseworthy where it means greater tolerance, questionable where it tends toward apotheosis.

It is not inappropriate here, perhaps, to invoke the noble shade of the knight of the sad countenance, who has for centuries served as the paradigm of the man who lives by his illusions, hallucinations, and delusions: Don Quixote. His nobility is predicated on his world of the imagination being nobler than the shabby reality around him, and on his willingness to give everything except his honor to prove that his fantasies have a deeper reality than that of the commonplace real, and that he could live up to these standards. Can the same be said of Black and his companions?

We have now traveled along route 1 for a considerable stretch. We have come quite close to our goal, but it has proved a long-winded road. How about the second route? We will now consider the content of the story as a projection of contents in the author's mind. We can do so for a simple and basic reason: the characters in the story do not exist except in the author's mind. This is true of all fiction, though to different degrees; least of all in historical fiction, moreso in realistic fiction, and to the highest degree in tales like "The Third Expedition." The characters' minds have no independent existence, because the characters themselves are only creatures of the author. They see, feel, think, and act the way they do because the author makes them see, feel, think, and act in that way, not because it is their nature.

This does not mean, of course, that an author necessarily shares his characters' perceptions and emotions. No writer worth his salt is limited to portraying himself. For instance, he may describe a man committing a crime, without ever having done so himself. Nevertheless, the thought of the crime must be in the writer; his mind must encompass the potential. He may fight it within himself, and the struggle may be the very reason why he describes it. To realize this is of particular importance for understanding delusions in literature. If John Black were living in a normal world, the idea of his brother changing into a Martian and killing him would clearly be a delusion, but he lives in an abnormal world. The truth of his idea is confirmed by events, so technically it is not a delusion. But the point is irrelevant. The author knows that the world into which Black has been flung is itself but a figment. He knows that Black's theory is delusion.

This can perhaps be made clearer if we look at the phenomenon from a morphological viewpoint. Whatever the character's perceptions, emotions, and reasoning in relation to reality—be it genuine reality or the "reality" of the story—they are illusions, hallucinations, and delusions in *form*. And just as a move in a game derives its significance only from the rules of the game, so here the form is what matters, because the reality has been rigged by the author. He has set the rules of the game. Because an author has stacked the cards against his characters, his work is resonant with irony. Eric Rabkin misses—or ignores—the point when in *The Fantastic in Literature* he speaks of "the sweetly lyrical romanticism of Ray Bradbury in *The Martian Chronicles*." The sweetness is only skin-deep. The flesh underneath writhes with horror.

The author's role may be obscured rather than elucidated by taking it for granted that "The Third Expedition" is science fiction, as is often done, merely because Bradbury is a science fiction writer. It is true, of course, that he is. But while it is convenient to pigeonhole an author in a specific genre, it is equally obvious that this is an oversimplification. Some of the finest science fiction stories are the work of celebrated "mainstream" writers (R. Kipling, E. M. Forster, E. B. White, and A. France come to mind), and science fiction writers have written nonscience fiction. We cannot say, "It's called science fiction, so it is science fiction." We must measure "The Third Expedition" against the criteria of a rational definition.

L. Sprague De Camp, in his *Science Fiction Handbook* (1953), offers this: "fiction based on scientific or pseudo-scientific assumptions (space travel, robots, telepathy, earthly immortality, etc.) or laid in a patently unreal although not supernatural setting (the future, another world, and so forth). . . ."[7] Even though De Camp cast his net wide, works like "The Third Expedition" would be caught. But that was a generation ago. Since then the genre has grown, branched out, matured. Sharper differentiation has become a necessity. There is consensus nowadays that science fiction should be distinguished from such adjacent types as fantasy, weird fiction, and the Gothic story. Even utopian fiction, long in eclipse, has recovered sufficiently to claim much of the territory that by default had gone to science fiction. The classical definition that H. Bruce Franklin gave in *Future Perfect* (1966) represents the prevailing modern thinking:

Science fiction seeks to describe reality in terms of a credible hypothetical invention—past, present, or, most usually, future—extrapolated from that reality; fantasy seeks to describe present reality in terms of an impossible alternative to that reality.... Science fiction views what *is* by projecting what not inconceivably could be; fantasy views what is by projecting what could not be.[8]

"The Third Expedition" makes "pseudo-scientific assumptions," uses a "patently unreal setting," "projects what could not be." It is science fiction by criteria of times past, not by current criteria. This is important because it sheds light on the author's intentions, or at least on what intentions he does not have. He does not care to explore scientific developments or future human societies. He does not contribute to any of the educational or uplifting effects ascribed to science fiction: better understanding of the world we live in through better understanding of science, enthusiasm for the marvels that the future holds in store for the human race, etc. He carefully leaves such opportunities unexploited. For example, we hear next to nothing about the actual space trip, nothing about the real Mars, and nothing about the spacemen's equipment (except that they have "guns" and "atomic weapons"). Moreover, the density of oxygen in the Martian atmosphere is one-thousandth of what it is in ours. Although this was learned only through recent space probes and earlier estimates were much higher—as much as one-hundredth of ours—still, it was evident that men would not be able to breathe on Mars without special apparatus. Bradbury must have known this, yet, he chose to ignore it. He is not interested in the air the men breathe, the soil under their feet, or the ship they came in. He is interested in what goes on inside them.

The key is in his method. His technique of projecting his characters' inner life, of making it visible to his readers, is to describe events that happen in the characters' minds as though they were happening in the outside world. Obversely, what he presents as occurring on the outside—in the "reality" of his tale—is actually what goes on in the minds of his characters, and nothing else. "Out of sight, out of mind" has been reversed into "out of mind, out of sight." This method has not been much studied and does not seem to have a name yet, perhaps because it seems to be an innovation of the post-realistic era, although it is actually quite old. We find it in ancient fairy tales, in works of the Romantics, and in such modern writers as Hermann Hesse (who experimented with it brilliantly in *Demian* and *Steppenwolf*) and Franz Kafka. We are not told, for instance, that Gregor Samsa in *Metamorphosis* thinks he is a cockroach; we are told that he is changed into a cockroach (or whatever species of "vermin" best fits Kafka's description). The claim that this is the specific method of these writers, and that the Bradbury of "The Third Expedition" is one of them, is admittedly bold. It is based on nothing more solid than subjective impression, but it proves its worth by providing the foundation for a coherent interpretation. I know of no other approach that can.

What does the writer really do? What makes him do it? What gift does he have? These questions are of great interest to psychologists, but for a long time they were leery of tackling them. Without the concept of the unconscious, the questions could not even be approached. Freud had too much respect for the Muses to be hasty about studying them. When the collapse of the seemingly stable European civilization in World War I compelled psychology to look at problems beyond individual scope, Paul Federn, a "first generation" psychoanalyst, coined this formulation in a book published in 1919: "What we can observe in early childhood as contents of fantasies and objects of anxiety works as unconscious forces hidden in the adult, to come to light misshapen in the delusion of the ill or well-formed in the work of the artist."[9] Much exploration has been done since then, but Federn's terse pronouncement has stood up. It fits "The Third Expedition" amazingly well.

Pertinent observations could, of course, be made before. When Goethe was unhappy in love and Charlotte married another man, he did not shoot himself. He wrote the story of Werther, who did. Charles Morice, a French art critic, wrote an article in 1885 reviewing the work of Odilon Redon who had produced astounding graphics, the counterpart in art of what works like *The Martian Chronicles* represent in literature (the best science fiction art is not necessarily found in illustrations of science fiction stories). Morice speaks of the double meaning of the word "dream." (Obviously it means one thing when we think of what we dreamt last night and when Martin Luther King, Jr., says, "I have a dream.") Morice says: "The meaning we must give the word "dream" is neither that of colloquial speech and prose (involuntary visions in sleep), nor the rare and poetic one (voluntary visions while awake). It is this and it is that, it is waking and sleeping. It is in truth the dream of a dream, the voluntary ordering of involuntary visions."[10] It is this ordering of the disordered that makes the art we are dealing with what it is.

NOTES

1. Ray Bradbury, *The Martian Chronicles* (New York: Bantam, 1976), p. 51. All page numbers will refer to this paperback edition.

2. It was actually published in *Planet Stories* (Fall 1948) under the title "Mars is Heaven," two years before the book appeared.

3. Jörg Hienger, *Literarische Zukunftsphantastik: Eine Studie über Science Fiction* (Göttingen: Wandenhoeck & Ruprecht, 1972), pp. 224–28.

4. E. P. Bernabeu, "Science Fiction: A New Mythos," *Psychoanalytic Quarterly*, 26 (1957), 529.

5. Mary Ann O'Roark, "I Have Never Again Been Afraid of Death," *McCall's*, Nov. 1976, p. 96.

6. Arthur Schnitzler, *Flight into Darkness*, trans. William A. Drake (New York: AMS Press, 1972). This is a reprint of the 1931 edition.

7. Quoted in Bernabeu, p. 528.

8. Franklin M. Bruce, *Future Perfect: American Science Fiction of the Nineteenth Century* (New York: Oxford Univ. Press, 1966), p. 3.

9. Paul Federn, *Zur Psychologie der Revolution: die vaterlose Gesellschaft* (Vienna: Anzengruber-Verlag, 1919), p. 17.

10. Charles Morice, "La Semaine," *Petite Tribune Républicaine*, 2 April 1885; quoted in *Odilon Redon, Dessins, Eaux-fortes, Lithographies* (Paris: Le Bâteau Lavoir, 1969), n. pag.

GEORGE R. GUFFEY

The Unconscious, Fantasy, and Science Fiction: Transformations in Bradbury's Martian Chronicles and Lem's Solaris

[A writer] floats on the heavenly lake; he steeps himself in the
nether spring. Thereupon, submerged words squirm up, as when a
flashing fish, hook in its gills, leaps from water's depth.

—Lu Ki, *Wen-fu*

A writer psychoanalyzes himself, not with a psychiatrist, but with
tens of thousands, hundreds of thousands, or maybe millions of
readers.

—Larry Niven, *Science Fiction Voices #2*

Those of us who come to fantasy and science fiction after years of studying the poetry and prose of the earliest periods of English and American
history do so with considerable delight. We are delighted, first, because a
substantial amount of the fantasy and science fiction published since 1950
is quality literature. We are delighted, second, because of the rich research
opportunities the field offers.

Shivering and squinting in dark, dank cubicles, we in the past studied
the crabbed, ambiguous handwriting of minor church functionaries, hoping
thereby to settle longstanding arguments about the birthplaces and birthtimes
of literary figures of major and minor importance. Similarly, we laboriously
collated faded manuscripts of doubtful authority against multiple copies of

From *Bridges to Fantasy*, edited by George E. Slusser, Eric S. Rabkin, and Robert Scholes, pp.
142–59, 213–15. © 1982 by the Board of Trustees of Southern Illinois University.

67

badly printed folios, quartos, and duodecimos, with the modest hope of learning something, no matter how little, about the creative imagination of Shakespeare, Dryden, or even Traherne. As we went about our scholarly tasks, we now and then pictured in our mind's eyes the relative affluence of colleagues who had chosen to specialize in more modern periods. Surrounded by holograph manuscripts, galley proofs, personal letters, and taped interviews, those happy devils, in our imaginations, clucked and chortled to themselves as their typewriters rattled away.

Although on the whole exaggerated, that picture of modern scholarly affluence does contain a significant amount of truth. Our age, unlike the Middle Ages or the Renaissance, not only places a high premium on the works of the individual writer, but also attempts in general to preserve as much of his personal history as possible. Many modern authors are, of course, uncomfortable about the dogged attention paid to their lives and therefore cover their tracks whenever and wherever possible. They destroy their juvenilia, refuse interviews, and go to great lengths to avoid personal contact with the reading public. To the delight of critics and scholars interested in the creative process, a few, and here fantasy and science fiction writers seem generally to fit, happily write autobiographical articles for magazines, mingle with their fans at conventions, and grant interviews of various sorts. It is with provocative comments made by some of these writers in recent interviews and articles that I wish to begin my essay.

1

One of the staples of fantasy and science fiction magazines, amateur and professional, is the interview with a successful writer in the field. Because many readers of these magazines are themselves would-be writers, the interviewers tend to focus on the practical problems of writing, especially the writing of novels. In other words, although they may or may not delve deeply into the educational backgrounds, political philosophies, or reading tastes of the writers they are interviewing, they almost always ask the two questions of most interest to beginning writers of fantasy and science fiction: Where do you get your ideas? and How carefully do you work your stories out before you begin to write?

The answers elicited by these and similar questions fall roughly into two categories. A few writers say that a considerable amount of conscious preparation is necessary before they actually begin to write. Here, for example, are the responses of Poul Anderson to questions about his writing habits:

> Writing a novel is a complicated task. Once I determine, in
> a general sense, what I'm going to do, I'll sit down and start

planning it in great detail. I'll try to figure everything out I possibly can about the world I'm trying to build. After I've calculated the mathematic skeleton of the story, I'll work on several more arbitrary things, such as drawing maps, identifying place names, researching life on the planet. I'll usually end up with pages and pages of closely written notes, just on that one planet, getting down to elaborate descriptions of flora and fauna. Then I'll start developing individual characters.[1]

Anderson, a fabricator of "hard" science fiction, is well aware that some writers work in a less conscious, less systematic way. In an autobiographical article published in *Algol*, he has distinguished two extreme methods of composition:

Some artists proceed in a kind of frenzy, unheeding of what they are about until the project is finished. This is not necessarily bad. A numbe[r] of our finest works have been created thus. No two makers have identical methods. Of course, if he's any good, the headlong artist has all the skill and understanding that he needs; they just operate less on the conscious level for him than they do for most people.

   At the opposite pole we find the completely cerebral person who plans everything out beforehand, takes careful note of what he is doing while he does it, and afterward goes back to ponder over each smallest detail and revise until he is satisfied. People of this kind also produce their share of greatness.[2]

Lester del Rey, although not given to extensive revision, seems in general to follow a procedure similar to Anderson's. In an interview which appeared in *Science Fiction Review*, he says of his writing practices: "I know what my story is going to be before I ever write it. This I work out in great detail. I'm never surprised by the development of a character because I've known that before I ever put it on paper, because I've planned that all out ahead of time. . . ."[3] And, interestingly enough, L. Sprague de Camp, generally a producer of fantasy and science fantasy, appears to be one of Anderson's "cerebral" writers, not one of his "frenzied" ones. "I'm one of these meticulous outliners," he says. "Some people sit down and the whole thing pours out. . . . I don't work very much that way. I have a general idea, and then gradually fill it out, add more detail, add more complications and the like."[4]

   Although Poul Anderson, Lester del Rey, and L. Sprague de Camp evidently construct their stories with the rationality and efficiency of an aircraft engineer working out the design of a new jet engine, a great many of the fantasy and science fiction writers interviewed during the last four or five years have indicated that their own creative processes are neither very rational nor very efficient. Gregory Benford, for one, notes that, knowing he is a scientist, many of his readers suspect him to be a "very rationalist writer, like Fred Hoyle." Actually, he says, "it seems to me that I'm a little more of a subconscious sort of writer." He does not, he adds, know where the "stuff" of his stories "comes from," and he is only able to put large chunks of his material together over long periods of time. A good case in point is his novel *In the Ocean of Night*, which grew out of previously published pieces of short fiction. He describes the making of that novel:

> I knew I was going to write the book for a long time, but I had to work out the details. . . . In the summer of '75, I sat down and tried to start on page one and go through and modify everything . . . and try to pull it together. It was mostly a subconscious process because I actually didn't know how major things in the book connected up with other major things. It was a series of revelations. I was in the middle of the book and just going along thinking about the plotline that I had laid out, and about 300 words before it happened I discovered that Nigel Walmsley's wife, Alexandria, was going to rise from the dead. I didn't know that! I suddenly realized that all that had been planted before, was all set up, and I hadn't even realized that I was planting it. . . . It was that kind of assembly work in which you slowly understand what is going on. . . . This seems to be the way that I have to write books. It takes a long time to put together the ideas and figure out what it means.[5]

According to the Jungian school of psychology, a frequently appearing symbol for the unconscious is the ocean.[6] In light of the large part that Benford's unconscious seems to have played in the creation of *In the Ocean of Night*, the title he chose for his book is peculiarly fitting. Among the various words one might use to characterize the unconscious, "ocean" and "night" would have to be at the head of the list.

Writing in *Algol*, Joe Haldeman recently discussed at length the problem of "getting ideas" for science fiction stories. Before suggesting a solution for writer's block, he described R. A. Lafferty's theory of artistic inspiration:

> R. A. Lafferty, than whom there is no more original writer in science fiction, claims that there's no such thing as an original idea, and writers who think they sit down and go through some rational

process to arrive at a story are kidding themselves. He claims that all ideas float around as a kind of psychic public property, and every now and then one settles on you. That sounds dangerously mystical to me, subversive, but I think it's true.[7]

Again, the image is Jungian: ideas "float around" in a psychic ocean, which is accessible to everyone. Surely we are here only a half-step away from Jung's theory of the archetypes and the collective unconscious. At times a writer finds that his, in Haldeman's words, "imagination has frozen solid," that "no ideas come floating down" to him. Here is Haldeman's solution to that, for a writer, most vexing problem:

Start typing. Type your name over and over. Type lists of animals, flowers, baseball players, Greek Methodists. Type out what you're going to say to that damned insolent repairman. Sooner or later, perhaps out of boredom, perhaps out of a desire to *stop* this silly exercise, you'll find you've started a story. It's never taken me so much as a page of nonsense. . . . [8]

The science fiction writer who seems to have thought most about the part the unconscious plays in the creative process is A. E. Van Vogt. His introduction to the subject came about, he tells us, as a result of his attempts to find a successful treatment for a chronic medical disorder:

I fell out of a second-storey window when I was age two and a half, and I was unconscious for three days, near death. Later, using hypnosis, and then still later, dianetics, in an effort to reduce the trauma of those three days, I discovered that unconsciousness has "on it" (in it) endless hallucinations. The normal part of my brain has probably spent a lifetime trying to rationalize the consequent fantasies and images. This could explain a lot about my bent for science fiction.[9]

Over the years, Van Vogt, who like Haldeman and most other writers at times suffered from writer's block, developed a unique way of freeing his blocked unconscious and thereby initiating stories or resuming halted ones. Noting that when he went to bed after a period of unsuccessful labor he often later in the night awoke with a solution to the problem which had frustrated him, Van Vogt, in order to prime his creative imagination, embarked on a demanding regimen: "Thereafter, I used an alarm clock to awaken me every one and a half hours. Throughout my career as a writer, I awakened myself by an alarm clock—and later with an industrial timer—about 300 nights a year. Thus, I enlisted my subconscious . . . in my ceaseless search for ideas and story solutions."[10] Eventually, Van Vogt's ruminations on the workings of the unconscious led him to a full-blown theory of composition which included, in addition to aspects of aesthetics, elements of archetypal epistemology and metaphysics as well:

> I had the theory that every grain of sand, every rock, every living cell contains within it a record of its ancient origin. The theory postulated that if we could but "read" that record, we could know the beginning of all things, and their subsequent history. Obviously, science has long attempted to use its methods to comprehend this record. My method, however, was more exotic. At a certain point in each science fiction story, I would let my subconscious mind freely associate within the frame of the ideas of that story. My hope was that, as time went on, as more stories were written, my subconscious would progressively spew forth ancient images; and that a picture of the truth of the universe would gradually emerge.[11]

I could quote numerous additional fantasy and science fiction writers on the subject of the role of the unconscious in the creative process, but time and space will allow for only two more. When an interviewer recently asked Stephen R. Donaldson where he got ideas for his stories, Donaldson replied, "Where? from the un- or sub-conscious recesses of my own mind. . . . When I'm receptive, they can be fished to the surface [that Jungian image, again] by almost any kind of external stimuli (one whole sequence in *The Power That Preserves* was triggered by a can of disinfectant in a restaurant washroom)."[12] A little later in the interview, he added, "The single most crippling obstacle to this process is self-consciousness: Self-consciousness blocks receptivity."[13]

Finally, in describing the origin and completion of *Sword of the Demon*, Richard Lupoff emphasized not only the contribution of his "personal" unconscious, but also the indirect contribution of the racial unconscious, through the materials he first absorbed from Japanese myths and then subsequently incorporated into his novel. The following is his description of the complete process:

> The very opening of the book, the first chapter of it, just occurred spontaneously. It had no particular source that I knew of. The famous wellsprings of the subconscious, or whatever. I had no awareness of it having come from any place in particular, it was just there. And I didn't know where to go with it. It sat in my

desk untouched for a couple of years because of that. Finally, I was looking through *The Larousse Encyclopedia of Mythology* and spent about the next six months reading Japanese cultural mythology. Just *submerged* [my italics] myself in it. All the characters and most of the incidents in the book are taken from Japanese mythology, but the book itself is not a literal retelling of any one particular story.... This book was produced by turning my head into some sort of solvent and filling it up with Japanese mythology until I got a supersaturated solution, and this book is the precipitate.[14]

Most lovers of literature find such vivid, personal statements about the creative process intrinsically interesting. What makes these statements especially interesting, however, is the remarkable way they echo key passages in C. G. Jung's most influential book, *Symbols of Transformation*. In the second chapter of that book, Jung's primary goal is the distinction of two fundamentally different kinds of thinking. One kind he calls "directed thinking"; the other he calls "fantasy thinking."

Directed thinking is, above all, verbal: "If we ... follow out an intensive train of thought—the solution of a difficult problem, for instance—we suddenly notice that we are *thinking in words*, that in very intensive thinking we begin talking to ourselves, or that we occasionally write down the problem or make a drawing of it, so as to be absolutely clear." Directed thinking, Jung adds, is logical thinking. It is difficult, even exhausting. It copies reality and produces adaptation to it. Certainly, the "clearest expression of modern directed thinking is science and the techniques fostered by it."[15]

On the other hand, "What happens," Jung asks, "when we do not think directly?" "Well," he answers, "our thinking then lacks all leading ideas and the sense of direction emanating from them. We no longer compel our thoughts along a definite track, but let them float, sink or rise according to their specific gravity." Unlike directed thinking, this kind of thinking (fantasy thinking) does not tire us, and it "leads away from reality into fantasies of the past or future."[16]

Although directed thinking is a conscious phenomenon, most fantasy thinking, according to Jung, goes on in the unconscious. For the clearest, most concise description of this fantasy activity and of the two parts of the unconscious psyche—the personal unconscious and the collective unconscious—we must resort to another of Jung's works, "The Psychology of the Child Archetype":

Modern psychology treats the products of unconscious imagination as self-portraits of what is going on in the unconscious, or as statements of the unconscious psyche about itself. They fall into two categories. Firstly, fantasies (including dreams) of a personal character, which go back unquestionably to personal experiences, things forgotten or repressed, and can thus be completely explained by individual anamnesis. Secondly, fantasies (including dreams) of an impersonal character, which cannot be reduced to experiences in the individual's past, and thus cannot be explained as something individually acquired. These fantasy-pictures undoubtedly have their closest analogues in mythological types. We must therefore assume that they correspond to certain *collective* (and not personal) structural elements of the human psyche in general, and, like the morphological elements of the human body, are *inherited.* . . . the fantasy-products of the second category (as also those of the first) arise in a state of reduced intensity on the part of consciousness (in dreams, delirium, reveries, visions, etc.).[17]

Very clearly, then, the first group of writers I quoted—Anderson, del Rey, and de Camp—are, in the language of Jung, "directed thinkers." Highly conscious and highly logical artists, they perform mathematical calculations, do extensive research, draw detailed maps, and make elaborate outlines before they actually begin to write their stories. The second group of writers—Benford, Haldeman, Van Vogt, Donaldson, and Lupoff—are, to varying degrees, what Jung called "fantasy thinkers." Less conscious and less logical as artists, they depend greatly on the promptings of the unconscious.

2

At first glance, the two books I wish to examine in some detail in the remainder of this essay would appear to have little in common. Ray Bradbury's *Martian Chronicles* is notable chiefly for its masterful stylistic effects. It holds our attention with its sensuous diction, its hypnotic sentence rhythms, and its skillful onomatopoeic devices. The scientific and technological materials of the book are unfortunately not so impressive; they are not only frequently self-contradictory, but they are also often in conflict with those of the world we actually inhabit. Stanislaw Lem's *Solaris*, on the other hand, is a masterpiece of philosophical fiction. In dealing with matters scientific and technological, it is always informed and sophisticated. Its rigorous and detailed epistemological speculations are in the main successfully integrated with fascinating character portraits and suspenseful incidents.

Surprisingly enough, these very different books do have, as we shall see, some significant points of contact. Those points of contact, I shall argue, are largely the result of the strong influence of the unconscious of each writer during the creative process. To begin, I must turn to the public statements Bradbury has made about his own methods of composition.

If his public comments about his methods of composition are to be trusted, Bradbury is a determined practitioner of what Jung called "fantasy thinking." In a speech in 1975, he rejected the notion that the conscious part of the mind should play a significant role in the creative process: "I have had a sign by my typewriter for the better part of twenty years, now, which says, 'Don't think.' I hate all those signs that say Think. That's the enemy of creativity." Melville, the author of the greatest American novel, did not intellectualize; he relied on emotion. "Emotion, emotion wins the day. Intellect can help correct. But emotion, first, surprises creativity out in the open where it can be pinned down! Learn from Melville!" Like Melville, and Plato's Ion, for that matter, Bradbury is, he says, at the mercy of his Muse when he writes. He is not in control. Having written, however, he is better balanced, better adjusted: "I've only been to a psychiatrist once in my life. I don't happen to believe in it. . . . I think good friends, or the act of creativity itself, sustains us and saves us more often than not."[18]

In an interview published only last year, Bradbury again emphasized that, for him, writing is essentially an undirected process: "I never plan ahead. Everything is always spontaneous and passionate. I never sit down and think things out. I also do a great deal of daydreaming. Oh, I do some thinking in-between, but it's a very loose thing. I'm not super-intellectual. If it feels right, then I'll do it." How does he get ideas for stories? "Basically, I just go [into my office] with the idea of writing something. I usually start off the day with poetry. I go through a process of free association. I do the same thing with short stories."[19]

Like many fantasy and science fiction writers, Bradbury admits, then, to a significant amount of daydreaming. To a psychoanalyst the daydreams of an individual are at least as significant as his nightdreams. When an individual daydreams, his psychic energy (or libido) manifests itself as a stream of images linked by association, a stream which flows freely in the direction of least resistance. Good writers such as Bradbury differ from ordinary daydreamers, of course, by possessing an ability to abstract ideas from their fantasies and objectify them in good literary form. Before analyzing Bradbury's finest achievement as a writer of fantasy, *The Martian Chronicles*, I must first place one of its dominant themes in a more general context.

One of the most common themes in nightdreams, daydreams, and myths is that of transformation, or metamorphosis. All of us have had nightdreams in the course of which inanimate objects, plants, animals, or people have changed into very different inanimate objects, plants, animals, or people. Among the materials collected and published by Freud and Jung, numerous examples of such transformations can be found. Here, for instance, is a short transformational nightdream collected by Jung and printed in his *Essays on a Science of Mythology*: "A white bird perches on a table. Suddenly it changes into a fair-haired seven-year-old girl and just as suddenly back into a bird, which now speaks with a human voice."[20] Another dreamer provides a longer, even more intriguing example:

> We go through a door into a tower-like room, where we climb a long flight of steps.... The steps end in a temple.... The temple is of red stone. Bloody sacrifices are offered there. Animals are standing about the altar. In order to enter the temple precincts one has to be transformed into an animal—a beast of the forest.... On the altar in the middle of the open room there stands the moon-bowl, from which smoke or vapour continually rises. There is also a huge image of the goddess, but it cannot be seen clearly. The worshippers, who have been changed into animals and to whom I also belong, have to touch the goddess's foot....[21]

As far as transformational daydreams are concerned, the ones most familiar to us are those involving wish fulfillments. In our reveries we are often temporarily transformed into powerful heads of state, heroic soldiers, world-class athletes, celebrated musicians, prize-winning authors, glamorous moviestars—the list of possibilities is virtually endless. Freud and Jung frequently touched on the subject of daydreams, and Jung even went so far as to publish a number of the most significant ones he had collected. Of those printed by Jung in *Essays on a Science of Mythology*, one, from a woman "in middle life," is especially relevant to the thrust of this essay. Richer, more bizarre than the transformational daydreams of most of us, it is especially interesting for its ending:

> A magician is demonstrating his tricks to an Indian prince. He produces a beautiful young girl from under a cloth. She is a dancer, who has the power to change her shape or at least hold her audience spell-bound by faultless illusion. During the dance she dissolves with the music into a swarm of bees. Then she changes into a leopard, then into a jet of water, then into a sea-polyp that has twined itself about a young pearl-fisher. Between times, she takes human form again at the dramatic moment. She appears as a she-ass bearing two baskets of wonderful fruits. Then she becomes a many-coloured peacock. The prince is beside himself with delight and calls her to him. But she dances on, now naked, and even tears

the skin from her body, and finally falls down—a naked skeleton. This is buried, but at night a lily grows out of the grave, and from its cup there rises the *white lady*, who floats slowly up to the sky.[22]

This daydream is interesting not only because of the number and variety of transformations it contains, but also because of the mythlike transfiguration at the end of it. The death and burial of the beautiful young girl and her subsequent rebirth in the form of a flower are, of course, paralleled by similar events in numerous well-known myths. In his *Metamorphoses*, Ovid, in fact, organized much of the mythology of Greece, Rome, and Babylonia around the theme of transformation; and, among the many different kinds of transformation he described, those involving the death of an individual and the subsequent rebirth of that individual in the form of a flower were amply represented. Because of their popularity with Renaissance poets such as Shakespeare, Milton, and Marvell, the Ovidian stories involving such myths (those about Narcissus, Hyacinthus, and Adonis, for example) are the best-known today. Overall, the tranformations depicted in *Metamorphoses* are more numerous and more varied than some of us will remember them to be: Chaos is transformed into an ordered universe, the coral "plant" into a rock, Syrinx Daphne into a reed, Daphne into a tree, the Thracian women into oaks, Ascalaphus into an owl, the nephew of Daedalus into a partridge, Daedalion into a hawk, Cadmus into a snake, Lyncus into a lynx, Lycaon into a wolf, Callisto into a bear, Galanthis into a weasel, Atlas into a mountain, Cyane into a pool, Arethusa into a spring, a dog into a marble statue, a city into a heron; nymphs are transformed into islands, ships into nymphs, and on, and on.

Over a hundred years ago Nietzsche suggested a relationship between our dream thinking and what he called the "whole thought" of primitive man. On the basis of dream analysis, Freud came to a related conclusion; he held that myths are the "distorted vestiges of the wishful phantasies of whole nations, the [age-long] dreams" of primitive man. And, finally, Jung himself wrote, "The conclusion that the myth-makers thought in much the same way as we still think in dreams is almost self-evident."[23] With these ideas about the nature and functions of nightdreams, daydreams, and myths in mind, we are now ready to turn to Bradbury's *Martian Chronicles*.

Near the middle of "Usher II," one of the stories in *The Martian Chronicles*, Mr. Stendahl, lover of fantasy and re-creator of the House of Usher, says of his architectural accomplishments, "I nurtured a medieval atmosphere in a modern, incredulous world."[24] Apt though they are for describing the house and grounds Stendahl created on Mars, Stendahl's words would have made an even more appropriate epigraph for *The Martian Chronicles* itself. Although superficially a book about a technologically superior world of the future, *The Martian Chronicles* is in reality a collection of atavistic daydreams, daydreams which derive much of their power from mythlike transformations.

One of the most mythlike stories in the book is "The Martian," a haunting tale of a Martian "boy" capable of changing his shape to accommodate the desires of the settlers from Earth. In what seemed like, in the words of the narrator, a "repeated dream,"[25] he moved among the settlers, assuming the shapes of their dead relatives and acquaintances. Always fearful of being "trapped" by the settlers, he eventually met his end beside a Martian canal, as members of a hysterical crowd struggled to hold him: "Before their eyes he changed. . . . He was melting wax shaping to their minds. They shouted, they pressed forward, pleading. He screamed, threw out his hands, his face dissolving to each demand. . . . They snatched his wrists, whirled him about, until with one last shriek of horror he fell."[26] This story, of course, reminds us of the myth of Proteus. A shape changer who also had to be constantly on guard against being caught and forced to satisfy the desires of his captors, Proteus, a god of the sea, sometimes assumed "the shape of a young man, at another transformed into a lion; sometimes he used to appear . . . as a raging wild boar, or again as a snake . . . or else horns transformed him into a bull."[27]

In "The Third Expedition," a spaceship from Earth lands near what appears to be a small Martian town. The commander of the ship is Captain John Black. A man eighty years old, Black, "through the grace of God and a science that . . . knows how to make *some* old men young again," is as agile and alert as the chronologically younger men accompanying him. Nearing the town, he and two of his men hear someone "softly, drowsily," playing "Beautiful Dreamer" on a piano. Minutes later, exploring the "dreaming" afternoon streets of the town, the Earthmen find that it appears to be in every way identical to the small, Midwestern towns of their youth; and shortly, in an "amazing dream of reality," Black is happily reunited with his long-dead "brother," "father," and "mother."[28]

But during the night, lying beside his "brother" in a bedroom like the one they shared as children, Black begins to awaken from his "dreaming hypnosis": "Suppose these houses are really some *other* shape, a Martian shape, but, by playing on my desires and wants, these Martians have made this seem like my old home town, my old house. . . . Sometime during the night, perhaps, my brother here on this bed will change form, melt, shift, and become another thing, a Martian. It would be very simple for him just to turn over in bed and put a knife into my heart." By morning, the Martians have, in fact, killed all sixteen men from the rocket ship. At their funeral, the "mayor" of the town, "his face sometimes looking like the mayor, sometimes looking like something else," makes a sad speech, while the faces of Black's crying "relatives" melt from familiar shapes "into something else."[29]

The transformations witnessed by Captain Williams and his crew in a different story, "The Earth Men," are even more bizarre than those encountered by Captain Black in "The Third Expedition." Taken for a hallucinating psychotic because he claims to have come from Earth, Williams, along with his crew, is locked in a Martian insane asylum, where he must spend the night surrounded by constantly metamorphosing "paranoids":

> A man squatted alone in darkness. Out of his mouth issued a blue flame which turned into the round shape of a small naked woman. . . .
>
> The captain nodded at another corner. A woman stood there, changing. First she was embedded in a crystal pillar, then she melted into a golden statue, finally a staff of polished cedar, and back to a woman.
>
> All through the midnight hall people were juggling thin violet flames, shifting, changing, for nighttime was the time of change and affliction. . . .
>
> Little demons of red sand ran between the teeth of sleeping men. Women became oily snakes. There was a smell of reptiles and animals.[30]

Convinced that Williams is a highly imaginative Martian who has transformed himself into a startlingly effective image of an Earthman, a Martian psychologist excitedly envisions a scientific paper on Williams's feat: "I'll write this into my greatest monograph! I'll speak of it at the Martian Academy next month! *Look* at you! Why, you've even changed your eye color from yellow to blue, your skin to pink from brown. And those clothes, and your hands having five fingers instead of six! Biological metamorphosis through psychological imbalance!"[31] Finally, having judged Williams's case incurable, the Martian psychologist resorts to euthanasia, only to find that, even after the death of Williams, his supposed hallucination, his Earthman's body, continues to exist.

An exhaustive account of the many kinds of transformation taking place in the other stories in *The Martian Chronicles* would require more space than I have been allotted for the rest of this essay, but perhaps I can at least suggest their variety and number before turning to similar materials in Lem's *Solaris*. In the stories and the bridges between the stories, a frosty Ohio winter is transformed into a brief summer by the heat from the exhausts of a rocket ship; Spender, a sensitive archaeologist, is (in spirit, at least) transformed into a Martian; Benjamin Driscoll, a latter-day Johnny Appleseed, turns a Martian desert into a green paradise; Pikes, a man of ten thousand faces, is able to transform himself into "a fury, a smoke, a blue fog, a white rain, a bat, a gargoyle"; Stendahl's guests, after being forced to don masks, are "transformed from one age into another"; a Martian woman, slain by the vulgar and crass Sam Parkhill, turns into "ice, snowflake, smoke," and is blown "away in the wind"; and, at the end of the book, the Hathaway family, having destroyed the rocket ship which brought them to Mars, become "Martians."[32] This list might be considerably extended, but it should suffice.

Finally, before leaving *The Martian Chronicles*, I must say something about the book's special use of metaphor and simile. All metaphors and similes are, of course, by their very nature transformational. If I, for example, say that "my love is a soft, soft cloud," I am, at *some* level of understanding, for a brief moment at least, transforming her. What is unusually interesting about the metaphors and similes of *The Martian Chronicles*, however, is the high frequency of what I shall call "biomorphic" figures of speech—metaphors and similes with inanimate tenors and animate vehicles. And among the many biomorphic figures of the book, those of greatest interest to me are the figures in which the tenors are machines.[33] Here are a few examples: "the ... house ... turned and followed the sun, flowerlike"; "From [the evil weapon] hordes of golden bees could be flung out with a high shriek"; "Up and down green wine canals, boats as delicate as bronze flowers drifted"; "the rocket had bloomed out great flowers of heat and color"; "[the rocket] had moved in the midnight waters of space like a pale sea leviathan"; "The rockets came like locusts"; "It was a machine like a jade-green insect, a praying mantis, delicately rushing through the cold air"; and "the great ships turned as lightly as moon thistles."

In interviews during the 1950s, 1960s, and 1970s, Bradbury repeatedly stated that he had never flown in an airplane, that (whenever possible) he avoided riding in automobiles, and that he disliked telephones and television sets.[34] Consistent with Bradbury's openly negative attitude toward machines, Mr. Hathaway at the end of *The Martian Chronicles* says of life during the last half of the twentieth century, "Science ran too far ahead of us too quickly, and the people got lost in a mechanical wilderness. . . ."[35] Only last year in an interview, Bradbury insisted, "We must learn to humanize the machine."[36] In light of his general mechanophobia, it is not, I think, therefore surprising to find in *The Martian Chronicles* and in Bradbury's other works numerous, probably unconsciously generated, biomorphic figures of speech.

According to Jung, fantasy thinking, although mainly a spontaneous product of the unconscious, contains elements of consciousness. The degree of influence an individual will allow his unconscious is dependent on the degree of rationalism prevailing in his immediate environment. Today, the countries officially most committed to a rationalist position are the socialist states of Europe and Asia, and the most read and most admired socialist writer of fantasy and science fiction is Stanislaw Lem of Poland. In recent public statements about his stories, Lem has revealed that, although he is officially a staunch rationalist, his attempts to rationalize the creative process have hitherto met with failure:

> I have tried all thinkable, rational, optimization procedures (tactics of writing). All in vain. I do not know where my ideas come from. . . . They come in dreams, but this is very rare; sometimes while reading scientific papers, especially mathematical ones. But then, there is no evidence of a rational linkage between a new idea and the said paper. . . . And truly I never know what I am writing—if it will be a short story, a novel, a serious thing or something grotesque—what problems may emerge, and so on. This is one hell and damnation, especially since I AM a rationalist, but it is so.[37]

Of even greater relevance to the concerns of this essay, though, are Lem's statements about the composition of his best novel, *Solaris*:

> I had no knowledge, not an atom of it, when I wrote the first chapter, what Kelvin would encounter on Solaris Station. I went forward in the same way that Kelvin went, and spoke for the first time with Snow, not knowing what was going on. Then, as I approached the end, again I did not know how to end the story, and it took a whole year—one day there came this illumination, and so it was. I do not like this kind of creative work, because I am myself a rationalist, and I would prefer to write in a planned, "rationalistic" way. . . . There were no plans, no elaborated preconceptions, no tactics, no nothing. . . . [38]

Surprisingly enough, then, Lem's metaphysical masterpiece appears to have been just as much the product of fantasy thinking as Bradbury's less intellectually challenging *Martian Chronicles*. All the extrinsic evidence supports that conclusion.

In addition, considerable intrinsic evidence can be marshaled in support of the same proposition. To begin—throughout *Solaris*, as throughout *The Martian Chronicles*, a dreamlike atmosphere prevails. Kelvin has, in fact, hardly set foot upon Solaris Station when he exclaims, "I must be dreaming. All this could only be a dream!"[39] Shortly thereafter, he encounters

Gibarian's nightmarish mistress in a corridor of the space station and his long-dead wife, Rheya, in his own room. At first, he is convinced that he is only dreaming of Rheya, but little by little he begins to entertain the possibility that she is real:

> My first thought was reassuring: I was dreaming and I was aware that I was dreaming.... I closed my eyes and tried to shake off the dream.... I thought of throwing something at her, but, even in a dream, I could not bring myself to harm a dead person.... the room, Rheya, everything seemed extraordinarily real. A three-dimensional dream.... I saw several objects on the floor.... When I wake up, I told myself, I shall check whether these things are still there or whether, like Rheya, I only saw them in a dream.... We kissed.... Was it possible to feel so much in a dream, I wondered.... Was it then that I began to have doubts? I went on telling myself that it was a dream, but my heart tightened.[40]

To further complicate matters for Kelvin, Rheya herself begins to dream doubtful dreams: "I have dream.... I don't know whether they really are dreams. Perhaps I'm ill."[41] And then, ironically, Kelvin, who had earlier tried to convince himself that he was dreaming, now dreams of Gibarian trying to convince him that he is awake: "Oh, you think you're dreaming about me? As you did with Rheya? . . . No, I am the real Gibarian. . . ."[42]

While Kelvin sleeps, the sentient ocean which inhabits Solaris probes his unconscious, and its invasive presence is reflected in the erotic, terrifying imagery of his nightmares. Two of these nightmares are vividly transformational. The first comes approximately halfway through the novel: "The night transfixed me; the night took possession of me, enveloped and penetrated me.... Turned to stone, I had ceased breathing.... I seemed to be growing smaller.... I tried to crawl out of bed, but there was no bed; beneath the cover of darkness there was a void. I pressed my hands to my face. I no longer had any fingers or any hands. I wanted to scream...."[43] Even more horrifying is the dream near the end of the book:

> Out of the enveloping pink mist, an invisible object emerges, and touches me.... I feel this contact like a hand, and the hand recreates me.... Under the caress of the hesitant fingers, my lips and cheeks emerge from the void, and as the caress goes further I have a face, breath stirs in my chest—I exist. And recreated, I in my turn create: a face appears before me.... This creature—a woman?—stays near me and we are motionless. The beat of our

hearts combines, and all at once, out of the surrounding void. . . . steals a presence of indefinable, unimaginable cruelty. The caress that created us . . . becomes the crawling of innumerable fingers. Our white, naked bodies dissolve into a swarm of black creeping things, and I am—we are—a mass of glutinous coiling worms . . . and I howl soundlessly, begging for death and for an end.[44]

In these nightmares, Kelvin undergoes transformations symbolic of the painful transformation he must in reality suffer on Solaris. That transformation begins when he first steps from his space capsule, which resembles a "burst cocoon," onto the space station.[45] After a series of tense encounters with Snow, Sartorius, and the "visitors" sent to the station by the ocean, Kelvin expresses his doubts and fears to Rheya in language not unlike that which he employs in describing his frightening transformational dreams: "After what has happened already, we can expect anything. Suppose tomorrow it turns me into a green jellyfish! It's out of our hands."[46] Much later, at the end of the novel, a more subdued Kelvin stands on the shore of the ocean and repeatedly reaches out to the waves which, without actually touching them, envelop his hand and his feet. Eventually, the ocean tires of this "game," but Kelvin, having undergone a kind of baptism, has been radically changed. His attitude has now become one of complete and total acceptance: "Although I had read numerous accounts of it, none of them had prepared me for the experience as I had lived it, and I felt somehow changed. . . . I . . . identified myself with the dumb, fluid colossus; it was as if I had forgiven it everything, without the slightest effort of word or thought."[47]

While Kelvin dreams his transformational nightmares and slowly metamorphoses into the sadly wise man who at the end of the novel waits patiently for another chance, for another "time of cruel miracles," the ocean itself is "engaged in a never-ending process of transformation, an 'ontological autometamorphosis.'" This "Polytherian form" of the category "Metamorph," this "mass of metamorphic plasma," is capable of infinitely varied "matter transformations."[48] Most of the time it busies itself with the shaping and unshaping of unique forms, for which a Solarist had in the past created the broad taxonomic categories of "extensor," "mimoid," "symmetriad," and "asymmetriad"; but, in the course of the novel, the protean ocean also at one time or another assumes the shape of a garden, a huge building, an enormous child, distorted tools, and, most important of all, the "visitors."

Of the last group, the "visitors," only two are ever very fully revealed to the reader—Gibarian's giant, steatopygic Negress and Rheya. Near the beginning of the novel, Kelvin characterizes the former as a "monstrous Aphrodite," and near the end of the book, Snow partially repays the compliment (or insult?) when in the presence of Kelvin he sardonically addresses Rheya as "fair Aphrodite, child of Ocean."[49] Both applications of the name are apt. Aphrodite, the Greek goddess of sexual love and beauty, was literally born from the sea, and the myths about her all exemplify the power of love.

Also apt are the names of the spaceships which figure in the novel. The *Laakon* and the *Ulysses*, for example, remind us of ancient myths about the sea. In one, Laocoön, a priest of Poseidon, the god of the sea, angers Apollo, who sends two huge sea serpents to kill Laocoön and his sons. In another, Ulysses, sailing a troubled sea, frequently runs afoul of Poseidon, Lord of Proteus, the old shape changer. In light of these and other mythic resonances within the novel, Kelvin's speculative question near the end seems particularly acute: "Are we to grow used to the idea that every man relives ancient torments, which are all the more profound because they grow comic with repetition?"[50]

Although in many ways very different, *The Martian Chronicles* and *Solaris* are, then, alike in at least one demonstrable way. Both incorporate significant amounts of dreamlike and mythlike transformational materials. An obvious question now comes to mind: are such transformational elements ubiquitous in works of fantasy and science fiction? Certainly, additional examples are easily adduced—the transformation of the animals into beast men and back into animals in *The Island of Dr. Moreau*, the transformation of the robots into human beings in *R. U. R.*, the transformation of individual Gethenians alternately into "males" and "females" in *The Left Hand of Darkness*, the transformation of Mrs. Grales into Rachel in *A Canticle for Leibowitz*, the transformation of the Mark IV computer into Mike in *The Moon Is a Harsh Mistress*, the transformation of the world's children into the Overmind in *Childhood's End*, the transformation of David Bowman into the Star Child in *2001*, the transformation of matter into various forms in *Cosmicomics*, and on, and on. A definitive answer to this intriguing question would obviously, however, require the transformation of this essay into a monograph, and, for the time being at least, I shall let it rest *in embryo*.

NOTES

1. Poul Anderson, quoted in Jeffrey M. Elliot, "Poul Anderson: Seer of Far-Distant Futures," in *Science Fiction Voices #2*, ed. Jeffrey M. Elliot (San Bernardino, CA: Borgo Pr., 1979), pp. 44–45.

2. Poul Anderson, "Poul Anderson Talar Om Science Fiction," *Algol* 15, no. 3 (1978): 14.

3. Lester del Rey, quoted in Darrell Schweitzer, "An Interview with Lester del Rey," *Science Fiction Review* 5, no. 3 (1976): 8.

4. L. Sprague de Camp, quoted in Darrell Schweitzer, "L. Sprague de Camp," in *Science Fiction Voices #1*, ed. Darrell Schweitzer (San Bernardino, CA: Borgo Pr., 1979), p. 60.

5. Gregory Benford, quoted in Nancy Mangini and Jim Purviance, "Interview with Nebula Nominee Gregory Benford," *SF & F 36: A Science Fiction Fanzine*, no. 6 (1978): 8, 7.

6. "In dreams and fantasies the sea or a large expanse of water signifies the unconscious" (C. G. Jung, *Symbols of Transformation: An Analysis of the Prelude to a Case of Schizophrenia*, 2d ed. [1956; reprint ed., Princeton: Princeton Univ. Pr., 1974], p. 219).

7. Joe Haldeman, "Great Science Fiction About Artichokes & Other Story Ideas," *Algol* 15, no. 3 (1978): 21.

8. Ibid.

9. A. E. Van Vogt, quoted in Jeffrey Elliot, "Interview: Van Vogt," *Galileo*, no. 8 (1978): 11.

10. Ibid., p. 10.

11. Ibid., pp. 8–9.

12. Stephen R. Donaldson, quoted in Neal Wilgus, "An Interview with Stephen R. Donaldson," *Science Fiction Review* 8, no. 2 (1979): 29.

13. Ibid.

14. Richard Lupoff, quoted in Jim Purviance and Nancy Mangini, "Interview with Nebula Nominee Richard Lupoff," *SF & F 36: A Science Fiction Fanzine*, no. 6 (1978): 14, 15.

15. Jung, *Symbols of Transformation*, pp. 11, 21.

16. Ibid., p. 17.

17. C. G. Jung, "The Psychology of the Child Archetype," in C. G. Jung and C. Kerényi, *Essays on a Science of Mythology* (New York: Pantheon, 1949), pp. 102, 103.

18. Ray Bradbury, "How Not to Burn a Book; or, 1984 Will Not Arrive," *Soundings* 7, no. 1 (1975): 19, 22, 13.

19. Ray Bradbury, quoted in Jeffrey M. Elliot, "Ray Bradbury: Poet of Fantastic Fiction," in *Science Fiction Voices #2*, ed. Jeffrey M. Elliot (San Bernardino, CA: Borgo Pr., 1979), pp. 21, 24.

20. Jung, "The Psychological Aspects of the Kore," in Jung and Kerényi, p. 241.

21. Ibid., p. 235.

22. Ibid., p. 238.

23. Nietzsche and Freud quoted by Jung. Jung, *Symbols of Transformation*, p. 24.

24. Ray Bradbury, *The Martian Chronicles* (New York: Bantam, 1975), p. 108.

25. Ibid., p. 126.

26. Ibid., p. 130.

27. Ovid, *Metamorphoses* (Baltimore: Penguin, 1967), p. 198.

28. Bradbury, *The Martian Chronicles*, pp. 35, 39, 43.

29. Ibid., pp. 46, 47, 47–48.

30. Ibid., pp. 26, 27.

31. Ibid., p. 29.

32. Ibid., pp. 110, 112, 138.

33. Ibid., pp. 2, 11, 14, 32, 78, 80, 140.

34. See, for example, Richard Donovan, "Morals from Mars," *The Reporter*, 26 June, 1951, pp. 38–40; Matt Weinstock, Los Angeles *Mirror-News*, 11 July, 1955, p. 10; Lawrence Lipton, "The Illustrated Man: Ray Bradbury," *Intro Bulletin 1*, nos. 6,

7 (1956): 9; Maggie Savoy, "Ray Bradbury Keeping Eye on Cloud IX," *Los Angeles Times*, 15 Mar., 1970, sec. E, p. 1.

 35. Bradbury, *The Martian Chronicles*, pp. 179–80.

 36. Bradbury, quoted in Elliot, p. 26.

 37. Stanislaw Lem, quoted in Daniel Say, "An Interview with Stanislaw Lem," *The Alien Critic* 3, no. 3 (1974): 8.

 38. Stanislaw Lem, "Stanislaw Lem, Krakow Poland," *SF Commentary* 24 (1973): 28.

 39. Stanislaw Lem, *Solaris*, trans. Joanna Kilmartin and Steve Cox (New York: Berkley Medallion Books, 1971), 16.

 40. Ibid., pp. 60, 61, 62.

 41. Ibid., p. 117.

 42. Ibid., p. 141.

 43. Ibid., p. 99.

 44. Ibid., pp. 187–88.

 45. Ibid., p. 11.

 46. Ibid., p. 153.

 47. Ibid., p. 210.

 48. Ibid., pp. 17, 24, 26, 30, 82, 211.

 49. Ibid., pp. 37, 192.

 50. Ibid., p. 211.

WILLIAM F. TOUPONCE

Reverie and the Marvelous

In this chapter and the next we will examine two of Bradbury's early
attempts at fantasy in the marvelous and Gothic traditions. I am not so
much interested in linking them to these traditions as examples of it as
I am in showing how reverie is present as a softening and transforming
influence. The first story contains an object reverie and the second an
exploration of the splittings and doublings that accompany the *anima–
animus dialectic* of reverie. A typical object reverie involves a fathoming
of the object in its material intimacy which then offers us a world. Most
of us have had the experience of the revelation of a marvelous interior by
certain objects: one discovers flowers and figures in the intimacy of frost
or crystal, a play of sculpture and design in stone. The object reverie typi-
cally goes in a multiple trajectory from exterior to interior, from interior to
exterior. Among the objects which privilege this sort of dynamic dreaming consciousness are of course sea shells, and our first story is about the
discovery of a fantastic world through inhabiting one. The doublings of
the self in reverie are characteristically less harsh and demonic than those
of the Gothic, reverie itself being dominated by images of feminine repose.
Our second story involves a fantastic world imagined by a woman frustrated by and afraid of her lover in the real world, though she is nonetheless a prodigious dreamer of mutual idealization.

From *Ray Bradbury and the Poetics of Reverie: Fantasy, Science Fiction, and the Reader*, pp.
21–41, 113–14. © 1984, 1981 by William Ferdinand Touponce.

It is no accident that both stories take place on occasions ideal for reverie and reading itself in the real world—vacations, periods of recuperation from illness, and lazy, rainy afternoons. In these early stories Bradbury is exploring his strategy for reverie which will later culminate in *The Martian Chronicles* and *Fahrenheit 451* where a whole kaleidoscopic array of reveries is presented to the reader. These novels are in themselves largely self-contained fantasy worlds, not marked by transitions from the ordinary to the fantastic (though it could be argued that *Fahrenheit 451* moves from a fantastic world to a real one). In any case the modern fantastic, as written by Bradbury, does not merely involve the laying bare of Gothic props and supernatural conventions. As always with Bradbury's poetics of reverie, it is a question of having the reader respond to a world and it is this which must be studied.

"The Sea Shell" (1944) was first published in the pulp magazine *Weird Tales*, of interest now because it introduced us to so many American authors of weird and horror fiction: H. P. Lovecraft, Robert Bloch, Clark Ashton Smith, and Bradbury himself, to name just a few.[1] It is one of Bradbury's earliest stories exploring childhood and reverie, creating both suspense and surprise as part of its overall discovery-structure. Because of the typical trajectory of this discovery-structure, "The Sea Shell" is practically an allegory of the reader's task in texts based on reverie and consequently we will want to examine it in some detail. It also contains one of the essential themes of the self in nineteenth-century fantastic literature according to Tzvetan Todorov: metamorphosis or rebirth to another self.[2]

Readers aware of the Romantic tradition will perhaps already have in mind from the title Wordsworth's poetic dream in the fifth book of *The Prelude*. As W. H. Auden points out in his archetypal poetic mediation on this dream of Wordsworth, *The Enchafed Flood*, the siren voice of the poetic shell calls men to the sea, the double kingdom, to put off their human nature and be trolls.[3] This prospect is alluring to the child in our story (and a rebirth motif is very much in evidence, though subtly handled), but he is not faced with the adult dilemma of the romantic hero according to Auden, which is the danger of becoming through this transformation a purely self-conscious ego. His problem is really the essential problem of adolescence, "that fever of time in human life," as Bachelard says.[4] Initially, his impatience appears to be due to an inability to sublimate in the Freudian manner, deferring his immediate desires with the substitution of another, more socially acceptable object. But actually the sublimation involved is that of reverie for the object does not give rise only to intellectual constructs. It gives rise to a fantastic world. We may call this problem the Omar Khayyam complex, since it is brought out consciously by the boy's mother and therefore the adult perspective, as such. She manifests a wistful kind of sadness towards him, no doubt because she knows what the adult world will do to her boy's dreams. In terms of oneiric criticism, she becomes a kind of anima figure (a feminine character who transmits the reverie object, or helps the reader/dreamer discover his own capacity for reverie, and guides him in that process) as she transmits the reverie object to her son, which provides the means for his escape.

"The Sea Shell" is an allegory of reverie and the reading process because the child's fidelity to the sea shell (often a symbol of psychic transformation and therefore familiar ground in the repertoire) and his persistent daydreaming of it during his convalescence, allows him to transcend the boredom of his harassed confinement in an act of pure transcendence and flight from the real world. As it turns out, the reader himself has to imagine through a surprise ending how this transcendence came about, but it is nevertheless subliminally prepared for him in descriptions of the child's inner world given by the narrator. In terms of oneiric criticism, this surprise has a later integrative phase, that of Bachelardian reverberation, in which the surprising aspects are seen in connection with what has gone before, with the whole drift of reading experience. In short the reader is brought to a confrontation with his own constitutive activity.

In this manner a dynamic dialectic of inside and out, of familiar and unfamiliar, is generated by the spirals of the reverie object. Primarily we see things from the child's limited point of view. That the child may be carried *too* far away is certainly suggested, since the alluring voices that come from the shell seem to anticipate his reactions. Some readers may feel uneasy about the prospect of the child being trapped in a world so different from that of an adult, but this reaction stems from our sharing of the mother's point of view. Bradbury's basic strategy is to present through a fantastic event the inadequacy of our adult view of things. This in turn releases the reader's spontaneity to seek a deeper understanding of the relationship between childhood imagination and reality.

The plot which underlies this transformation is realistic and straightforward, concerned with the everyday activities of parents and children in the midst of warm domesticity. We are surrounded by what is obviously an American small-town landscape. Johnny Bishop is an eleven-year-old who is simply too impatient to wait a week for his cold to take its natural course. He wants to be out of bed, and outside to play pirate with his friends. The action of the Omar Khayyam complex organizes for the reader all those images and suggestions of compulsive hurrying that appear in the time-flow of reading. The norms of the adult world, the world of constraints on desire and deferral of satisfaction, are represented in the text by the mother. She gives her son a sea shell "to have fun with," hoping that it will ease his impatience. But this only leads to more questions on the part of the boy. The mother finds that she cannot frame an answer to his naive questions about the value of these defer-rals. In this manner two very different perspectives are set in a hermeneutic tension and revolve around the sea shell. In the solitude and repose during the next day and night, Johnny begins to inhabit the world of the shell, by listening to the sounds of the imaginary ocean contained in it. This landscape comes more and more to dominate the real world, until supernatural voices beckon the boy to come away. Finally the mother discovers that Johnny is not in his room, and, thinking that he has disobeyed her in running off to play with his friends, she picks up the shell. She hears Johnny playing in the surf when she puts it to her ear.

Having discussed the repertoire and strategies of this text, we can now proceed to treat it as an allegory of our theory of reading. It should be stressed for the sake of clarity however that in general and in all cases where we are dealing with imagistic acts of consciousness produced from a text, to objec-tivate does not mean to reify. I am simply thematizing and bringing out for analysis those acts of consciousness which were operative in passive syntheses during reading in order to reveal how the process of consistency-building is built up and destroyed, giving rise to the experience of the imaginary and the reader's released spontaneity. Those acts of consciousness described remain dynamic and functional for other readers. Since the story is short, I will quote extensively from it in order to give the reader the all-important sense of con-text within which reverie develops. It begins by formulating a desire:

> He wanted to get out and run, bounding over hedges, kicking
> tin cans down the alley, shouting at all the windows for the gang
> to come and play. The sun was up and the day was bright, and
> here he was swaddled with bed clothes, sweating and scowling,
> and not liking it at all. (p. 388)

As we are made familiar with the world of this story in this opening paragraph, we can already sense the presence of a self (or complex) in a child-hood landscape and certain magical acts, emotive images, relating to that landscape. There are, in fact, two opposing landscapes that can be observed on closer inspection. One is imaginary and desired, the other is real and frus-trating. Thus a subliminal suspense, a tension of inside and out, is generated at the outset. The landscape of activity the boy desires is outside; to escape to it he transforms the frustrating situation inside by recourse to imaginary acts (which are also emotive intentions) that evoke the presence of objects from that desired landscape: an alley, tin cans to kick, windows to shout at, friends to play with. The objects are given as having value within the horizon of his imaginary play on this sunny, bright day. In the imaginary landscape the boy can move freely, without resistance from the pragmatic world. The real world reveals itself as confining, and the boy is "not liking it at all."

The swaddling clothes, objects which resist his activity, also hint at the rebirth motif and at the fact that for the moment he is a helpless baby, a prospect at which he scowls. Because the situation is difficult and he has no means of escape as yet, the boy has unreflectively invested the world with frustration and is living it as such. The swaddling clothes are his sweating confinement. It is the world which appears frustrating. However, by an emotional and magical act negating his situation, the boy has also made imaginatively present to us another landscape. There is a strong subliminal link here with the body as landscape. As we shall see, the boy will act on his own sublimatory "lost" body in reverie in order to escape this frustrating situation (in the real world, the fever effectively separates him from his body, makes him self-conscious of it).

The story continues to present more familiar objects of the inside convalescent world subtly transformed by the child's imagination: perfumes (his mother's, orange juice and medicine) evoke the presence of objects that have passed through the atmosphere and are now absent. This scent-laden atmosphere is expressive of a passive mind saturated with emotion and memory, against which the boy rebels. The day is "up," and a shaft or sunlight strikes *down* at him. The patchwork quilt appears to shout at him, just as he imagines shouting at the windows outside. Objects of this world magically shout back at him:

> The entire lower half of the patch-work quilt was a circus banner of red, green, purple and blue. It practically yelled color into his eyes. Johnny fidgeted.
> "I wanna go out," he complained softly. "Darn it. Darn it." A fly buzzed, bumping again and again at the window pane with a dry staccato of its transparent wings.
> Johnny looked at it, understanding how it wanted out, too. (p. 233)

A circus is a world of brightly clashing colors which creates at times the magical illusion of flying apart. A multi-colored banner rippling in the wind and sun is its metonymic emblem. The important thing about this emblem (besides the formal tension of its colors) is, phenomenologically, the implied spatial structure which is operative here. The banner is always placed at the top of a pole or mast, overlooking the circus world. The raised position of the banner literally expresses ex-*alta*tion, or the desire to heighten one's life by raising it above the normal level (sublimation in the Bachelardian sense).

Generally, a banner is a sign of victory or self-assertion, but poor Johnny seems wrapped in a defeat which yells color at his eyes. He finds an equivalent for his situation in a not-so-antiseptic creature that normally belongs to the outside world also. The fly "shouts" against the window with its transparent wings that suggest magical flight. As we are made familiar with these objects (the window, the bed-quilt, etc.) we also take over these subliminal, emotive image-structures which appear transformed subtly again in the following sequences (especially the last, where they serve to ground the familiar world which is then abruptly transformed, and through an object with which we are going to be made very familiar: the sea shell).

The mother brings Johnny the bad news that he will have to remain in bed for another two days, a fact that arouses his consternation. He resents having to drink more "healthful" fluids, even if the taste is disguised with orange juice, but the mother offers no medicine this time, only an unfamiliar object:

> "This time—no medicine."
> "What's that in your hand?"
> "Oh, this?" Mother held out a round, spiralled gleaming object.
> Johnny took it. It was hard and shiny and—pretty. "Doctor Hull dropped by a few minutes ago and left it. He thought you might have fun with it." (p. 389)

It should be pointed out that the mother emerges into this conversation from a freshly polished hall shining from the care with which she has touched it. The house is her reverie object, and although she is an adult, as anima figure she still has the sensuous feel for objects that awakens reverie. There is a subliminal suggestion that the boy is already living within a polished shell. Be that as it may, we now find emerging here a network of intentionality surrounding the shell. The doctor sends it as an object intended to be healthful and to assuage the boy's impatience. For her part, the mother transmits these values and shows the boy how to imagine the shell in the next sequence. Because she is an adult, however, she does not transform the shell into a world, although she certainly invests it with value (perhaps she thinks of it as a distraction for her son). Her affective grasp of this object is therefore weak or delicate when compared to the boy's surprise.

The irony is, of course, that the boy will do more than just "have fun" with the shell in rejecting the norms of the adult world. The child will become so familiar with the gift that he genuinely surprises his mother (and us) at the end. He will transform his "Omar Khayyam complex" by living it completely, by transcending it towards a childhood world without parental complexes.

For the moment, however, let us note that the shell forms the center of a developing narrative network embracing all the characters. Johnny's first perception of the inanimate shell is from the outside; it is seen as having a humanly-defined lure of prettiness whose resistant textures (hard and shiny and spiralled) invite a loving caress. But the boy is dubious, perhaps because the object *is* unfamiliar, and he needs to classify it before he will accept it:

> Johnny looked palely dubious. His small hands brushed the slick surface. "How can I have fun with it? I don't even know what it is!"
>
> Mother's smile was better than sunshine. "It's a shell from the sea, Johnny. Doctor Hull picked it up on the Pacific shore last year when he was out there."
>
> "Hey, that's all right. What kind of shell is it?"
>
> "Oh, I don't know. Some form of sea life probably lived in it once, a long time ago."
>
> Johnny's brows went up. "Lived in this? Made it a home?"
>
> "Yes."
>
> "Aw—really?"
>
> She adjusted it in his hand. "If you don't believe me, listen for yourself, young man. Put this end—here—against your ear."
>
> "Like this?" He raised the shell to his small pink ear and pressed it tight. "Now what do I do?"
>
> Mother smiled. "Now, if you're very quiet, and listen closely, you'll hear something very, very familiar."
>
> Johnny listened, His ear opened imperceptibly like a small flower opening, waiting.
>
> A titanic wave came in on a rocky shore and smashed itself down.
>
> "The sea!" cried Johnny Bishop. "Oh, Mom! The ocean! The waves! The sea!"
>
> Wave after wave came in on that distant, craggy shore. Johnny closed his eyes tight black and a smile folded his small face exactly in half. Wave after pounding wave roared in his small pinkly alert ear.
>
> "Yes, Johnny," said Mother. "The sea." (p. 389)

Another landscape (still distant because the child is not immersed in it as yet) has been made imaginatively present. The mother's magic (the magic of the Other in transforming *my* world) is to transform Johnny's world from the outside.[5] She shows him the very familiar in the unfamiliar, teaching him to discover the marvelous by patient listening to the reverberation of images (Bachelard's *retentissement*). The sea shell is indeed a marvelous reverie object because it contains within it an intimate immensity—the boy can hold the ocean in the palm of his hand. At the beginning of this passage the shell is somewhat of an empty schema for the child. He has no knowledge of it other than what is given in perception or from his mother who guides him through this reverie experience. He is given some knowledge of it from her (she tells him it is from the Pacific shore) which he then fills in with affective intentions in order to transform his situation. The shell is first hypothesized as containing life (the waves have the activity and weight of bodies here)—which the child initially disputes. The boy is dubious about any living creature wanting to live in such a confined space. But then he is asked to listen (imagine for himself) in order to discover that life. He discovers to his surprise the internal landscape of the sea within it. Magically, the sea shell works a kind of spell on him. Coming from the Other, and yet being safe, it shatters the pragmatic order of the day by disrupting his expectations.

But Johnny also acts unreflectively on himself. He "lives" this illusion in which the world seems changed. He is able to inhabit this magical world in an instant, through the phenomenon of belief created by the incantation of the waves pounding on the beach. Now, these imaginative acts are already a transformation of the world which has become too difficult for him. They are the means by which he apprehends this new and unfamiliar object. Imagination in reverie is therefore not merely the filling in of empty schemas of knowledge with images. It is also the magical emotive transformation of those objects as we would like them to be (and just for the sake of oneiric verisimilitude, Bradbury has us learn in the next section that the boy has never *seen* the ocean but is working from analogies of a local lake by exaggerating images. Exaggeration, according to Bachelard, is the surest sign of wonder).

Normally, we learn about new objects through perception, that is, by *degrees*. They offer solid resistance to our attempts to know them; they are never (or rarely) seen as totalities, only as given in perspective, in facets. In fact the boy expresses his *impatience* with this perceptual process. How can I have fun with it, he says, if I don't know what it is, as if only those things which offer instantaneously the promise of a world (namely, images) are worthy enough to hold a world of freedom. The mother hopes to teach the boy patience by listening, but we can see that he has discovered that reverie negates a problematic world of frustration and setbacks (the adult world) by offering an instantaneous transformation in which we "live" our desires. And it must be persistently believed in, dreamt with fidelity, if it is to rival the real world. As we shall see, that is exactly what Johnny does in the following sequences.

But what of the reader's role thus far? Has his capacity for reverie been activated? Bachelard himself was extremely fond of shells, but he points out in *The Poetics of Space*, where he devotes an entire chapter to them, that the material imagination suffers a kind of defeat before this beautifully formal object. For Bachelard the shell would seem a triumph of the formal imagination, nature herself having dreamt pure geometry in a spiral that nevertheless represents the life force itself. How is it possible, Bachelard wonders, to surpass nature in her own dream? Perhaps, Bachelard suggests, we should begin phenomenologically with the naive observer, the child, before the object which will invite his daydream. Now, because the shell is a hollow object that once contained life, it has borne the traditional associations of the allegory of body and soul. In order to avoid these scholarly accretions therefore what one needs to consider is the "function of inhabiting" these objects. This will counter the classifying tendencies of the conchologist.

Then, says Bachelard, a lively dialectics of childhood wonderment emerges. In the textual play of his own meditation Bachelard considers many descriptions of melusines and fantastic monsters that dreamers have imagined to inhabit empty shells. He comments on fantastic texts where wondrously large creatures, like elephants, emerge from small shells, activating a dialectics of large and small. The phenomenologist's imagination is also stimulated by the dialectics of creatures that are free and others that are in fetters. Bachelard notes however that this exercise often leads to a fear–curiosity complex. We want to see what is in the shell, but we are afraid of what might leap out at us:

> These undulations of fear and curiosity increase when reality is not there to moderate them, that is, when we are imagining. However, let's not invent, but rather give documents concerning images which have actually been imagined or drawn, and which have remained engraved in precious and other stones. There is a passage in the book by Jurgis Baltrusaitis in which he recalls the *action* of an artist who shows a dog that "leaps from its shell" and pounces upon a rabbit. One degree more of aggressiveness and the shell-dog would attack a man. This is a clear example of the progressing type of action by means of which imagination surpasses reality. For here the imagination acts upon not only geometrical dimensions, but upon elements of power and speed as well—not in an enlarged space, either, but in a more rapid tempo. When the motion picture camera accelerates the unfolding of a flower, we receive a sublime image of offering; it is as though the flower we see opening so

quickly and without reservation, sensed the meaning of a gift; as though it were a gift from the world. But if the cinema showed us a snail emerging from its shell in fast motion, or pushing its horns toward the sky very rapidly, what an aggression that would be! What aggressive horns! All our curiosity would be blocked by fear, and the fear–curiosity complex would be torn apart.[6]

It should now be apparent that we have not been wandering from our topic, the reader's role, as might first have seemed. The undulating spiral of fear and curiosity is not allowed to increase (as yet) because reality *is* there in our story in the form of a generalized schema of a shell to moderate it. The mother is guiding the reader as well, by assuring him that Johnny is going to find something very very familiar in the shell. We are assured that no fantastic animal is going to suddenly leap upon us—as perhaps would happen in some weird or horror stories. Our imagination is not allowed aggressively to surpass reality.

Furthermore, the fear aspect of this reading complex is softened by the narrator's flower image, which offers to the reader the promise of a safe refuge in inhabiting the shell. We can describe phenomenologically how this feeling is established for the reader by passive syntheses in the following manner. The reader has first of all to build up a series of equivalences between flower and shell. A flower is a formal image, equivalent to a shell in that respect, but unlike the shell it is rapidly opening, suggesting a certain dynamism. An open image is the only image sure to bring about reverie. Second, Johnny's ear opens imperceptibly. We are not asked to perceive, but to imagine a small flower opening, waiting. The flower image is not just a static metaphor, but suggests an equivalent to Johnny's experience which is in the nature of a guarded, protected opening to an as yet strange and unfamiliar world. The reader's further imagination of Johnny's ear as another kind of shell, small and pink, is thus mediated by an oneiric image, hence its central position in this passage.

Thus the oneiric level of the text aids us imperceptibly in integrating two dimensions of experience, self and world. The flower image presents the reader with interiority that invites intimacy; it gives him the assurance that he is going to link up oneiric relations that reverie will make inexhaustible in this new world. In short, the flower defines the reader's imaginative position in an instantaneous act of consciousness: the reader is centered as in the center of a flower, surrounded by rays of color in the delicately nuanced petals of meaning. And if we now consider Bachelard's fantasy about the rapidly opening flower, then this surprise image of offering can be linked back oneirically to the doctor's and the mother's gifts. This surprise linking introduces an oneiric level of significance to narrative consciousness, tells us that the reverie world offers itself as a flower to us, and assures us that we will inhabit this world without fear.

At the end of this sequence, when the waves wash refreshingly again and again over it, Johnny's ear is practically a small pink creature inhabiting the shell. If he is then a creature "in fetters" in the large shell of the house, then one definitely gets the feeling that he is going to prepare this small space as a means of dynamic escape. His ear is now "pinkly alert," that is, now that the equivalence of the house and shell have been established by an oneiric logic of invention (if the entire sea can be contained in such a small space, why not a boy?). Johnny closes his eyes "tight black," smiling broadly, no longer wanting to consider the shell in formal imagination. No longer respecting form or color (those stable things) he is seized by a conviction of a refuge in which life can be concentrated and then transcended by leaping to meet the in-coming waves.

Let us now summarize the passive syntheses that we have made thematic in the past few pages. Initially, the boy is seduced by the unfamiliar formal and sensuous beauty of the shell. He wants to classify it in order to play with it in an exterior fashion. This is as far a Freudian sublimation would go—the limit of the concept. The shell is then hypothesized as containing life, but the boy is dubious about any creature wanting to inhabit such a small space. It seems a very small and confining world indeed. The mother/anima figure then guides the boy by putting the shell to his ear so that he can "believe" in the statement she has made. Then, as we have seen, this gesture activates the fantasy of rebirth to another world. Johnny finally leaves behind the formal imagination (which, as Bachelard says, defeats the production of images) and establishes an imaginative grounding in *matter*, the water which will underlie and sustain the play of surface imagery in the third sequence. Johnny can hear the play of his friends outside:

> Their voices seemed so far away, lazy, drifting on a tide of sun. The sunlight was just like deep yellow, lambent water, lapping at the summer, full tide. Slow, languorous, warm, lazy. The whole world was over its head in that tide and everything was slowed down. The clock ticked slower. The street car came down the avenue in warm metal slow motion. It was almost like seeing a motion film that is losing speed and noise. Everything was softer. Nothing seemed to count as much.
>
> He wanted to get out and play, badly. He kept watching the kids climbing the fences, playing soft ball, roller skating in the warm languor. His head felt heavy, heavy, heavy. His eyelids were

window sashes pulling down, down. The sea shell lay against his ear. He pressed it close.

Pounding, drumming, waves broke on a shore. A yellow sand shore. And when the waves went back out they left foam, like the suds of beer, on the sand. The suds broke and vanished, like dreams. And more waves came with more foam. And the sand crabs tumbled, salt-wet, scuttling brown, in the ripples. Cool green water pounding on the sand. The very sound of it conjured up visions; the ocean breeze soothed Johnny Bishop's small body. Suddenly the hot afternoon was no longer hot and depressing. The clock started ticking faster. The street cars clanged metal quickly. The slowness of the summer world was spanked into crisp life by the pound-pound of waves on an unseen and brilliant beach. (p. 390)

Insofar as I have been able to determine, this is the earliest example in Bradbury's fantasy of a deliberately narrated daydream. As such, it is an exemplary illustration of a dreaming subject going into image-making reverie in an imaginary landscape unseen yet brilliant. It unfolds in three phases which are coherent deformations of each other. The dozing style of the first phase seems to me to evoke the mingling of memory and imagination. It suggests long solitary hours spent lying idle on the beach at Fox Lake, where we know the boy has vacationed before. It is the recollection of a real landscape of gently lapping water that gradually immerses the real world with the help of the boy's imagination. Once he finds this element he wants to develop it further, to sublimate it further from small lake to ocean. As the boy half shuts his eyes in the lazy warmth, the two landscapes, real and imagined, seem to melt into each other. The world seems bathed in the languorous yellow light of this remembered daydream; indeed, it appears to be underwater (suggesting the pastness of the past), and objects of the familiar outside world are being slowed down by the resistance of the tide of liquid sun. Notice especially the "far away" perception of objects that are softened by reverie into meaning less than they normally do as utensils in the real world. The metal of the street car is on the verge of a surreal deformation.

The same phenomenological psychology that was operative before is again operative here—he finds the world difficult and tries to escape, this time by falling back into a reverie he had experienced long ago, one which has been reactivated by his discovery of the sea shell's reverberating interiority. It is thus the reverie object which activates the archetype of watery rebirth, but I am not arguing for any causal determinism here. The real world in fact appears to be losing speed and time—and its grip on him. No doubt the boy has something of a fever, but convalescence here is simply a metaphor for reverie (in one of his aphorisms Bachelard asks us: is not every convalescence a childhood?). The body is again the substratum for reverie. The text gives us a humorous comparison of the boy's eyes closing like window sashes shutting out the unreachable desired world of play outside. It is a familiar enough metaphor, but appropriate to the hypnagogic phases of reverie where acts of consciousness may take on a dramatized form. Of course the whole point of the metaphor is to show us that the boy does not *want* to fall asleep where he would be something less than an active subject pursuing his own intentions.

The only recourse is to evoke a world of activity, and when the boy puts the shell to his ear in the second phase, we enter reverie proper. The beach is described as an independent world, as brilliant yet unseen. No transition is given by the narrator; the world is magically *there*, rivalling the real world through the incantation of its waves. The shell recalls the yellow sand shore of its origin, and takes the boy with it. The water of the sea is, however, unlike that of the lake. It is a force which produces new images, thousands of them. The archetypal foam is full of bubble-dreams, visions of worlds possible if evanescent.

All of this shows us that once the imagination touches matter in reverie, it produces multivalent, excessive beauty, and psychic well-being. Notice, for example, the healthful activity of the little sand crabs who are so obviously seen as aggressively tanned by the sun. Reverie has dislodged and jostled the very adjectives that describe their behavior out of their familiar positions: they are imagined as dynamic and moving, tumbled, salt-wet, scuttling brown. If given free rein, reverie often plays with words in this fashion, creating surprise by new syntactic relationships among words, but there are never any violent eruptions of nonsense which are irreducible to meaning. In the unconscious field we may experience a complete lapsus of the word; in reverie the archetypal element, the substance being imagined, controls the play of linguistic signs. In this world the cold splash of the waves provides a material resistance and meaning stimulating to the imagination, a kind of joyful intentionality that experiences a force in directing itself towards an object. It is altogether different from the sweating adversity of the boy's bed clothes.

In the third and final phase, Johnny returns to the real world which is seen as refreshed, and moving faster from his reverie activity. The ocean breeze has soothed his body—again, an indication of how the unreflective emotive intentions of reverie act magically to transform the world by influencing the body. The summer world is spanked into crisp life, a metaphor of rebirth, of course, but perhaps also recalling the image of the doctor who picked up the shell. There is not as yet a completely independent fantastic world however. It is only the real world which has been rejuvenated. But by virtue of this experience of imaginary meaning sustained by acts of consciousness based on archetypal matter, by the fact that its beautiful and new images are born in the dreamer's solitude away from the real world of perception, by virtue of the fact that the dreamer ventures far away to recover these riches, and by virtue of the well-being it creates, we can call this passage a successful reverie. That the child is a persistent day-dreamer is indicated in a narrator's summary that follows this passage, a passage which estimates the value of the shell in days to come. It is a means to keep temporality flowing onwards toward the future.

There is one aspect of reverie which we first mentioned in our brief summary in the introduction that as yet we have not discussed, namely, its cosmic power of origination. This is actually the most important dimension of reverie, but I have put off discussion of it until the fourth narrative sequence because it is made thematic for the reader there. The fourth sequence is a cognitive attempt at a "philosophy of childhood." The reader is asked to consider the child's desire and imagination in a much larger context which reflects the possibilities of man as a conscious being. There is an allusion from the repertoire to the *Rubaiyat* of Omar Khayyam (whose verse form, the *ruba'i*, was said to have been accidentally discovered by a poet who overheard the gleeful shout of a child at play and adopted it) to aid the reader in understanding the problem of the conflict or problematic opposition of the world of childhood and the adult's world. The dialogue takes the form of a lesson about the necessity, from the adult's point of view, of acquiring the attributes of maturity: waiting, planning, and above all being patient (there is probably a pun on being a patient and impatience). Yet there is no doubt where the sympathy of the reader should lie, because the mother herself feels the loss of her own childhood in the eyes of her son, which are wide and full of the blue light of his imaginary ocean. Her lesson is therefore somewhat reversed on her.

Now, the boy has learned through the persistence of his daydream the power of cosmic origination in reverie. With that power the boy can say "no" to the adult world even as the new world of reverie opens up for him (symbolically expressed by the shell which he keeps listening to and putting against his ear throughout the lesson). He is no longer completely captive in the world of adults, and we have seen him play with this new-found power (which some parental readers may find anxiety-provoking) in the narrated daydream of the third sequence. Iser might say that what the child has learned, though he cannot at this stage explicitly formulate it, is that his acts are not determined. Imaginative acts of consciousness are caused by nothing but consciousness itself; indeed, they are the characteristic free functioning of childhood consciousness (as readers, we share these acts of imaginative consciousness and spontaneously give our own as well, so it can be said that they are characteristic of adult consciousness as well—a point which I will elaborate in my summary of the reader's discovery in this text). Johnny is a free, if perhaps not entirely responsible, agent. His great discovery is that there is a world of oneiric possibility superadded to the world of reality. The boy is not restricted to the real, for he can enter at will the realm of the ideal through the reverie object. He has the power to negate the actual and actualize the merely possible. Why should he not be intoxicated with this magic power (the sea foam is compared to suds of beer, we remember) and be very reluctant to give it up. Most importantly, however, the child's accession to the freedom of reverie is a break with reality, a rupture which refuses the adult world in creating its own. Johnny's questioning and contrary attitude in this sequence is an important indication that he finds the adult world inadequate and incomplete. The child's imagination is not, therefore, perception revivified, but a characteristic function of human consciousness which transforms the world by the power of negation.

As the end of the third sequence, Johnny had asked his mother about going to the seashore as soon as possible (he imagines the sea as being better than Fox Lake) not being willing to wait for his father's two-week vacation in July. Now the mother tries to teach him patience:

> Mother sat down on the bed and held his hand. The things she said he couldn't understand fully, but some of them made sense. "If I had to write a philosophy of children, I guess I'd title it impatience. Impatience with everything in life. . . . You're a tribe of potential Omar Khayyams, that's what." (p. 391)

She reminds him of the attributes of maturity and he responds:

> "I don't wanna be patient. I don't like being in bed. I want to go to the sea shore." (p. 391)

The mother tries to mediate the problem of childhood by offering an example from her own childhood:

> "I remember, I saw a doll once when I was a girl. I told my mother about it, said it was the last one for sale, I said I was afraid it would be sold before I could get it. The truth of the matter is there were a dozen others just like it. I couldn't wait. I was impatient, too."
>
> Johnny shifted on the bed. His eyes widened and got full of blue light. "But Mom, I don't want to wait. If I wait too long, I'll be grown up, and then it won't be any fun." (p. 391)

Obviously, the mother does not want the boy to lie about how well he feels, but the boy's remark about the adult world stifling the fun of things (it doesn't matter how *many* dolls, or sea shells, there are in truth, he seems to say, what matters is having one as a reverie object for one's childhood—otherwise, what would one have to look back on from adulthood if one was never allowed to develop reveries during this precious time) brings the mother to the brink of tears:

> " . . . Sometimes I think you're—right. But I don't dare tell you. It isn't according to the rules—"
> "What rules, Mom?"
> "Civilization's. Enjoy yourself, while you are young. Enjoy yourself, Johnny." She said it strong, and funny-like.
> Johnny put the shell to his ear. "Mom. Know what I'd like to do? I'd like to be at the seashore right now, running towards the water, holding my nose and yelling, 'Last one in is a double-darned monkey!'" Johnny laughed.
> The phone rang downstairs. Mother walked to answer it.
> Johnny lay there, quietly, listening. (pp. 391–392)

Teaching the reader an unexpected lesson about the necessity of childhood reverie, the mother's attempt to mediate the values of civilization and its discontents (the renunciation of reverie, if not of instinct) to the child has backfired. The equivalences she offers as a bridge of understanding all fail before the boy's desire. She must listen to the pragmatic voices of the adult world, symbolized by the telephone, while her son listens to the call of the sea. Putting the shell to his ear, the child again makes a gesture of commitment to his reverie world. This kind of reversal of intention will be repeated at the end of the last sequence when the mother puts the shell to her ear and hears supernatural voices; in fact she hears the exact same words: "Last one in is a double-darned monkey." This doubling or echoing shatters the framework of everyday reality as her own son becomes a supernatural Other transforming her world from the "outside," that is, from the world within the shell. Thus the reader is made familiar here with a challenging phrase that will return to surprise and perhaps mock him in a fantastic mode. It could be argued that this repetition brings about an uncanny effect of meaning in the reader, but it is actually more in the nature of a fulfillment of meaning postulated as an empty intention earlier.

Certainly it intensifies the problem of a "philosophy of childhood" of whose meaning we might have thought ourselves master. We learn that the language and attitude towards the problem of childhood expressed by the mother, while pretending to be univocal, actually admits to having a double meaning. Children are a potential tribe of Omar Khayyams, always wanting to shatter the schema of things and refashion it closer to the heart's desire (the XCIX stanza of the *Rubaiyat*). Thus the phrase "to have fun with," repeated several times in the story, comes to mean quite different things to the mother than to the boy. The mother thinks that the schema of things, the harsh rule of the reality principle and civilization, cannot be broken, but in the story's marvelous ending, they are. This surprise causes the reader to reexamine the nature of the relationship between imagination and reality, to reconsider a philosophy which represses what childhood reverie does with language, and to formulate for himself the ways in which that schema, which seems so solid, can be broken together with the value of breaking it.

The mother/anima figure raises the possibility that a philosophy of childhood could be written. Bachelard's texts affirm that it can, although in ways subtly subversive of philosophic conceptual mastery itself. We ourselves have been reading (or rather writing about) this story as if it were an allegory of childhood and reverie, as if the entire text had the effect of being an illustration of that idea. As Todorov points out, this procedure is a meta-reading which to an extent falsifies the all-important temporal and experiential structure of fantasy texts. Knowing the end destroys the function of hesitation on which the genre seems to depend.[7] For Todorov, the fantastic is a genre of "emphatic temporality." It is essential in his view that a reading of the fantastic follow that of the reader in his identification with a character step by irreversible step. We too want to follow the flow of reading and not to impose artificial constructs, yet this procedure is justified here because the reader's double role in "The Sea Shell" directs him to reconsider retrospectively and reflectively the relationship of imagination to reality he held prior to reading. In philosophical terms, when the empty schema of the shell is marvelously "filled in" with supernatural voices at the end, we wonder how the boy manages to be absent from the world yet present in language at the same time. Our allegorical reading does not therefore destroy the effect of the fantastic, so much as it does thematize how that effect is brought about through the experience of the imaginary, the ontological significance of which the reader has to search for at the end. Let us therefore consider how the themes and elements of the fantastic emerge in the fifth sequence.

There is first of all the reader's hesitation (constituting what in Todorov's view is the evanescent theoretical genre of the pure fantastic) about the supernatural voices that emerge from the shell. Is the boy imagining them or are they real? The narrator gives us no indication but records the character's own surprise and hesitation on hearing them. We are still very much in the adult scheme of things at the beginning of this sequence. However, a dynamic tension between two landscapes is again conveyed through an oneiric window-metaphor: stars are caught in the squared glass corrals of the big window. This suggested equivalence brings about a child's view of the night sky's constellations as brightly moving animal figures that have been imprisoned, and lends a sense of cosmic sympathy to the boy's situation. But from this confining boundary or frame to the end of the story, the events move away from the world of everyday reality to end in what Todorov would classify as a fantastic-marvelous situation, defined as a hesitation between the real and the imaginary where the supernatural has not yet been accepted.[8] Following the character's emotive intentions, the reader has thus far assumed that Johnny was imagining that shore inside the shell, but now autonomous voices appear:

> Johnny closed his eyes. Downstairs, silverware was being clattered at the dinner table. Mom and Pop were eating. He heard Pop laughing his deep laughter.
>
> The waves still came in, over and over, on the shore inside the sea shell. And—something else.
>
> "Down where the waves lift, down where the waves play, down where the gulls swoop low on a summer's day—"
>
> "Huh? Johnny listened. His body stiffened. He blinked his eyes.
>
> Softly, way off:
>
> "Stark ocean sky, sunlight on waves. Yo ho, heave ho, heave ho, my braves—" It sounded like a hundred voices singing to the creak of oar-locks.
>
> "Come down to the sea in ships—"
>
> And then another voice, all by itself, soft against the sound of waves and ocean wind. "Come down to the sea, the contortionist sea, where the great tides wrestle and swell. Come down to the salt in the glittering brine, on a trail that you'll soon know well—"
>
> Johnny pulled the shell from his head, stared at it.
>
> "Do you want to come down to the sea, my lad, do you want to come down to the sea? Well, take me by the hand, my lad, just take me by the hand, my lad, and come along with me!"
>
> Trembling, Johnny clamped the shell to his ear again, sat up in bed, breathing fast. His small heart leaped and hit the wall of his chest. (p. 392)

The presence of these legendary voices is full of the dynamic activity the child desires. They could be pirates or Sinbad the sailor's men, a tribe of potential

Omar Khayyams. Interacting with the sea by rowing rhythmically, they chant of magical pathways among the waves. But we do not respond merely to linguistic speech acts. There is again the attraction of shining, gleaming, glittering things from a landscape brilliant but unseen. Bright colors, pungent smells, and seductive words and gestures call for the boy to immerse himself in their collective action. Then a single voice separates itself from this chanting and invites him to come down to the "contortionist" sea "on a path that you'll soon know well." The very idea of the sea as a contortionist suggests the acrobatic transformation of the self into some extraordinary fantastic position. The ordinary and regular paths of the adult world (which the boy has spent so much time emotively negating) are to be magically replaced by a trail the boy will soon know well by some slight of hand. Clearly, the voice anticipates his inmost desire, surprising and shattering his expectations. The voice comes from the realm of the supernatural Other, but it is nevertheless a guiding voice that tells him he will soon be very familiar with something. It thus quickly establishes its benign nature by mimicking the anima's safe and gradual guidance. It may be demonic, but the surrounding voices are soft, insistent, and Johnny's small heart leaps at the thought of taking part in such rhythmic activity, and by this we know he is already magically transforming his body to meet it. The dialectics of inside and out takes one more step in telling Johnny that the path to the sea-water world lies in the mysterious imagination of the shell's exterior form (the mother had directed his attention to the inside after luring him with exterior prettiness):

> "Have you ever seen a fine conch-shell, shaped and shined like a pearl corkscrew? It starts out big and it ends up small, seemingly ending with nothing at all, but, aye lad, it ends where the sea-cliffs fall; where the sea-cliffs fall to the blue!" (p. 392)

These internally rhyming lines contain the pleasure of novelty and surprise (in seeing words dissimilar in meaning appear similar in sound) while creating a kind of enclosing spell. The spiral is a synthesis of both big and small, a path of infinite imagination that only seems to end up with nothing (complete negation and loss of the real) but actually reveals its own world in the frozen image of a wave at play. Johnny recognizes that the shell points in an imaginary direction, out of this world:

> Johnny's fingers tightened on the circular marks of the shell. That was right. It went around and around and around until you couldn't see it going around any more.
> Johnny's lips tightened. What was it mother had said? Children. The—the philosophy—what a big word! of children!

> Impatience. Impatience! Yes, yes, he was impatient! Why not?
> His free hand clenched into a tiny hard white fist, pounding
> against the covers. (p. 393)

The last gesture is indeed a magical action! Johnny's hand has become a
wave pounding on the beach. He has transformed his mother's philosophy of
children into action, by making his hand into the image of a wave. Why not,
he thinks, negating the adult world, and the reader may find that he himself
has accepted these supernatural events as marvelous, as Johnny seems to
here. At any rate, we can understand why he chooses to hide the precious
shell from his father when he comes to say goodnight. The world of the
child should remain separate from the adult world, we feel.[9] Yet the reader's
fear–curiosity complex is aroused. In the mother's philosophy, the shell can
always be removed from one's ear, one's impatience having been temporarily
assuaged, and it is therefore an object belonging to the larger instrumental
complex of the adult world. But if the shell is itself a world, then the boy is
lost to us. As I have mentioned, some readers may feel a strong sense of menace in the way these voices seem to anticipate his reactions. However, I find
the subliminal suggestion of fear so softened by the boy's obvious enjoyment
and well-being in the reverie world that I do not fear for him at all. My fear
and surprise are rather for the mother in the last sequence.

The sixth and final sequence is told from the mother's point of view,
that is, from the point of view of one who possesses the *philosophic* attributes of maturity, but also an embarrassed sympathy for the child's imagination. At the end of the fifth sequence, we are held in suspense, wondering
whether the voices will be seen to be illusory or not. We carry forward our
hesitation into this last sequence, which at first seems to modulate towards
what Todorov calls the supernatural explained (the uncanny). But the story
then spirals down to a surprise ending—a quality which is difficult to capture in quotation. First of all the boy is absent from the scene, we do not
as yet know where, but all the familiar objects the boy has invested with
emotive intentions return. Through a succession of empty objects that are
nevertheless subliminally suggested as filled (and this juxtaposition leads
the reader, but not the mother, to the oneiric level) we can feel that the boy
has escaped:

> The bed was empty. There was nothing but sunlight and
> silence in the room. Sunlight lay abed, like a bright patient with
> its brilliant head on the pillow. The quilt, a red-blue circus ban-
> ner, was thrown back. The bed was wrinkled like the face of a
> pale old man, and it was very empty. (p. 393)

Daydreaming sunlight, which emanates from the outside world, has taken Johnny's place. The circus banner that confined him is thrown back, abandoned, which reveals the bed itself as transformed to an old man, wrinkled and empty. These images go beyond the obvious rejection-of-adulthood motif—they hint at a transformation of self to a world where youth is forever preserved against the onset of adulthood. They suggest a world transcended. The mother hypothesizes that the child has run outside to play with "those neighbor ruffians." As the mother begins to adjust the quilt into place (trying to rearrange things back to the paths of the ordinary and orderly world) and to smooth the sheets, she discovers that the bed is *not* empty. The shell is there. It appears again as unfamiliar in perception. The mother brings forth "a shining object into the sun." This image hints again at the rebirth motif, for a child is unfamiliar to its mother at birth. She smiles, recognizing it as familiar, and perhaps to remember her own childhood or her son who she assumes is now absent, puts the shell to her ear "just for fun" and receives the shock of her life:

> The room whirled around in a bright swaying merry-go-round
> of bannered quilts and glassed run.
> The sea shell roared in her ear. (p. 394)

The mother's sudden vertiginous loss of reality, the shattering of the adult scheme of things, is conveyed by the rapid motion of the merry-go-round, an object which itself bears connotations of the return of childhood time. We feel that she is instantaneously thrown into this fantastic world, which the narrator now presents without comment, leaving an ellipsis or indeterminacy for the reader at the end:

> Waves thundered on a distant shore. Waves foamed cool on a far
> off beach. (p. 394)

So far, these images are very much like those Johnny discovered in his reverie of the shell, and they could be her reverie, but:

> Then the sound of small feet crunching swiftly in the sand. A
> high young voice yelling: "Hi! Come on, you guys! Last one in is a
> double-darned monkey!"
> And the sound of a small body diving, splashing, into those
> waves . . . (p. 394)

So the story ends, on a fantastic-marvelous event. As Tolkien would perhaps say, the sea shell was no more us than we were it. The reader's spontaneity has been released; the child has become totally Other, transforming the mother's world from the outside (which is also, of course, the inside of a shell). A reverie object of the inside familiar world suddenly reveals its potential to shatter the scheme of things, teaching the mother a lesson in the "philosophy of childhood." The sea shell was an instrument of deferral in the hands of the mother, a world of reverie to the boy, and a means of marvelous escape to whatever supernatural beings seemed to inhabit it. The reader is left with the impossibility of accepting this event as a hallucination—we are given too much of a grounding in the familiar world of the mother to believe that *she* is sick or feverish. Neither can we acquiesce in the pure marvelous, as in a fairy tale, where events of this nature would provoke no surprise. It seems to me that the reader is left with a problem of working out for himself the relationships of imagination and reality that have played back and forth throughout this story.

Summarizing the reader's double role, we can say that the sea shell of our story receives different imaginative values from two perspectives: that of the adult and that of the child. As the story progresses, it functions as a center for intentional acts of consciousness that are instrumental in building up Johnny's sublimative reverie world and in destroying the limited perspectives of the adult world. With the surprise ending the reader is directed towards the oneiric level of the text from which he must build up an adequate "philosophy of childhood." Offering a transcendent vantage point, this level allows the reader to explore existentially his own capacity for reverie. Just as in the experience of the fantastic according to Todorov, the implied reader of "The Sea Shell" is required to judge certain events while identifying himself with a character. Yet these events are so structured by the text that recollecting and anticipatory acts of consciousness on the part of the reader lend it a kind of reflective depth that Bachelard calls reverberation. The reader must built up a system of equivalences between the two perspectives that culminates in the emergence of the aesthetic object, the shell as world. Our surprise at this world "fills in" the passive and provisional syntheses that went before with a more active significance.

Because the shell is only a schema in a story (picking up our allegorical reading again), it solicits us to imagine it, as imagined by the characters of the story who represent the norms of the adult and childhood worlds in conflict. The sea shell reverberates with this conflict as it comes to consciousness in the reader's mind. We reexperience their intentions, but the shell itself remains a beautiful formal object. Only its significance changes, due to the affective intentions, strong or weak, of the characters. As long as we remain on the emotive level (which is basically unreflective) we live this story by our own imaginative acts of consciousness. But reverie becomes a magical world *for us*, we double ourselves in the midst of the pragmatic world we have for the moment suspended. The story would not be able to have the effect on us that it does (the search for the meaning of childhood imagination) if we did not constitute it, however unreflectively, for ourselves first. In that regard, we can agree with Todorov. But the last magical transformation of the shell defeats our expectations, surprises us. We are confronted with our own emotive acts of consciousness as magical,—the very ones we used to constitute a fantastic world—and as we see the mother's world transformed into a dizzying merry-go-round by the supernatural Other. We realize that the shell has been made to conform to the child's ideal image of it, that is, as a world of oneiric activity apart from the adult world, containing him—what he wanted it to be all along. The boy's feelings, we realize, have remade the world closer to his heart's desire. How this occurrence came about we are not told, the text remains in the fantastic-marvelous, and we must re-search the problematic relation between the real and the imaginary.

The reader's unreflective imaginary possession of this story and its reverie object, the sea shell, will lead him later to several discoveries about reverie itself, which we are now prepared to summarize. First of all, we can say that "The Sea Shell" has enriched our understanding of the relationship between the imagination of childhood and the largely perceptual (or so Bradbury presents it) world of adults. Perceptual objects, like the shell, yield themselves only by degrees, never all at once, as in the magical image. There is great pleasure in considering objects for their formal beauty, but their real value can be discovered only by inhabiting them. Second, we realize that should the sea shell have appeared unaccompanied by imaginative transformation, we would have experienced a singularly impoverished world. The childhood imagination in reverie seeks to change the merely perceived by making up for what is lacking in the adult world. Lastly, this magical and emotive transformation of things closer to the heart's desire *is* based on what is known in perception, but it is not merely a reproduction of it. In reverie the image-making powers of the mind are a synthesis of the emotive and the cognitive.

Considered as an objective verbal document, "The Sea Shell" is not the equal in style to some of Bradbury's later accomplishments with object reveries in the context of the family, which we will examine in later chapters. It has a tendency to make its theme—a philosophy of childhood—all too sentimentally obvious. Nevertheless, Bradbury does use those phenomenological elements of the reading process we have outlined—recognition and grounding in the familiar repertoire, expectation, imagistic surprise which then leads to discovery—to enable the reader to constitute one of the major themes of all his work, namely, a philosophy of childhood. The reader of "The Sea Shell" discovers a resultant world composed on the basis of the old and familiar adult world, but yet entirely new and unique, transformed by childhood imagination. As in all texts based on reverie, the reader is compelled to imagine an intimate relation with the cosmos and to wonder at the sudden illumination of the image which opens on another fantastic world.

A sophisticated reader might be inclined to smile at such childish enthusiasms. But Bradbury, in having the reader identify with his character, Johnny Bishop, really returns him to the thing itself, the sea shell, as constituted by a purely phenomenological consciousness, which, because of its extreme naiveté, is without preconceptions. We follow the naive consciousness of the boy imagining the sea shell and gather for ourselves images that suggest a sublimatory capacity for renewal. The reader discovers, in short, a rebirth of his own childhood imagination. Inside the small shell time speeds up in marvelous ways, distance is magically abolished, the reader's imagination bathes in the cosmic rhythms of the sea. Bradbury's formal re-imagining of the shell's spiral has generated a story which begins with traditional images and associations but which does not allow the reader to crawl slowly into the shell and subsist in repose. Johnny has left the sea shell behind, in the hands of the anima figure who gave it to him, for fun. He has transcended the parental "Omar Khayyam complex." He has gone on to dream in his element, water, and the reader may well surmise that the real hero of the story is the doctor, who must have known that a child who cannot imagine surely suffers a worse fate than one who can, no matter how ill, when he picked up the sea shell along the sounding shore.

NOTES

1. Ray Bradbury, "The Sea Shell," in *The Fantastic Pulps*, ed. Peter Haining (New York: Vintage Books, 1975), pp. 386–94. All further references are in the text.

2. Tzvetan Todorov, *The Fantastic*, trans. Richard Howard (Ithaca: Cornell University Press, 1975), p. 109.

3. W. H. Auden, *The Enchafed Flood* (New York: Random House, 1950), pp. 86–87.

4. Gaston Bachelard, *The Poetics of Reverie*, p. 110.

5. Jean-Paul Sartre, *Esquisse d'une théorie des émotions* (Paris: Herman, 1965), pp. 58–59. According to Sartre's phenomenological analysis of emotion, affective consciousness is in general a magical and transformative act. He distinguishes two situations in which emotion arises. In the first, I shatter the deterministic order of a world I find too difficult by unreflective acts directed at my body as object. In the second, the Other shatters the deterministic order by appearing magical to me.

6. Gaston Bachelard, *The Poetics of Space*, pp. 110–11.

7. Todorov, *The Fantastic*, pp. 89–90.

8. Ibid., p. 52.

9. Lahna Diskin, "Bradbury on Children," in *Ray Bradbury*, ed. Martin H. Greenburg and Joseph D. Olander (New York: Taplinger, 1980), pp. 127–55. Diskin explores Bradbury's general view of children and tends to confirm this view as the prevalent one in his work.

BEN P. INDICK

Stage Plays

As with his film and television projects, Bradbury has consistently used his own short stories as the basis of his many stage plays. A notable exception is the film, *Something Wicked This Way Comes*, which existed first as a screenplay, and was converted into a novel only when Bradbury could not convince anyone to produce it. Of all his published plays, only his Irish plays, collected as *The Anthem Sprinters*, are originals, some of them being rewritten later as short stories, "when I couldn't sell the plays."[30] There is, however, an ambivalency in Bradbury's fictional approach which works without harm in his stories, perhaps less so in his films, but which is evident and is a problem on the stage.

On the one hand, he is a writer driven to make certain philosophical points, as in his cautionary fantasy; when they are strong enough, they may dominate his characters, and detract from their individual reality. On the other hand, he genuinely likes and has a deep sympathy for people, as is clear in *The Anthem Sprinters*, which is entirely free of moralizing or warnings; the characters exist only for themselves. In a play, the audience is confronted with flesh and blood individuals, not descriptions on paper or pictures on a screen, where such factors as colorful writing or directorial skills can mitigate too obvious a motive. If an imbalance exists between these polarities on stage, the characters cannot seem real; they will be puppets, and the dramatic quality of

From *Ray Bradbury: Dramatist*, pp. 22–35, 39–41. © 1977, 1989 by Ben P. Indick.

the piece will be affected. We shall see where Bradbury has failed to reconcile the poles and where he has succeeded. For admirers acquainted only with his prose fiction, the quantity, depth, and love expressed within his plays may come as a revelation.

In his initial major stage production, *The World of Ray Bradbury*, it was to be expected that he would reveal himself in his most characteristic and renowned form, as a fantastist. He adapted three of his most famous short stories for this omnibus program: "The Pedestrian," "The Veldt," and "To the Chicago Abyss," and produced and financed the show himself. It opened in Los Angeles on October 1, 1964, and the reviews, he writes, were "all, I repeat *all*, excellent. If I had written them myself, they couldn't have been better."[31] It ran for twenty weeks, and was succeeded by an equally successful run of another Bradbury play, "The Wonderful Ice Cream Suit," which ran for twenty-four weeks. He decided to take the original trio to New York City, and opened it off-Broadway one year after the Los Angeles opening. Here he met with considerably less success. Howard Taubman, writing in *The New York Times* of October 10, 1965, appreciated the writer's belief in "fundamental things, joys of nature, need for fulfillment," but reported that the plays were "not primarily theatrical." They were like "lectures delivered with stark, linear pictures, supported by an assortment of familiar and eerie sound-effects." Indeed, Taubman seemed more appreciative of the "pendulum-sound" John Whitney had designed than of the dramas. The play closed after an abbreviated run, leaving the unhappy author/playwright poorer by $40,000. Bradbury blames "inferior casting, and a dreary theatre in a bad section of The Bowery, plus a newspaper strike,"[32] as the causative factors in the failure.

The failure was undoubtedly due to some if not all of these factors, but the real reason may have gone deeper than that. The problem with these plays goes back to the polarities we mentioned earlier. Taubman speaks of Bradbury's "beliefs in fundamental things," and these surely do play a part in most of his better fiction. Bradbury feels a deep compulsion to preserve that which is most important in our lives. One recalls *Fahrenheit 451*, "The Exiles," and the story "The Pedestrian," among others, all warning of a world where individualism and imagination have died or been suppressed; his early radio play, "The Meadow," is another example. The stories, deftly constructed in mood and poetry, are powerful prose fictions, and strike sympathetic chords within the reader. On the stage, however, even with stage directions which are themselves strong in mood and poignancy, the didactic element tends to overwhelm the characters. An audience does not, after all, *read* stage directions; and, as the famed film producer Samuel Goldwyn is alleged to have said, if he had "wanted to send a message he would have called Western Union."

Consider the language itself. It is, after all, the most direct approach to the audience, and, strangely, Bradbury has altered it to its detriment on its journey from page to stage. In the story version of "The Veldt," the psychiatrist McLean tells the parents (after they have closed off their children's wishes-come-true nursery) that their act means

" ... everything. Where they had a Santa Claus, now they have a Scrooge. You've let this room replace you and your wife in your children's affections. This room is their mother and father, far more important in their lives than their real parents.... No wonder there's hatred here. You'll have to change your life. Like too many others, you've built it around creature comforts. Why, you'd starve tomorrow if something went wrong in your kitchen ..."

On stage, the comparable speech loses the directly personal aspect, dealing with a specific act by specific parents, and becomes a polemic on the habits of our culture in general:

"George, Lydia, ... why do your children hate you so much? What kind of life do you live? Machines make your bed, shine your shoes, blow your noses for you. Machines listen for you, speak for you.... How long has it been since you got out of your car and walked with your children? ... flew a kite ... picked do-it-yourself strawberries? How long? How long?"

Maclean [sic] is not finished, either:

"when you force-grow flowers in a mechanical greenhouse, don't be surprised if you wind up with exotic orchids, strange tiger lilies, or Venus fly-traps."

In converting "The Pedestrian" into a play, Bradbury's compulsion to emphasize his point is at least as obtrusive. The story has only one human character, who, at least in terms of his own culture, is a misfit, an individual who prefers to walk the deserted streets at night. The people of his era, buried in mass-cult, huddle mindlessly before their television sets. An empty, robot-controlled police car accosts him, and finally arrests him as a "regressive" person. The menace in the story is nearly always hidden and understated; only twice does the hero reveal his feelings about the moribund culture which surrounds him, questioning in a soft whisper as he passes a house, just what

TV show it is watching. When the police car stops him, his sole defense is that he was just walking, "for air, to see and just to talk."

The strength of the story is its ability to make the reader insert his own questioning mind into such a civilization. It is, however, uncomfortable for an audience to watch a man simply walking and talking to himself. So Bradbury feels constrained to introduce a second character into the play. A friend of the hero is persuaded by him into the dangerous and forbidden act of taking a night walk. Now all the bitterness and rebellion of the hero may be expressed vocally to his friend (and thereby to the audience). In consequence, the play is nearly all exposition. The menace, when it appears, is no longer as disquieting as when our own imaginations were required to evoke it.

Bradbury is not unaware of what he is doing in these plays. In 1972 he wrote: "I cannot . . . accept a theatre that is devoid of ideas and poetry."[33] In 1975 he stated even more emphatically his feelings about the relative importance of idea and characters:

> What you have in most of my stories and plays then is rarely a highly individualized character (I blunder into these on occasion) but Ideas grown super outsize: Ideas that seize people and change them forever. So, I should imagine, in order to do my plays at all, you must become the Idea, the Idea that destroys, or the Idea that prevails.[34]

The problem with this otherwise admirable ideal is that audience identification with "Ideas" is immensely more difficult than identification with "Characters." When the language itself is emotionally and/or intellectually moving, it can work; when it is not of such a level, the idea will not seem important to the audience, and the play will seem to preach. Shaw likewise was interested in idea, but consider how it was cloaked in the most human terms in *Pygmalion* or *Man and Superman*. And the theatre of the absurd, which was so much in vogue in the 1960s, was based on ideas; the most successful of its works were those in which idea was cloaked by comedy, as in the plays of Eugene Ionesco, or by enigmatic indirectness, as in Harold Pinter's plays. Possibly the most seminal play of our time, Samuel Beckett's *Waiting for Godot*, is a play of idea alone, whose message is nearly impossible to fathom. This is, of course, the essence of absurdist theatre, since "absurd" here refers not to the play but to the universe in an existentialist sense. Beckett offers idea which is cloaked in mystery, never delineated. It works subconsciously on its audience. Bradbury, fascinated by idea, dislikes this type of theatre. Its plays, he writes, are "frail exercises, more often than not half-witted . . . lacking in the prime requisites of imagination and ability."[35] The question, then would seem to be the technique by which idea is imparted to the audience, and, when Bradbury allows his strong humanism to control him, he then is more likely to be successful.

The third play in *The World of Ray Bradbury* illustrates this formula. Anyone familiar with Bradbury's fiction is aware of his fondness for minutiae, those seemingly insignificant things of which life is ultimately constructed, like a grand melody composed of small, individual notes. "Kents, Kools, Marlboros," mumbles the old man of "To the Chicago Abyss," musing about the past in a shattered, post-cataclysmic world. "Those were the names . . . with the red slick small ribbon that ran around the top you pulled to zip away the crinkly cellophane . . . and the tin foil you saved as a big bright silver ball." Surely a young Bradbury was moved and forever influenced by Thornton Wilder's *Our Town* in 1938. Wilder had written an apotheosis of the beauty and importance of those aspects of daily life which are simply taken for granted. The discovery of the importance of such daily trivia is an idea, but a very human one, because it affects the heart as much as the mind. Bradbury used this sense of the importance of the commonplace in one of his finest short stories, "The Third Expedition," from *The Martian Chronicles*: astronauts from Earth discover on Mars what seems to be an entire town miraculously transported intact from their youth, with its small houses and picket fences, "Dad with his pipe . . . pink, plump mom," and phonographs playing remembered tunes. It is eventually revealed to be something quite otherwise, but the relevance is unchanged.

Even "The Fog-Horn" finds a moment for such musings (in both the original story and in the adaptation into a one-act play):

> I'll make a voice that is like an empty bed beside you all night long, and like an empty house when you open the door, and like trees in autumn the first night the leaves have gone away. A sound like birds flying south, crying, and a sound like November wind, and the sea on the hard, cold shore.

This is not merely poetry. However beautifully expressed it may be, there is always the danger that poetry as dialogue may sound stilted. But not in this instance. This is a record of what the inner eye sees and feels, truthful emotion, humanism at its most observant and insightful. When this appeal to an inner non-intellectualized truth becomes an inherent part of the "idea" play, it finds a response in the audience. "To the Chicago Abyss" is a direct exposition of this appeal, and does not attempt to conceal its purpose. The old man remembers sadly, and to the pain of others, who are also forced thereby to conjure up their own recollections, forgotten candy bars, vaudeville routines, automobile names. It is an immensely moving threnody because we recognize and sympathize with its truth. Yet, without violating its intellectual basis—what humanity can lose due to war—it can still look forward to a better time. The others on stage will not betray the old renegade, and at curtain, he is speaking to a boy: "Once upon a time . . ."

Bradbury employs the same motif in another short play, "Kaleidoscope" (partly derived from the more extensive screenplay discussed earlier). Here a group of astronauts are floating helplessly in space, outside their shattered spaceship, awaiting death.

> Remember those summer nights when you were a kid and stayed out in the middle of the street playing ball until you couldn't see it was so dark, not wanting to go home, and at last all the mothers calling from blocks around, blowing whistles, yelling, and, at last dragging their bats, scuffing their shoes, all the boys went home, sad, and hating it, as though summer would never come again, even though summer was the next night, and the next after that?

The juxtaposition of the adult men, dying sadly, bravely, in a wholly foreign environment, sustained by a memory which every member of the audience can share, produces a situation in which idea and emotion become one. It is direct enough that for the scene to work—the anguished faces and voices of the actors are sufficient.

In "Pillar of Fire" the author eschews the sentimental quality of the foregoing plays, employing something of a Huxleyan framework. In the latter's *Brave New World* a future "savage" is in essence our own contemporary. Bradbury's hero is a twentieth-century man, reborn after two centuries of death into a sterile imagination-hating state. It is, of course, a favorite theme of the author's, and, in fact, he has described the original story as a "rehearsal" for the novel *Fahrenheit 451.* The poetic style coalesces perfectly with the direct and even outrageous actions of the hero. People are murdered by him without even the saving grace of unbalanced emotions, as he strives to convince a populace which no longer fears the dark or the supernatural that horror may still exist. The darkness with its indwelling fear is a symbol for the inner mind, the imagination which can soar. Dead—and by the twenty-third century, forgotten authors—Poe, Baum, Tolkien, Lovecraft, and others, form a sighing chorus behind the desperate hero, more real in their agony of eternal and neglected death than the characters who are "living" in the play. "Such a world," the hero cries, as he faces destruction (neatly paraphrasing both Shakespeare and Huxley), is an "unbrave new world that has cowards in it!"

The title points up the idea of the play. In the biblical story of Exodus, the Hebrews, leaving Egypt, are led by God as a "pillar of fire" through the wilderness. In the play, the importance of the hero's message is the "pillar of fire," as well as being an ironic reference to an age which worships bright sunshine without its inverse, shadow.

There is a time for serious ideas, "for today, tomorrow and beyond tomorrow," as Bradbury subtitles both collections (*The Wonderful Ice Cream Suit* and *Pillar of Fire*). There is also a time for playwrighting for the joy of it, and to reveal those characters one has observed and simply loved just for themselves. The poetry is more overt in Bradbury's idea plays, as though they somehow required more formality, but it is still evident in the lyrical rhythms of the folk who inhabit his more realistic plays, and their humanity is congenial and warm. *The Anthem Sprinters* is a group of four plays Bradbury wrote after spending time on location in Ireland to film *Moby-Dick*. These "Irish" plays are perhaps only small exercises in capturing the naive but winning guile and simplicity of village Irishmen, but they have great character and humor. His ear has picked up the colorful and extravagant pattern of speech which has also been employed to great effect by playwrights Shaw, Synge, O'Casey, and Carroll, among others.

These are good-natured studies of the "locals" as a friendly outsider would see them, and the title play will serve as a good example. The author visits a village pub and discovers that the big "sporting event" is a unique race at the local motion picture theatre. "Any night, every night," he is told, "for tens of dreadful years, at the end of every damn fillum all over Ireland, in every cinema, as if you'd never heard the baleful tune before, the orchestra strikes up for Ireland!" The author is confused, recalls that in London he had heard "God Save the Queen" played after the film concluded; it could not be as well? "Here it's the National Anthem, it's all the same!" he is told. Prodded by his bar-mates he is able to guess (even in the vernacular) what must happen locally, that "if you're any man at all, you try to get out of the theatre in those few precious moments between the end of the film and the start of the Anthem." He is greeted with cheers: "He's nailed it! Buy the Yank a drink!—On the house!" Bradbury is obviously very fond of these people, and allows himself to be a butt and straight-man to their good-humored pranks and jokes. The results are warm and sometimes hilarious.

"A Medicine For Melancholy" is an unpublished Bradbury play which captures nicely the conversational quality of the original story, and which can be favorably compared to his Irish plays and the works of Yeats and Synge. Set in London "when Boswell's Johnson was alive," it is a fanciful tale about a young girl's growing into maturity, with a rollicking *soupçon* of humor about the inquisitive and acquisitive ways of humankind. The power of love proves finally (and not unexpectedly) to be a perfect medicine for melancholy.

"A Device Out Of Time" (also unpublished) is a one-act play which appeared on stage in 1965 with "The Wonderful Ice Cream Suit." It is a touching vignette of two boys encountering a very old man, Colonel Fairleigh, whose reminiscences of his life, including a grotesque account of a vaudeville bullet trick, a buffalo hunt, and a boyhood as a Civil War drummer boy, provide a veritable Time Machine for the wide-eyed boys. The old man (and the boys) appear in Bradbury's novel *Dandelion Wine*, and in the subsequent dramatization of episodes from the book, and he will also appear in a musical adaptation (still in the creative phase) of *Fahrenheit 451* [q.v.].

In a somewhat different mode is "The Day It Rained Forever," a robust, good-natured tale of a group of grizzled old-timers, set in an arid portion of the American Southwest. They are impatiently awaiting the annual single day of rain (as opposed to the situation depicted in "All Summer In A Day"). An old woman comes on-stage unexpectedly, carrying a steering wheel and a collapsed innertube. She has arrived in an automobile which quite literally falls to pieces (off-stage). This bit of slapstick, with appropriate noises and parts flying here and there, is highly reminiscent of the Laurel and Hardy heaps, as well as Jack Benny's famous Maxwell of radio days.

The old lady informs the astonished group that she is well, but "my car has suffered." Appropriately, a final rattle is heard. Slowly, the slapstick turns to nostalgia. She had never thought she might cry at the "death of an automobile," she tells them, but "things need names, and when you name them they're not things anymore. I called her Bess. I think I loved her very much." The others then confess that they too have given names to objects; a rifle, Ned; a radio, Pete; even an electric fan has a name, Sam. Bradbury has worked a magical transition here. The woman begins playing a harp bringing on the rain, as well as a sense of the glory of life. She delivers the moral of the play:

> "All my life, I've been so busy running from Beethoven to Bach to Brahms, I never noticed I was twenty-nine. Next time I looked I was forty. Yesterday, I was seventy-two. Oh, there were men, but they'd given up singing when they were ten and given up flying when they were twelve. I always figured we were born to fly, one way or another, so I couldn't stand most men shuffling along with all the iron of the Earth in their blood. I never met a man who weighed less than nine hundred pounds . . ."

Those familiar with the original story may be surprised to learn that, if anything, the play is even more alive, meaningful, and beautiful than the written word.

In "The Wonderful Ice Cream Suit" humor, warmth, and imagination combine to form a serene and confident stage presentation. Six Mexican men of similar build have purchased one beautiful white suit. Each is scheduled to wear it for a brief but special moment. Their attempts to insure that the suit remains undamaged provide the humor of the play, and their short luminous adventures provide the magic. The scenes are bathed in the poetry of hope, warm and sweet as a tropical evening. Finally, after a hectic and uproarious night, the suit is hung back on its hanger, safe and sound, to be admired by its owners. One of them sits back and reflects,

> "Funny, when I wear this suit I know I will win at pool like Gomez. I will sing and play the guitar like Villanazul. Be strong in the arms like Vamanes ... So, tonight I am Gomez, Manulo, Dominguez, Villanazul, Vamanes, everyone. Ay, ay ... if we ever get rich, it'll be kind of sad. Then we'll all have suits. . . . It'll never be the same."

The foregoing works have all been one-act plays of varying lengths, just as most of Bradbury's prose writing has been in the short story genre. However, three major themes, explicated in full-length plays, have occupied him for many years. The first to see production was the result of his obsession with Melville's great opus.

Moby-Dick went in Bradbury's transmogrification from a tale of the sea to a tale of the sea of space. *Leviathan '99*, originally a radio drama, was adapted to the stage as "a longer version, rewritten. We used projections, sound effects, and a basically empty stage."[36] It was presented in 1972 in Los Angeles. The play is a poetic metaphor of the *Moby-Dick* plot. While it is a "space" drama, it follows the familiar outline, even to opening with the protagonist's famous line, "Call me Ishmael." This traveller tells us that he was actually conceived in space by parents who had been among the first Earthfolk to voyage to Mars. Now, homesick, they are returning to Earth, "homeless between yestermorrow and noon's midnight."

An adult, Ishmael signs aboard the largest rocket ever built, the *Cetus* (i.e., whale). He meets Quell, the play's equivalent of Queequeg, encounters "the warning man," who reveals his name is Elijah here too, and attends a church as did Melville's whalers. Whispers tell of lost astronauts, while the preacher describes spacemen as "Jonahs traveling in the belly of a new metal whale." Aboard ship, the destination is revealed to be "a star in Cygnus about which might roll a planet, moist and green as Earth"; however, a monomaniacal Captain (known only by his rank) like Ahab also has an obsession. He has been physically blinded by exposure to the great comet, *Leviathan*, and he burns with a passion to destroy it. The comet, to him, is a "vast exhalation of mystery upon the Deeps. A pale bride with a flowing veil come back to bed her lost unbedded groom."

This is a daring analogy, even for poetic imagery. Advanced instrumentation might make a blind man a feasible choice for space pilot; and a flaming comet is perhaps as good a metaphor for imperturbable, uncaring Fate as a giant white whale (although for a mere space ship to attack a comet seems less presumptuous than foolish). The Captain's chief officer, Redleigh, tells him that the comet is "an outmouthing of God. . . . As well stop your own heart as try to stop that great pale beating." The fanatical Captain, however, has his own reasons: "But if both stop at once . . . will it not be victory?" The officer responds that "in rending it you rend your own flesh," to which the Captain spits out, "That flesh offends me! . . . That thing is lost and evil."

The play continues to follow the plot of the novel, even to encountering another spaceship which had come up against the comet and had lost a small life-rocket sent out to investigate the monstrous space wanderer. Finally, the *Cetus* meets *Leviathan*. As if to warn off the puny craft, the comet sends "a messenger ahead . . . a storm of gravities, atomic whirlwinds, cosmic explosions . . . and warpings of Space." The ship is twisted through Time, uncertain whether it be that of cavemen, Caesar or Napoleon, until at last it is returned to its own time and destiny. The comet is now a "great white holy terror that filled all the Universe and put out every star." Life ships set out from the *Cetus* to "destroy . . . and be destroyed." In a final explosion, the Captain himself and everyone except Ishmael are annihilated. Ishmael floats in Space on the coffin which Quell had made for himself, until at last he is rescued by the spaceship encountered earlier, the *Rachel*, "who, in her long search for her missing children, found but another orphan." Recently, Bradbury has been reworking the play into an opera, for which its portentous lines and static scene might work well, as set pieces. Meanwhile, it was performed as a play in Paris in 1985.

While the play was not a commercial success (nor had it been expected to be), it has intensity and beauty, and has earned staying power. In 1976, Bradbury followed *Leviathan '99* with a curious fragment, "That Ghost, That Bride in Time," its title obviously suggested by the earlier play. It is a very brief resume of the same story, with a blind Captain piloting a *Cetus*, and an Ishmael as narrator. Motivation for the Captain, though, is different. He believes that the comet will crash into the Pacific Ocean on Earth, and he seeks to halt it. The writing style is a strange, uncomfortable blend of pseudo-Shakespearean poetics, much given to pompous, flowing bombast and science fiction jargon.

When NBC television chose Richard Matheson to adapt Bradbury's most famous work, *The Martian Chronicles*, into a mini-series, there was cause to question the decision. Matheson is indeed an excellent writer of fantasy and has a fine record as an author of film and TV scripts, but there was already available a more-than-adequate theatrical treatment of the book, by Bradbury himself. The Studio Theatre Playhouse of Los Angeles had produced it in August 1977, to enthusiastic audiences and favorable critical response. Bradbury's adaptation included some of the favorite stories from the episodic novel. The first act chronicled the arrival of Earthmen on Mars and the eventual, accidental destruction of the last Martians. The second act, like the last stories, is an unhappy picture of the failure of Earthpeople to make of Mars something beautiful and idealistic, repeating instead the banalities and prejudices of Earth. Continuing wars on Earth force many of the settlers to return. Only a new generation at last will find Mars is truly their home and begin to regain idealism, and then perhaps look beyond. The mother of the first-born son on Mars asks whether her son's sons will be the first-born halfway to Andromeda, and if so, why? There is no simple answer, since humankind has proven to be so inadequate here on this first stop. She can only be told that "short man" has a "large dream," and that those who dream are "aching to hear a voice cry back along the universal Mall, We've reached Alpha Centauri, And we're tall, o God, we're *tall*!"

The Los Angeles production of *The Martian Chronicles* was brilliantly directed with settings, lighting, and sound by Terrence Shank, which, together with equally effective costumes and masks, converted the theatre into "a landscape decidedly foreign to anything we know."[37] The play was enormously popular and its sold-out run was extended after a brief hiatus.

The production, unfortunately, despite high hopes, did not travel to the East Coast. Possibly, in the final analysis, the script was still lacking. Sylvie Drake's review notes, after praising the splendid costumes and stage movement of the "Martians," that they and the setting "all conspire to create . . . a powerful total impact that makes Bradbury's philosophies pale in comparison. The metaphysical cuisine that he serves up is not always quite up to the lavishness of the service and setting."[38] She nevertheless has much kudos for the production. The characteristic dichotomy of Bradbury's theatrical writing is revealed in the last crucial scenes, in which realism battles with purpose in language self-consciously poetic. There is a place in the theatre, however, for noble experiment and creative staging. The play, with reconsidered text, may yet regain life on the highest professional levels.

It is precisely those levels which Ray Bradbury has been working to achieve with two of his most beloved novels, *Dandelion Wine* and *Fahrenheit 451*. For the former, whose nostalgia for the joys of boyish discovery is quintessential Bradbury, he has enlisted the services of Jimmy Webb, a composer who would appear to be particularly well attuned to such an emotion. Webb's major hit songs include: "Up, Up and Away," "Wichita Lineman,"

"Galveston," and "MacArthur Park." Still in early form, the play was scheduled for a reading in May 1989, at the University of Oklahoma.

If *Dandelion Wine* is the summation of the author's brand of nostalgia, *Fahrenheit 451* represents Bradbury in his cautionary phase, fearful for
the preservation of individualism and imagination in a world whose rulers
are frightened by these most human qualities, and are determined to destroy
them. Dissatisfied with the Truffaut film (see above), Bradbury had long
considered dramatizing the novel. He was approached by Georgia Bogardus
Holof, a lyricist, and David Mettee, her composer, who had already collabo-
rated on three Off-Off-Broadway musicals, and wished to convert the novel
into a musical play. Bradbury put aside his plan to dramatize the story and
enthusiastically agreed to join them. Inasmuch as the musicians are located
in New York City, and Bradbury in Los Angeles, their collaboration has been
one whose progress has been achieved through mailed drafts. However, the
play has gradually been reaching a definitive form.

In 1985 a private reading was held for director Maggie L. Herrer at
the prestigious Eugene O'Neill Theatre Center in Waterford, Connecticut.
Bradbury stated later that he was "in tears. I knew it was working."[39] The following year the collaborators were invited back for the next stage in the play's
development, a staged reading. Working with actors, observing the effects of
the lines, Bradbury made any script alterations deemed necessary by himself.
"He would run upstairs to his room and feed the rest of the group revisions
every twenty minutes."[40]

There were three performances for the public, in a converted barn, basically staged readings with the actors carrying scripts, and music supplied by a
piano. The very important special stage effects, while described in the program,
were of necessity left to the audience's imagination. In late 1988 the play, now
termed an "opera" by its author,[41] through basically still in the same musical
format of dialogue with songs, was fully staged at Fort Wayne, Indiana. It
had a full cast of thirty, with excellent scenic effects by Robert Sandmaier,
including fire. It is scheduled for a late 1989 production, still developmental,
following a pre-summer 1989 reading, by the Musical Theatre Works in New
York City. This is a non-profit group whose aim is to foster original operas
and musical theatre pieces.

A critique of the play can only be based on the O'Neill Theatre Centre
presentation, as this author has not seen the Indiana production. It has certainly gotten closer to a definitive form, but has not reached that status yet,
according to a conversation with Ms. Holof, who is, however, very optimistic
about its progress. The problems which must be resolved are in essence similar
to those which have been present in others of the author's plays.

Fahrenheit 451, reread as a novel thirty years after its original publication, still strikes one with the genius of the young Bradbury. He pinpointed so well Montag's desperate urgency in his brilliant but intellectually and emotionally sterile future world, a world where language still burns as brightly as the fires made by the books being burned. Consider, for example, the opening paragraph:

> With the brass nozzle in his fists, with this great python spitting its venomous kerosene upon the world ... and his hands were the hands of some amazing conductor playing all the symphonies of blazing and burning to bring down the tatters and charcoal ruins of history.

Such a literary *tour de force* presents a problem if it is to be staged without sounding pretentious. To place such beautiful but self-conscious prose in the mouth of a narrator (as Bradbury did in his previous plays) is as dangerous as placing straight exposition in the mouths of characters: it stops the live action dead in its tracks. To coin an expression, the page is not the stage. A musical, however, offers a way out: a song is a permissible mode of expressing one's thoughts and feelings. It is the equivalent of the hallowed but disused *soliloquy*. A piece of music may also serve as a *bridge* to cover action: thus, the play opens in lively fashion, with Firemen going out to perform their duty—burning books—while explaining their actions in song and choreography. Herrer's staging in Connecticut carried out these requirements very ably, with word and action alone. In a later scene, referring back directly to the book rather than the immediate needs of the story, the song "Porches" became a well-realized bit of Bradburyan nostalgia, recalling the familiar front porches of yesterday's houses. Had it merely been read, it might have seemed superfluous sentimentality; sung, its poignancy enabled the audience to visualize porch swings on a warm summer evening, and to feel regret for their absence in the uncaring, shiny metal world of the play.

Difficulties still remain, however. The first act is diffuse, touching on too many bases, without leaving a single strong impression or sense of direction. There is a certain lightness, even a blandness, which does not translate well the smoldering malevolence of the State.

Characterization also leaves something to be desired. Stereotyped characters are delineated on the basis of single attributes: the TV-bound housewife; a Colonel Fairleigh type; the fey, saccharine Clarice, whose off-stage demise at the O'Neill has fortunately been altered in the later version. Off-stage action is by definition unwise; an audience must *see* if it is to care. The

Fire Captain's off-stage death has also been changed so that it may now be shared by the audience.

Finally, the climax, while effective in the novel, is less so on stage. It is very important to the author to show these last few brave individuals, walking around reciting snippets from the books they have learned by heart in order to preserve them. In many ways their action is the heart of his story. However, they come off more like a convention of scholars, and while this might command the respect of some audiences, it is far less likely to stir their emotions. Apparently, Bradbury has been unwilling to tamper with this particular element of his story. Still, without diminishing the meaning, he could perhaps gain more dramatic impact by selective attention to dialogue, and by effective use of the musical idiom which should be the play's spine. A fine and successful example is the great chorale number which climaxes Leonard Bernstein's opera, *Candide*. Voltaire's innocent hero, having survived all the hardships and calamities of a cruel world, states simply enough after a lengthy speech by the fatuous Dr. Pangloss, "Tis well said but we must cultivate our gardens." Bernstein emphasizes its true significance with the aid of unforgettable music rising to a glorious crescendo.

Bradbury, a legend beyond the boundaries of the fantasy genre, was observed at the performance in Connecticut, attired in a sparkling "ice cream suit," seated in the first row, anxiously repeating and weighing each word spoken. At the curtain, the author bounded up to join the actors and to share in the final plaudits, as eager and proud as any young hopeful. He has triumphed in so many fields, but one goal remains elusive: a successful Broadway production.

This noisy, insular, chauvinistic venue remains indisputably the diadem of American Theatre. It is impossibly cruel. A major musical, especially a spectacle such as *Phantom of the Opera* or *Les Misérables*, cannot be brought in for an investment of less than $7 million. These great successes will return their investments many times over, and will be taken to theatres around the world. For others, the money may evaporate overnight, as was the case with *Carrie*, a musical based on the Stephen King novel, which received a critical chorus of nays, and closed almost at once, with a total loss of the original investment. Obviously, Bradbury's dictum, stated early in his career, that he preferred to do shows with his own people and his own money, is not workable in such a rarified atmosphere. When *Fahrenheit 451* appears for its most significant run-through yet on the modest stage of the Musical Theatre Works in the Big Apple itself, it will, one hopes, be able to demonstrate that it can face those same critics forthrightly, and take its place among the modern triumphs of the imaginative American stage.

Notes

30. Personal communication.
31. *The Wonderful Ice Cream Suit*, Introduction, p. vii.
32. Ibid., p. vii.
33. Ibid., p. ix.
34. *Pillar of Fire*, Introduction, p. xi.
35. *The Anthem Sprinters*, p. 153.
36. Personal communication.
37. *Los Angeles Times*, 8/9/77.
38. Ibid.
39. *New York Times*, 8/25/86. Interview with Dena Kleiman.
40. Ibid.
41. As described on the dust jacket of *The Toynbee Convector* (New York: Alfred A. Knopf, 1988).

Selected Bibliography

Published Plays of Ray Bradbury

"The Meadow," *Best One-Act Plays 1947–9*, M. Mayorga, Dodd, Mead.

The Anthem Sprinters, Dial Press, 1963. Includes:
    "The Great Collision of Monday Last,"
    "The First Night of Lent,"
    "A Clear View of an Irish Mist,"
    "The Anthem Sprinters, The Queen's Own Evaders."

The Day It Rained Forever, Samuel French, 1966.

The Pedestrian, Samuel French, 1966.

The Wonderful Ice Cream Suit and Other Plays, Bantam, 1973. Includes:
    "The Wonderful Ice Cream Suit,"
    "The Veldt,"
    "To the Chicago Abyss."

Pillar of Fire and Other Plays, Bantam, 1973. Includes:
    "Pillar of Fire,"
    "Kaleidoscope,"
    "The Foghorn."*

That Ghost, That Bride in Time, Roy A. Squires, 1976.

*Written variously. The text of this title spells it "Foghorn"; the back cover, "Fog Horn"; elsewhere the author hyphenates it, "Fog-Horn."

SUSAN SPENCER

The Post-Apocalyptic Library:
Oral and Literate Culture in Fahrenheit 451
and A Canticle for Leibowitz

At the dawn of widespread literacy in fourth-century Athens, Plato appended to the end of his *Phaedrus* a story that has often been perceived as, as Jacques Derrida puts it, "an extraneous mythological fantasy" (67). Derrida argues in *Dissemination* that there is nothing extraneous about the myth at all, but rather it is an expression of an important and timely idea with which the classical Athenians were concerned. Recent orality/literacy theory, as outlined by Eric A. Havelock, Walter S. Ong, and others, would seem to back him up. The story is that of the discovery of the technology of writing, a tale that Socrates claims is traditional among the Egyptians. According to Socrates, the god Theuth invented this technology and offered it to the king of Upper Egypt as something that would "make the people of Egypt wiser and improve their memories" (*Phaedrus* 274b). But the king scorned Theuth's gift, saying:

> by reason of your tender regard for the writing that is your offspring, [you] have declared the very opposite of its true effect. If men learn this, it will implant forgetfulness in their souls; they will cease to exercise memory because they rely on that which is written, calling things to remembrance no longer from within themselves, but by means of external marks. What you have discovered is a recipe not

From *Extrapolation* 32, no. 4 (Winter 1991), 331–42. © 1991 by Kent State University Press.

for memory, but for reminder. And it is no true wisdom that you offer your disciples, but only its semblance, for by telling them of many things without teaching them you will make them seem to know much, while for the most part they know nothing, and as men filled, not with wisdom, but with the conceit of wisdom, they will be a burden to their fellows. (275a,b)

The remark about "telling them . . . without teaching them" is evidently an expression of uneasiness with the idea of text as what Ong calls "unresponsive." In *Orality and Literacy: The Technologizing of the Word*, Ong sees one of Socrates's arguments as being "if you ask a person to explain his or her statement, you can get an explanation; if you ask a text, you get back nothing except the same, often stupid, words which called for your question in the first place" (79). While this idea is so commonplace to us as to go practically unnoticed, except when we are frustrated by a particularly opaque text, it was new and frightening to the Greeks. According to Havelock in "The Oral Composition of Greek Drama" (*Literate Revolution* 261–312), the late fifth and early fourth century B.C. was a period of relatively rapid change in literary style, as a direct result of the spread of popular literacy. Not only was an explanatory oral framework done away with, but also the old formulaic devices that helped oral composers keep their place and remember what they were talking about. "Compositionally, as plays began to be written with the expectation of being read, the composer would feel a reduced pressure to conform to certain mnemonic rules. The invented would be freer to prevail over the expected" (266). This, Havelock hypothesizes, created some tension in the Greek theater—a tension that can be traced in Aristophanes's *Frogs*, where the more conservative, more "oral" Aeschylus wins a contest against the more "literary" and startlingly original Euripides; and, as we can see (although Havelock does not mention it here), in the inherent uneasiness in Plato's *Phaedrus*.

Although "The Oral Composition of Greek Drama" was first published in 1980, some theory of postliterary tension was working its way into the intelligentsia several decades before. To quote Havelock again, in his 1950 book *The Crucifixion of Intellectual Man*, the myth of the Fall in Genesis, as a direct result of eating of the tree of knowledge, "gives poignant expression to that conflict within the civilized consciousness of man, between his sense of intellectual power and his distrust and fear of that power. . . . All the warmth and the richness of man's nature demand that he live in the protection of certain illusions in order to be secure, happy, and peaceful" (8). The "expected" rather than the "invented." The further the artificial "memory" created by textuality stretches back, and the more it can be built upon by an advancing science, the more that security fades away. Man becomes dangerous and also frightened. "Though our science may kill us, it will never allow us to retreat. Somehow we know that we would never burn enough books, nor eliminate enough intellectuals, to be able to return to the warm room" of blissful ignorance (9).

Within a decade of this assurance, two famous science fiction novels appeared dealing with the very attempt that Havelock had just pronounced futile: Ray Bradbury's *Fahrenheit 451* (1953) and Walter M. Miller's *A Canticle for Leibowitz* (1959). In *Fahrenheit 451* the protagonist, Guy Montag, is a "fireman"; that is, he burns forbidden books, and the houses that hide them, for a living. This is a busy job, considering the fact that just about all books are forbidden. There are a few rare exceptions, such as three-dimensional comic books, trade journals and, of course, rule books, those mainstays of any oppressive society. The rule book for the Firemen of America includes a brief history of the profession: "Established 1790, to burn English-influenced books in the Colonies. First Fireman: Benjamin Franklin" (30). According to the only available text, and to the voice of political authority, this is a glorious and time-honored profession, an idea that gives the firemen a sense of continuity and security . . . and, perhaps, allows Bradbury to make a comment on the fact that textual knowledge is power, even—or perhaps especially—false knowledge. Power becomes unbreachable if textual information is monolithic. According to the sinister but brilliant fire chief, Beatty, the main danger in books is that "none of those books agree with each other" (33, 54, 95). Very true, but a danger to whom? Peace of mind, he argues repeatedly. To one lawbreaker, kneeling despairingly amid her kerosene-soaked illegal books, Beatty cries, "You've been locked up here for years with a regular damned Tower of Babel. Snap out of it!" (33).

Inevitably, Montag becomes discontented with the status quo and curious about this nebulous "danger." Both his discontent and his curiosity are intensified when the woman mentioned above chooses to burn with her books rather than lose them. Beatty, seeing his distress when Montag feels "sick" and feigns illness, explains the real advent of the firemen in phrases that echo Havelock's concept of the loss of the "warm room" but takes it to its extreme limit:

> You always dread the unfamiliar. . . . We must all be alike. Not everyone born free and equal, as the Constitution says, but everyone made equal. Each man the image of every other; then all are happy, for there are no mountains to make them cower, to judge themselves against. (51)

On the literary side, he also echoes Plato on the "conceit of wisdom," and just how far that can be taken as a sort of leveling device:

Give the people contests they win by remembering the words to more popular songs or the names of state capitals or how much corn Iowa grew last year. Cram them full of noncombustible data, chock them so damned full of 'facts' they feel stuffed, but absolutely 'brilliant' with information. Then they'll feel they're thinking, they'll get a *sense* of motion without moving. And they'll be happy, because facts of that sort don't change. Don't give them any slippery stuff like philosophy or sociology to tie things up with. That way lies melancholy. (53–54)

These things are written, but they are not literature. The classicist may be reminded here of the problems associated with Linear B, the proto-Greek script found at Mycenae and Knossos. All of the inscriptions are "bald counting-house dockets," (Palmer 13), "a text of the greatest interest" being a tablet that "lists amounts of barley against various classes of craftsmen" (Palmer 104). There is no literature *per se*, unless one were to use the standard eighteenth-century definition of literature as "anything written." As a result, it is difficult to get students interested in learning Linear B. There is simply nothing interesting to read. The situation is described by Havelock as one of pre-literacy, in spite of the physical existence of written text: "whereas historians who have touched upon literacy as a historical phenomenon have commonly measured its progress in terms of the history of writing, the actual conditions of literacy depend upon the history not of writing but of reading" (*Literate Revolution* 56). One needs an audience. Get the audience to lose interest, and you can do away with the literate civilization. In *Fahrenheit 451* the reader has the feeling of moving backward in time to a preliterate society, and the content of the society's "literature," although here it is for political ends, strengthens this impression.

The last phrase of Beatty's pronouncement, "That way lies melancholy," with its literary overtones—very different from the plainer common speech of his subordinates—is not unusual for Beatty. In keeping with the idea that knowledge is power, Bradbury gives us several hints that the fire chief has had frequent access to the forbidden texts and that this is either a cause or a result of his being made chief (just which one is unclear). Like Kurt Vonnegut, Jr.'s short story "Harrison Bergeron," set in another disturbing dystopia where "everybody [is] finally equal" (7), some people are seen clearly to be more equal than others and thus enabled to wield power over their fellows. In Vonnegut's story, the ascendancy is physical: Diana Moon Glampers, the "Handicapper General," is the only citizen who isn't decked out in distorting glasses, distracting ear transmitters, and bags of birdshot to weaken her to the level of society's lowest common denominator. In *Fahrenheit 451*, the ascendancy is purely textual, but that is enough. Beatty's obnoxious confidence and habit of quoting famous works strikes the reader immediately and leads to a question that Bradbury never answers: why is this highly literate person permitted to survive, let alone hold a position of high authority, in an aggressively oral society? Something is rotten in the whole system. Evidently someone higher up, Beatty's shadowy superior, feels that there is some inherent value in a well-read man, in spite of all the political rhetoric. This probability is directly opposed to Beatty's frequent deprecation of texts (a protection of his own monopoly?) and claim that the eventual ban of almost all books was not a political coup accomplished by a power-hungry elite at one fell swoop. Beatty's explanation, which we are never called upon to doubt, is that an outraged people seeking complete equality called for more and more censorship as texts became more widely available to interest groups that might be offended by them: "It didn't come from the Government down. There was no dictum, no declaration, no censorship, to start with, no! Technology, mass exploitation, and minority pressure carried the trick" (51). As Plato warned thousands of years earlier, well-read man had become an offensive "burden to his fellows."

Bradbury closes the novel, however, with an optimistic view: the text *will* prevail, and man will be the better for it. This is shown symbolically in the escape from the city by Montag and Faber, the only two literate men in the story besides Beatty—who, also symbolically, perishes in the same manner as the many books he has burned. The ignorant oral-culture citizens, radios tamped securely in their ears, remain in the city to be blown up by an enemy they could easily have escaped, if it weren't for the fact that their monolithic media preferred to keep them ignorant and happy. Having taken up with a group of itinerant professors, haltingly trying to remember the text of Ecclesiastes, Montag takes the first steps toward realizing the dream he had as he blindly fled the government's persecution: "Somewhere the saving and the putting away had to begin again and someone had to do the saving and keeping, one way or another, in books, in records, in people's heads, any way at all so long as it was safe, free from moths, silverfish, rust and dry-rot, and men with matches" (125).[1]

The idea that it is safe only when locked away in memory is almost a startling one in this book that so privileges the literary text; it seems as if the author has come full circle to an oral culture and the need to circumvent the shortcomings of Theuth's invention. Yet Bradbury makes it clear that they will write everything down as soon as possible and will try to reconstruct a fully literate society again. This should not take long, and is certainly desirable. The concept of text is a progressive thing, not a cyclical, and as long as any remnants remain there is always a base, however small, on which to build a better and wiser world.

A far more ambiguous view is present in *A Canticle for Leibowitz*. The loss of literacy here is not a gradual, internal thing, but a reactionary disruption. The survivors of nuclear war, emerging from their fallout shelters to face a devastated world and irreversible chromosome damage, realize that they have been shut out of Havelock's "warm room" for good. And they're angry. So, like Bradbury's people, they seek comfort and revenge by destroying all texts and all individuals connected with learning, escaping into a simple agrarian lifestyle very different from Bradbury's high-tech nightmare. One technician, Isaac Leibowitz, escapes, and hides among a group of Cistercian monks with a contraband collection of written material he has managed to save from the general purge. Eventually he is found out by the mob and martyred. But the texts, without him as interpreter, survive and are handed down from generation to generation. As Leibowitz takes on the trappings of sainthood, the texts become holy items—not for what they communicate, but for what they are, something he died to protect. The collection is eclectic: half a physics book here, three charred pages of mathematical equations there, an old book of fairy tales—anything the monks can get their hands on. For centuries these are passed down, their meaning becoming obscured, and this is where Miller's narrative begins.

The novel is set up in three sections, each set six hundred years apart from its predecessor. The first, postulating a civilization very like the European Dark Ages, deals with a novice named Brother Francis, who inadvertently discovers some new texts in an ancient fallout shelter six centuries after what the new scriptures refer to as the second, or Flame, Deluge (to distinguish it from Noah's flood). The characters in part 1 are innocent and superstitious, very like the civilization that spawned such works as Caedmon's hymn (which is often read as an allegory for the literate Christian world superseding the oral world of the pre-Christian, preliterate "heathens"). The choice of Cistercians is an appropriate one: not only does it associate the Abbey of the Blessed Leibowitz with Monte Cassino, that similar repository of learning and text, but "the organizational principles of movements like the Cistercians [in the middle ages] were clearly based on texts ... Within the movement, texts were steps ... by which the individual climbed toward a perfection thought to represent complete understanding and effortless communication with God" (Stock 90).

As Brian Stock points out, "one of the clearest signs that a group had passed the threshold of literacy was the lack of necessity for the organizing text to be spelt out, interpreted, or reiterated" (91). Brother Francis has not yet reached this level. In fact, Miller uses this lack of sophistication to humorous effect, showing how the monks have created a new oral mythos around the limited literature they have. When Francis discovers the fallout shelter

(Maximum Occupancy: 15), he has enough literacy to read, but not to correctly interpret, the sign that identifies it:

> were not the monsters of the world still called "children of the Fallout"? That the demon was capable of inflicting all the woes which descended upon Job was a recorded fact ... [and] he had unwittingly broken into the abode (deserted he prayed) of not just one, but fifteen of the dreadful beings! (23)

The misinterpretation of the word "shelter" to mean a shelter *for*, rather than a shelter *from*, makes perfect grammatical sense. There is nothing wrong with Francis's reasoning, other than the fact that, as a semiotic critic would say, his sign system has broken down. When Francis runs into a similar problem over a memo reading, inexplicably, "Pound pastrami ... can kraut, six bagels" (33), the monks' painstakingly reconstructed "literacy" turns out to be a world of signifiers with no corresponding signifieds to give them concrete meaning. Words have truly been reduced to phonemes, units of sound; the morphological substructure is incomplete and inappropriate.

The papers in the shelter bear the name of I. A. Leibowitz, and, as relics, focus attention on the literary Memorabilia of a past era. The Blessed Leibowitz is canonized and so, in a way, are the newfound papers: they are incorporated into the canon of the Memorabilia, to be copied by generations of monks who do not always understand what they are copying. Brother Francis, for instance, spends fifteen years producing a gorgeous illuminated and gold-leafed copy of the blueprint for a circuit board, and literally gives his life for it in a world where there has been no humanly generated electricity for six hundred years. The fact that he begins by questioning the possible sacrilege of copying the original backwards (black on white rather than white on black) and is later relieved of his anxiety when he finds a fragment explaining blueprints and realizes that since "the color scheme of the blueprints was an accidental feature of those ancient drawings ... [a] glorified copy of the Leibowitz print could be made without incorporating the accidental feature" (89) is an additional semiotic joke on Miller's part. As they are copied, original documents are stored carefully away in lead-sealed, airtight casks, and faithful copies are made of the copies—with, of course, the occasional inevitable scribal mistake to provide a basis for future textual criticism.

Six hundred years after Brother Francis's discovery, the Abbey is still conducting itself along the same preliterate lines. Some advances in learning have been made, but not much of a practical nature. Although the naïveté is gone, it is still largely a case of learning solely for the disinterested sake of learning. There is a faint rumor of political conflict, but Hannegan, a local prince of Caesar-like ambition, is cheerfully illiterate and unlikely to show any interest in such an isolated area. This man has a literate cousin, however, who is very interested, indeed. Thon Taddeo receives permission to study the Memorabilia, and his "rediscovery" and interpretation of these hidden works prompts a renaissance of learning.

This is not altogether a good thing. The first indications of a theme of antiliteracy are, perhaps, in the portrayal of the character of the Poet who has taken up residence in the Abbey. He is crude and ill-mannered, a trial to the monks' calm and ritualistic existence. In this way he is very like poetry itself—that is, lyric poetry of the sort that reached its apex of popularity in our own Victorian period. One may recall John Stuart Mill's distinction between (mere) eloquence and poetry: "eloquence is *heard*; poetry is *over-heard*" (1038). The Poet is definitely of the overheard variety: "The Poet has always muttered," complains the prior (207). He is a highly literate character, as unpredictable and inventive—and despised—as Aristophanes's Euripides. Not too surprisingly, the only book that is mentioned in the entire novel as being read for pleasure is a book of "daring" verses that the abbot in part 3 pulls out, a book said to be written by "Saint Poet of the Miraculous Eyeball" (319), a reference to the Poet's glass eye. One might note that in part 3, when the world has become fully literate, the Poet is venerated as a saint, while in the semiliterate culture of part 2 he is regarded with mistrust and even dislike, for the most part. Marshall McLuhan identifies a similar mistrust in Pope's *Dunciad*, written at a period of increased circulation, and thus an increased reading audience, resulting in a stream of "self-indulgent" emotional poetry with no didactic purpose. He claims that "Book III [of the *Dunciad*] concerns the collective unconscious, the growing backwash from the tidal wave of self-expression. . . . Wit, the quick interplay among our senses and faculties, is thus steadily anaesthetized by the encroaching unconscious" (259). A similar annihilation occurs with the loss of the socially instructive function of poetry, the direct descendant of preliterate eras when Achilles and Agamemnon and Jesus Christ were presented as patterns for behavior.

In part 2 of *Canticle*, books are still either to be copied in the scriptorium or read aloud at communal meals (which, perhaps significantly, the Poet does not generally attend). Upon Thon Taddeo's arrival he is treated to a reading aloud of a scriptural account of the Flame Deluge, in highly ritualistic style: "But one of the magi was like unto Judas Iscariot, and his testimony was crafty, and having betrayed his brothers, he lied to all the people, advising them not to fear the demon Fallout" (198). The lesson contains a number of veiled warnings against the hubris of learning and the misuse of power, but Taddeo sweeps them all aside, disregarding everything but the archaic oralist language. He dismisses the warning as quaint, and heads for the library even as his retinue of soldiers begin sketching the Abbey's fortifications to report back to Hannegan its usefulness as a potential fortress—an action even more chilling when we consider it in the light of our own ill-conceived assault on Monte Cassino in 1944, a raid in which Miller took part and which was the partial genesis of *A Canticle for Leibowitz* (Ower 441). This secular influx, it is clear, bodes no good for the store of learning. A further note of foreboding is sounded when the Poet quits the monastery, leaving his glass eye with Taddeo: the abbot explains that as he was in the habit of removing the eye whenever he was about to do something outrageous, the brothers and the Poet himself have come to refer to the eye as "the Poet's conscience." Taddeo replies, "So he thinks I need it more than he does" (237).

There are other parallels with our own literary history that come out in part 2, although Miller reverses the traditional role of the church vs. secular forces. Even as it is not writing, but reading, that defines a literate culture, in many ways it isn't so much writing, but *not*-writing, that is the political act. In a conference paper in 1981, Ong pointed out that "the totality of existence-saturated time is simply too much to manage" ("Oral Remembering" 13). The author has to pick and choose, simply by nature of his medium. Ong illustrates this with a quotation from the book of John: "There are still many other things that Jesus did, yet if they were written about in detail, I doubt there would be room enough in the entire world to hold the books to record them" (21:25). In this case, the choice is clear: "the author picks from Jesus's life what is particularly relevant to human beings' salvation" ("Oral Remembering" 13). The issue of what gets preserved is a similar one. Jeff Opland reminds us in his book on *Anglo Saxon Oral Poetry* that much of what is reported about poetry, and what poetry we have, is inextricably tied up with church politics and what the Catholic Church deemed worthy of preservation. Basically, it comes down to a situation of who has the vellum.

The extreme of this is, of course, Orwell's *1984*, but it is also an aspect of preliteracy. The Sapir-Whorf hypothesis—the idea that our language shapes our perceptions of reality—is most easily observed in preliterate cultures. Their values, their thought, and even their vocabulary is much more homogeneous: "Sapir-Whorfian notions of cultural relativity in distinctions encoded within differing languages apply more obviously to cultures which have remained primarily oral . . . since oral cultures, lacking dictionaries, delete from the lexicon as well as create distinctions within it according to the criterion of current social usefulness" (Durant 337).

Miller's monks are aware of this in a subconscious sort of way, and attempt to maintain a homogeneity of cherishing everything equally. To them, all texts are holy, and they continue to treasure their illuminated grocery lists long after they have grown sophisticated enough to realize that these texts are likely to be of doubtful utility. Text is above utility or politics and has entered the realm of the sacred, taking on almost the mystic quality of runes, or the writing on a well-known Greek cup dating back to preliterate days: "Whoso drinks this drinking cup straight-way him / Desire shall seize of fair-crowned Aphrodite" (Havelock, *Literate Revolution* 195). Writing itself has the power, rather than the person who exploits it. Taddeo never realizes this. Even as he travels toward the Abbey he explains to the nomad tribes which are providing him with an escort that he is seeking "*incantations* of great power" (174; italics are Miller's) that will be of tactical use for him.

By not giving privilege to any particular genre or subject, the monks have effectively depoliticized the medium, a situation that comes to an abrupt end when Taddeo comes along to make distinctions between what is useful and what is not. Thus Taddeo's rediscovery of the Memorabilia is not just a renaissance of science but also a revolution in the role of text as communication rather than text as object. The change in role is not accomplished without some trepidation on the part of the more conservative monks, in particular the librarian: "To the custodian of the Memorabilia, each unsealing represented another decrease in the probable lifetime of the contents of the cask, and he made no attempt to conceal his disapproval of the entire proceeding. To Brother Librarian, whose task in life was the preservation of books, the principal reason for the existence of books was that they might be preserved perpetually" (209–10).

The librarian is the extreme case, but even the abbot is concerned about such an abrupt and complete dissemination of texts, as he confides to Taddeo in one of the most important passages in the book:

> You promise to begin restoring Man's control over Nature. But who will govern the use of the power to control natural forces? Who will use it? To what end? Such decisions can still be made. But if you and your group don't make them now, others will soon make them for you. Mankind will profit, you say. By whose sufferance? The sufferance of a prince who signs his letters X? (238)

This is the turning point. As Alan Durant remarks, "literacy leads to a diversification of, and contradictions within, previously homogeneous 'oral' cultures, as readers are differentially influenced by earlier stages of the cultural record, interpret them differently, and use them to support divergent versions of aspiration and intent" (337). This is what Beatty was warning of in *Fahrenheit 451*, and now it is what Thon Taddeo opens up. When the abbot pleads with him to slow down his investigations and keep destructive information out of Hannegan's hands, Taddeo characteristically misinterprets him and believes that he is forcing religion down his throat. "'Would you have me work for the Church?' The scorn in his voice was unmistakable" (239).

As a result of Taddeo's reintroduction of the Memorabilia to the general public, six centuries later "there were spaceships again" (258) and electric lights and newspapers and all manner of technological marvels. When we first meet the third and final abbot he is being held at bay by an "Abominable Autoscribe," a machine that converts oral text to written (and, if necessary, into a foreign language, to boot). The fact that it doesn't work is indicative of the difficulties of all writing: having lost the ability to communicate orally—the abbot is trying to write a letter to a cardinal who doesn't speak his language—he finds himself at the mercy of an imperfect technology. Yet he admits that "I don't trust my own Anglo-Latin, and if I did, he'd probably not trust his" (266). As Socrates's King of Egypt predicted, the medium that was meant to increase memory has actually decreased it, with potentially disastrous results: the aborted letter was a request for orders concerning Operation Peregrinatur, a plan to evacuate selected members of the Order to the off-world colonies on Alpha Centauri, since it has become obvious that history has repeated itself and mankind is once again manufacturing nuclear weapons.

Inevitably, war does come and the Operation is put into effect. Having lost their function as guardians of the Memorabilia, the monks spend all of part 3 desperately trying to escape its effects. As "the visage of Lucifer mushroom[s] into hideousness above the cloudbank, rising slowly like some titan climbing to its feet after ages of imprisonment in the Earth" (355), the starship lifts into the sky with a cargo of twenty-seven monks, six nuns, twenty children . . . and the Memorabilia, preserved *in toto* on microfilm. "It was no curse, this knowledge, unless perverted by Man, as fire had been, this night" (303). But of course it will be, eventually. Text, with the seeds of destruction encoded within it, follows Man like a recurring damnation. Man, the textual animal, will Deconstruct the universe.

Both *A Canticle for Liebowitz* and *Fahrenheit 451* end with a nuclear apocalypse and a new literacy springing from the ashes. Bradbury's positive, progressive view of literary history contrasts sharply with Miller's negative, cyclical view, just as Bradbury's depiction of a predominately oral culture as mind-numbing contrasts with Miller's depiction of orality as the preserver of ritual and collective human values. One might conclude this paper with the Unanswerable Question so popular with medieval bards at the ends of their stories: "Which point of view is the correct one?" And, as it has always been, the correct answer is "both."

Note

1. This, of course, is a Biblical echo: "lay up for yourselves treasures in heaven, where neither moth nor rust doth corrupt, and where thieves do not break through nor steal" (Matthew 6:20).

Works Cited

Bradbury, Ray. *Fahrenheit 451*. New York: Ballantine, 1979.

Derrida, Jacques. *Dissemination*. Trans. Barbara Johnson. Chicago: U of Chicago P, 1981.

Durant, Alan. "The Concept of Secondary Orality: Observations about Speech and Text in Modern Communications Media." *Dalhousie Review* 64 (Summer 1984): 332–53.

Havelock, Eric A. *The Literate Revolution in Greece and Its Cultural Consequences*. Princeton, NJ: Princeton UP, 1982.

———. *The Crucifixion of Intellectual Man*. Boston: Beacon Press, 1951.

McLuhan, Marshall. *The Gutenberg Galaxy*. Toronto: U of Toronto P, 1962.

Mill, John Stuart. "What is Poetry?" *Norton Anthology of English Literature*. Vol. 2. Ed. M. H. Abrams et al. New York: Norton, 1986.

Miller, Walter M., Jr. *A Canticle for Leibowitz*. London: Black Swan, 1984.

Ong, Walter S. *Orality and Literacy: The Technologizing of the Word*. New York: Methuen, 1982.

———. "Oral Remembering and Narrative Structures." *Analyzing Discourse: Text and Talk. Georgetown University Round Table on Languages and Linguistics 1981*. Ed. Deborah Tannen. Washington, DC: Georgetown UP, 1982. 12–24.

Opland, Jeff. *Anglo Saxon Oral Poetry: A Study of the Traditions*. New Haven, CT: Yale UP, 1980.

Ower, John B. "Walter M. Miller, Jr." in *Science Fiction Writers: Critical Studies of the Major Authors from the Early Nineteenth Century to the Present Day*. Ed. E. F. Bleiler. New York: Scribner, 1982. 441–48.

Palmer, Leonard R. *Myceneans and Minoans: Aegean Prehistory in the Light of the Linear B Tablets*. New York: Knopf, 1962.

Plato, *Phaedrus*. Trans. R. Hackforth. *Plato: Collected Dialogues*. Ed. Edith Hamilton and Huntington Cairns. Princeton, NJ: Princeton UP, 1961.

Stock, Brian. *The Implications of Literacy*. Princeton, NJ: Princeton UP, 1983.

Vonnegut, Kurt, Jr. "Harrison Bergeron." *Welcome to the Monkey House*. New York: Dell, 1970. 7–13.

JONATHAN ELLER

The Body Eclectic:
Sources of Ray Bradbury's Martian Chronicles

There is an intriguing five-year gap between the time that Ray Bradbury first envisioned a book about people on Mars, and the time that he rediscovered that intent and produced his remarkable first novel, *The Martian Chronicles*. Bradbury's new introduction to the Fortieth Anniversary Edition recalls the crucial moment of rediscovery, a New York luncheon in June 1949 with Don Congdon, Bradbury's literary agent, and Doubleday editor Walter I. Bradbury (no relation). At the urging of radio writer and producer Norman Corwin, the twenty-nine-year-old author had traveled to New York from Los Angeles with fifty new stories and enough money to stay at the YMCA for a week. It was an exciting time for Bradbury—O. Henry Prizes in 1947 and again in 1948 were leading to recognition beyond the secondary market of the pulp magazines. He had already published a horror story collection with August Derleth's specialized Arkham House imprint; now, Bradbury and Congdon used the New York trip to showcase his stories for the major publishing houses.

But Bradbury found that story collections by bright new writers weren't selling; Walter Bradbury was the last in a long line of editors that week who asked "Is there a novel in you somewhere?" Like so many times before, Bradbury found himself explaining that he had always been a short story writer,

From *The University of Mississippi Studies in English*, New Series 11–12 (1993–1995): 376–410.
© 1995 by the University of Mississippi.

and probably always would be. The other editors had shown no interest, but this time the response was different:

> Walter Bradbury shook his head, finished his dessert, mused, and then said:
> "I think you've already written a novel."
> "What?" I said, "and *when?*"
> "What about all those Martian stories you've published in the past four years?" Brad replied. "Isn't there a common thread buried there? Couldn't you sew them together, make some sort of tapestry, half-cousin to a novel?"
> "My God!" I said.
> "Yes?"
> "My God," I said. "Back in 1944, I was so impressed by Sherwood Anderson's *Winesburg, Ohio,* that I told myself I must try to write something half as good, and set it on Mars. I sketched out an outline of characters and events on the Red Planet, but soon lost it in my files!"
> "Looks as if we've found it," said Brad.[1]

Although the outline was long forgotten, Anderson's masterpiece may have served as a subconscious pattern for the Martian stories which followed; indeed, in his extensive interviews with Professor David Mogen in 1980, Bradbury observed that despite the five-year hiatus, the developing concept of *The Martian Chronicles* "was all due to *Winesburg, Ohio.*"[2]

But to assume that in 1949 Bradbury simply plugged his Martian tales into the Winesburg formula is misleading. During the summer of that year, he heavily revised a select group of his Martian stories, added new stories, and wrote eleven bridging chapters for the new book. Even then, Bradbury sensed that the chronicles were something entirely different from the original plan:

> By the time our first daughter was born in the autumn of 1949, I had fitted and fused all of my lost but now found Martian objects. It turned out to be not a book of eccentric characters as in *Winesburg, Ohio,* but a series of strange ideas, notions, fancies, and dreams that I had begun to sleep on and waken to when I was twelve. (*MC* 40, ix)

The textual history of *The Martian Chronicles* remains the great untapped source of information about Bradbury's creative process in writing his first novel. Viewed as a process, the transformation of these tales helps to define the structural and thematic unities of the book, and to determine just what kind of book it is.

* * *

The earliest of Bradbury's fancies and dreams about Mars dates to his juvenile reading. By 1932, he had discovered and consumed the romantic Martian tales of Edgar Rice Burroughs; that year, at the age of twelve, he wrote a short story titled "John Carter of Mars" on his toy typewriter.[3] But he envisioned a different Mars when, in 1940, he wrote his first serious Martian story, "The Piper." It appeared (under the pen name of Ron Reynolds) in the fourth and final issue of *Futuria Fantasia*, the amateur "fanzine" which he had created and edited since his graduation from Los Angeles High School in 1938. The story is lyrical and dream-like, a cautionary tale which describes the exploitation of Mars by Earthmen of the future. Though short (barely 1200 words), "The Piper" anticipates a central theme of *The Martian Chronicles* and is clearly a forerunner of Bradbury's unique stylistic approach to the genre, but the story was too unconventional to earn a professional sale. With Julius Schwartz, an agent well-known to science fiction editors, Bradbury re-wrote "The Piper" to the fast-action formula required by most of the science fiction pulps, and placed it in the February 1943 issue of *Thrilling Wonder Stories* for the then-significant sum of $60.00.[4]

But three more years would pass before Bradbury published another Martian story. His experience marketing "The Piper" revealed that his evolving style was not what the science fiction magazines were looking for. He continued to place occasional fast-action stories in the science fiction pulps, but the encouragement of mystery/detective fiction editor Ryerson Johnson led Bradbury to write for detective magazines during the remaining war years. From 1943 through 1945 he placed 43 professional stories, but only one out of every four was a science fiction tale, and most of these were formula pieces.

There were, however, discoveries during these years which would lead to *The Martian Chronicles*. In 1943 Bradbury wrote a fine space story, "King of the Gray Spaces," and placed it in the year-end issue of *Famous Fantastic Mysteries*. With this story, Bradbury first realized the themes of the space frontier which would inform much of his best science fiction. This stylistic maturity and thematic sophistication began to appear in his horror and fantasy work as well. With "The Wind" (1943), "The Lake" (1944), and "The Jar" (1944), Bradbury hit his stride as a master of the thriller.

Sometime in 1944, fellow writer and longtime friend Henry Kuttner told Bradbury about *Winesburg, Ohio*, and this discovery led to an outline titled "Earthport, Mars." The outline, which still exists, lists Winesburg-like title characters for twenty-one stories about Martian settlers from Earth.[5] At this point in his writing, the connection was a natural one—the lonely, half-mad piper of his first Martian story was a grotesque figure of dream-like proportions, rallying the displaced of Mars to rise up and drive out the Earth men. Such characters would appear in later Martian tales, but more and more the emphasis would center on the theme of exploration, of sacrifice, achievement, and the dangers inherent in the desire to make over new lands in familiar images. These themes would subsume the isolated grotesques and center most of the subsequent Martian stories on explorers, settlers, exploiters, and idealists.

The full canon of Martian tales produced during the late 1940's is not too difficult to define. Between 1946 and the publication of *The Martian Chronicles* in May 1950, Bradbury published twenty-two Martian tales in various magazines. Most of these were sold to the pulps, but Don Congdon (who became Bradbury's agent in 1947) managed to place reprints in major market slick-paper magazines and fiction anthologies. Three new stories appeared in the first edition of *The Martian Chronicles*, and two more were added to some later editions. Seven more Martian stories were published between 1950 and 1982, but all were written with the others in the late forties. Add to these thirty-four at least four extant story typescripts and three story fragments for Martian tales which never reached print. All of these materials were on hand in some form when Bradbury made his June 1949 trip to New York (Appendices A–C).

The A-Chronology

On the evening after his luncheon with Walter Bradbury, he returned to his room at the YMCA and spent most of the night going over the raw materials in his mind:

> It was a typical hot June night in New York. Air conditioning was still a luxury of some future year. I typed until 3 A.M., perspiring in my underwear as I weighed and balanced my Martians in their strange cities in the last hours before the arrivals and departures of my astronauts. (*MC* 40, ix)

In the morning he gave Walter Bradbury the outline and received in return a contract and a $750 advance. This outline—perhaps the original, but more likely a subsequent draft—still exists, providing invaluable clues about the long night's work. It bears no title other than "chapters," but for purposes of analysis it can be called the "A-Chronology" in order to identify its priority over later documents. The A-Chronology identifies seventeen numbered chapters with titles that are traceable to actual stories in all cases, with possibly one exception. Five of the chapters are identified as "unfinished." The completion status of the various titles, their order in the A-Chronology, and the content of the sixteen identifiable stories come together to reveal just how Bradbury first envisioned the completed project.

As his comments indicate, he spent much time that night on the opening third of the book, which relates to Mars at the moment of first contact between Earth men and the ancient, wiser, but extremely xenophobic Martians of Bradbury's imagination. He selected encounters of four kinds, three of which were already in print: " ... And the Moon Be Still as Bright," a novelette from the June 1948 issue of *Thrilling Wonder Stories*; "The Earth Men," a shorter work from the August 1948 issue; and the chilling "Mars Is Heaven!" from the Fall 1948 issue of *Planet Stories*. In their original forms these three encounters represented completely unrelated tales of first contact; the only common thread was the Martian culture itself, which was already forming in Bradbury's mind as an identity so alien that most Earthmen would not be able to understand it—or even to perceive its deadly instinct for self-preservation. In both "The Earth Men" and "Mars Is Heaven!," Earth's astronauts are destroyed by their own inability to sort out illusion from reality. The Martians of " ... And the Moon Be Still as Bright" are long dead, but the tension between those Earthmen who would preserve the planet's past and those who would grind it underfoot nearly destroys this expedition as well.

Preceding these titles, Bradbury typed the name "Ylla" from yet a fourth encounter with the Martian culture, an as-yet unpublished tale which subsequently appeared in the 1 January 1950 issue of *Maclean's* (Canada) as "I'll Not Look for Wine." Ylla is the central character of this story, a Martian woman, estranged from her husband, and who receives the thoughts of Nathaniel York of Earth's first Martian expedition, still several day's journey out in space. She is terrified, then drawn to the alien consciousness until her husband, sensing the telepathic relationship, seeks out the landing site and kills York and his crew-mate. The story is one of the best Martian tales, written late enough in the sequence that Bradbury had fully developed his vision of a bronze-skin, golden-eyed race with exotic art forms and jaded temperament. By placing this story first, Bradbury had decided to open the book with a long and fascinating look at an ancient civilization on the verge of extinction, a culture clearly unable to assimilate what Earthmen would bring.

The first third of the A-Chronology included two more titles. "Rocket Summer" (identified in A as unfinished) would become the first of the eleven bridge passages, opening the novel with an emotionally charged prelude to the new voyages of discovery. The failed voyages of "Ylla," "The Earthmen," and "Mars Is Heaven" appear in that order, followed by "The Death Disease,"

a bridge which Bradbury wrote as an explanation for the death of the Martians prior to the action of " . . . And the Moon Be Still as Bright." As Ylla's
husband succumbs to "The Death Disease," he realizes that it was carried to
Mars by the very Earthmen he had killed. In outline, these first four stories
and two bridges chronicle the demise of the Martian culture, leaving Earth's
explorers with a precarious claim to the legacy of the Red Planet.

The A-Chronology also indicates that Bradbury had a good idea of the
final portion of the book very early on. For the climax of the chronicles, he
selected three of his previously published tales which, though independent,
share the situational irony of a colonial society whose cultural lifeline is sev-
ered by the ravages of atomic war back on Earth. These stories appear in the
outline under their original titles: "The Off-Season," (*Thrilling Wonder Stories*,
December 1948), "The Long Years," (*Maclean's* (Canada), 15 September 1948),
and "The Million-Year Picnic," (*Planet Stories*, Summer 1946). Between "The
Off Season" and "The Long Years," Bradbury placed a new story titled "There
Will Come Soft Rains." This unpublished story eventually appeared in the 6
May 1950 issue of *Collier's*, just prior to publication of *The Martian Chronicles*.
One of the most anthologized of Bradbury's stories, "There Will Come Soft
Rains" describes the last day in an automated house of the future which has
miraculously survived total atomic war only to die, part by robotic part, in the
flames of a freak natural accident.

"There Will Come Soft Rains" is not about Mars at all, but it brings
the parallel chronology of the mother planet into focus at the moment when
war of unimaginable proportions drastically alters the future of the Martian
colonies. It follows "The Off-Season," the story of Sam Parkhill's bittersweet
realization of the American dream on the eve of Earth's war. He opens the
first hot-dog stand on Mars at a lonely crossroads, envisioning a booming
business from future waves of migrant laborers; but before his gaudy neon
lights can attract a single customer, representatives of the ancient Martian
culture emerge from hiding to offer Parkhill a "gift." Fearing the loss of his
stake in the new world, he kills most of his visitors before realizing that the
gift is a deed to vast tracts of the planet. Parkhill cannot comprehend why
the Martians have offered him the opportunity to become a "true" Martian
until he sees the explosions of Earth's war in the night sky. He is left in shock,
while his wife sarcastically describes the tragedy in business terms—they are
in for a very, very long "off-season."

"There Will Come Soft Rains" brings home the mindless destruction
of those distant explosions with visceral impact, and sets up a timeline for
the two alternate future views of Mars which conclude the collection as first
planned. "The Long Years" tells the story of Doc Hathaway, the physician
and archeologist who is marooned on Mars when Earth recalls all colonists

during an atomic war back home. A rescue ship from a rebuilt Earth finds an aging Hathaway twenty years later, but the crew is mystified that his wife and three children have not aged at all. Hathaway suffers a fatal heart attack from the excitement of rescue, and the crew soon discovers that his "family" is really a marvelous robot family built as exact replicas for the wife and children he had lost years before to plague. The rescuers bury Hathaway, but cannot bring themselves to terminate the lifelike robot family; they are left to continue their ritualized family routine, an endless illusion of life on a dead planet. "The Million-Year Picnic" offers a positive alternative to the death and sterility of "The Lonely Years." This final tale chronicles a post-holocaust family which comes to Mars not as conquerors, but as refugees. These new "Martians" establish a "Million-Year" future on their new planet by adopting it rather than exploiting it. "The Million-Year Picnic" was the first of his Martian tales to reach print after "The Piper," but even at this early conceptual stage there are glimpses of the same ancient but incredibly fragile Martian culture that he would develop in the later stories. Bradbury returned to this early vision of the encounter between Earth and Mars to close out the new book with a sense that mankind still has a chance to start over.

From the beginning, conceiving and organizing the middle section of the book presented the most problems. Seven titles appear in this section of the A-Chronology, six of which are readily identifiable. But only three of these stories—"The Martian," "Usher II," and "Way in the Middle of the Air"—would find their way into the first edition of *The Martian Chronicles*. The tentative nature of this section is reinforced by Bradbury's own notation that the other four stories—"The Fathers," "The Naming of Names," "Love Affair," and "The October Man"—were unfinished when the outline was prepared. In fact, none of these seven had as yet reached print, and only three—"The Naming of Names" (*Thrilling Wonder Stories* August 1949), "The Martian" (*Super Science Stories* November 1949, as "Impossible") and "Usher II" (*Thrilling Wonder Stories* April 1950, as "Carnival of Madness") would see print before book publication. A survey of all seven titles provides some clues to Bradbury's initial plan for the heart of the book.

Although unfinished at this point, "The Fathers" eventually became "The Fire Balloons," one of four stories leading off this section of the A-Chronology which involve contact with aboriginal Martian "survivors." In "The Fathers," the Jesuit Father Peregrine and a companion search for God among the Martian hills, and find a benign lifesaving force which defies analysis and torments the searchers with hopes that God might once again walk with man. "The Naming of Names" presents a community of settlers which has named and claimed a new frontier, but soon finds itself marooned on Mars by atomic war on Earth. The planet itself becomes proactive, subconsciously implanting a racial memory of the ancient Martian language and a desire to assume the identities of the native names and homesteads. Mars slowly transforms the settlers into Martians, and a rescue ship arriving five years later finds only dark and golden-eyed Martians living far from the colonial settlement. The new crew surveys and names the major landmarks; in this way, "The Naming of Names" begins all over again.

In sharp contrast to the primeval Martian powers of these two stories, "The Martian" portrays a survivor who is tempted by loneliness to enter a human home, using his powers of illusion to appear as the lost son of an old couple living on the edge of a colonial settlement. A fatal journey into the settlement reveals that any strong human memory will trigger a shape-change; the helpless Martian dies in an agony of metamorphosis, overloaded with the identities of long-lost loved ones from the desperate dreams of the humans around him.

"The Love Affair" is the only story other than "Ylla" listed in the original chronology that is written from the Martian point of view. Like "Ylla," it is a story of a secret sharer, in this case a Martian boy, perhaps the sole survivor of his race, who braves the threat of the Death Disease to meet the isolated Earth woman that he has loved from afar. Although the reader knows that she is a prostitute on vacation from the settlements, this factor only adds more possibilities to the moment of meeting—a meeting which Bradbury leaves to the reader's imagination. The final two stories from the middle section focus entirely on Earthmen who come to Mars to escape repression. "Way in the Middle of the Air" is Bradbury's pre-1950s vision of freedom for Black Americans, who rise up not in rebellion but rather in a successful attempt to leave the old order behind in a new Exodus to Mars. In "Usher II," a future where imaginative literature is banned drives a rich eccentric to Mars to recreate Poe's House of Usher. When the authorities follow to tear down his creation and burn his books, he is ready for them, with a vengeance worthy of Poe himself.

Poe may also be "The October Man" of the A-Chronology. This title represents the only mystery in the first list of chapters; it appears nowhere else in Bradbury's manuscripts or published stories, but there are clues. In "Usher II," Bradbury's obsessed millionaire recreates on Mars the perpetual autumn environment of Poe's House of Usher, an "ancient autumn world" which is "always October." Eventually, Bradbury came to see his own Poe-esque horror and suspense stories as fantasies set in "The October Country," and collected his best early thrillers under that now-famous title in 1955. But the most compelling clue surfaces in the next chronology, where a second Poe story does appear in the middle of the outline in place of "The October Man."

At some later date, Bradbury returned to the mid-portion of the A-Chronology and wrote in two more titles—"Grandfathers" and "Night Meeting." Neither appears in the next Chronology, although they surface again in the third. Their appearance as holograph additions to A may underscore the tentative nature of the original mid-book titles, but it is more likely an indication that Bradbury was working with both the first (A) and second (B) chronologies as he made the substantial revisions to this section which are evident in the third (C) chronology.

At least initially, it appears that Bradbury was more interested in examining the "displaced" than the "displacers" in the central section of the book. The first three stories in the middle section of A are imaginative explorations of the consequences of the social Darwinism and egocentric attitudes that the first Earthmen bring to Mars to replace the fragile Martian culture. The fourth is a love story told, like "Ylla," from the Martian point of view. "The October Man" is problematic, due to the tenuous nature of its identity. Only the final two stories turn to the pressures that drive men outward from Earth's civilization, and the frontier imperatives that lead to exploration and settlement. The progressive chronology of discovery, exploration and settlement promised by "Rocket Summer" doesn't carry through the center of the A-Chronology. For this section at least, more than revision would be required in the months ahead.

The B-Chronology

The A-Chronology provides an excellent baseline by which to measure the succeeding stages of large-scale restructuring. The next stage is also recorded in an extant outline, probably prepared not long after Bradbury returned home to California in late June 1949. This "B-Chronology," as we may call it, includes twenty-one entries. Two titles are dropped from the A-Chronology; six new ones are added. Significantly, the B-Chronology entries have date prefixes similar to those that Bradbury would settle on in lieu of chapter numbers for the first edition text, differing only in the span of years he would identify as inclusive to the final structure of the book. In B, these dates run chronologically (with two typographical errors) from "July 5th, 1985" to "Fall 1999."

In this phase, Bradbury retained in order the six titles which open his original concept of the chronicles. He even highlighted the chronology by annotating the stories of exploration following "Ylla" as the second, third, and fourth expeditions. In the case of "Mars Is Heaven," the subtitle "Third Expedition" would eventually become the new title. Bradbury gives this story the date April 3rd, 1986, while "The Death of the Martians" takes place the next day, indicating that in B he already envisioned a strong link between

Earth's three ill-fated expeditions and the cultural extinction of his Martians by human bacteria.

Bridges between major sections of the book begin to appear in B. A bridge tentatively titled "Threat of War on Earth" provides a new transition into the final apocalyptic chronicles. Not surprisingly, this section remains largely unchanged, with one major exception. "The Silent Towns," which had recently appeared in *Charm* (March 1949), was inserted between "There Will Come Soft Rains" and "The Long Years." The addition proved very effective. Like "The Long Years," "The Silent Towns" is a story about the few lonely colonists left behind when the settlers return to friends and families on war-torn Earth. But the sense of loss and brooding isolation in "The Long Years" is effectively balanced by the grotesque characterizations and darkly humorous accommodation to an empty world that is central to "The Silent Towns." In this story, an itinerant miner named Walter Gripp returns from the hills to find that all the settlements have been abandoned in the rush home. He amuses himself by playing both vendor and consumer in a ghost town where everything is free, but even the eccentric Gripp soon discovers a craving for human company. His ultimate wish is fulfilled when the sultry voice at the other end of a phone call leads him to the only other human on the planet. His odyssey ends in the presence of Genevieve Selsor, a plump chocolate-chewing nightmare; Gripp flees in a panic, never realizing that she is no more grotesque and mannerless than he is.

B clearly shows that the opening and closing sections remained essentially unchanged; but Bradbury was still far from satisfied with the mid-portion of the book. A new bridge, tentatively titled "The Settling In," leads into the core of the book, but the rest of this section varies significantly from A. "The Love Affair" and "The October Man" drop out (as do the holograph entries for "Grandfathers" and "Night Meeting"). "The Naming of Names," "The Fathers" (retitled "The Priests"), "Way in the Middle of the Air," "The Martian," and "Usher II" remain, but appear in this new order. Three new titles appear in the center of this grouping: "Sketch: what happened to Negroes?"; "Mr. Edgar Allan Poe Comes to Mars"; and "The Passing Years."

These changes suggest that Bradbury was still looking for an arrangement of material which would give focus and continuity to the entire work while carrying it beyond the scope of a story collection. Two of the new titles play off of material developed in the original chronology. "Sketch: what happened to Negroes?" may be a companion piece to "Way in the Middle of the Air." The earlier story ends as American Blacks head off to the rocket ports for Mars, leaving the traditional White society to sort it all out. "Sketch" appears to be either a bridge, or Bradbury's initial idea for a follow-up piece; if the former, it becomes "The Wheel" bridge of the C-Chronology; if the latter, it evolves into "The Other Foot," a story of prosperous Black settlers on Mars who, after a nuclear war on Earth, are confronted with the ironic situation of having to take in a White refugee from war-torn Earth. The story concludes with backlash hatred melting into compassion when the shoe is on "the other foot."

The book-burning behind the plot of "Usher II" shows that Bradbury was already shaping the material which would bear fruit in *Fahrenheit 451* several years later. Both Poe and book-burning resurface in the next new story of the B-Chronology. "Mr. Edgar Allan Poe Comes to Mars" is most likely a planned revision of "The October Man" of the A-Chronology; the new title provides convincing evidence that it would become "The Mad Wizards of Mars," a story which eventually appeared in the 15 September 1949 issue of *Maclean's* of Canada. It is closer to whimsical fantasy than any other story considered for *The Martian Chronicles*. Here Bradbury envisions a writer's graveyard—the mass burning of Earth's literary treasures sends the ghosts of all the great writers to exile on Mars. On the eve of a first expedition to Mars, Poe's ghost leads the other literary masters in an attempt to telepathically terrorize the crew into turning back. They fail, and when the Captain burns the last copies of the masterworks from his ship's library, the ghosts themselves dissolve away.

"The Passing Years" may be the first interior bridge for this section of the book. The title and its date—twelve years after the preceding entry—suggests that the stories of early settlement were to be set off from those chronicling the evolving colonial identity on Mars. But such changes are still tentative in B—in spite of the date entries, there is very little bridging or true chronological depth to the material.

The B-Chronology shows a shift of emphasis in its middle titles; with the deletion of "The Love Affair," only three remaining stories in this section deal with the old Martians. Although we cannot be sure of their content at this early outline stage, the Poe fantasy and the Negro sketch seem to add to the stories concerned with the transfer of Earth's culture to a new world. As work progressed, Bradbury would continue this trend in his stories as well as his bridging chapters.

The C-Chronology

The last surviving record of revision appears to be the final chronology that went forward to the publisher with the manuscript; if so, it probably dates from November or December 1949. The most striking changes involve the dating prefixes and the significant expansion of titles—now totaling 29. Bradbury moved the point of departure to the eve of the new century, and expanded the scope of *The Martian Chronicles* to cover a full quarter century of colonization. (Oddly enough, the perspective of time shows that Bradbury's dates approximate today's tentative timetable for NASA's projected manned Mars missions.)

Even in outline, the C-Chronology appears far more complete than the earlier chronologies. In preparing C, Bradbury deleted three stories from B, but retained the remaining eighteen titles—five bridges and thirteen stories—with some title revisions. Most significantly, he added eleven new titles—five stories and six bridges—and completely reshaped the sequence of stories in the middle portion of the work.

The C-Chronology adds only one story to the opening section, and none to the closing section of the outline; this evidence confirms that Bradbury's initial vision of man's exploitation of a dying culture, and the eventual "second chance" to redeem man's mistakes on Mars, were firmly rooted in the earlier chronologies. The major addition in C is "The Summer Night," which appeared in the Winter 1949 issue of *The Arkham Sampler* (as "The Spring Night"), just as Bradbury was finishing his revisions for *The Martian Chronicles*. "The Spring Night" is, in effect, a 900-word bridge between "Ylla" and "The Earth Men"; the internal evidence of the magazine text indicates that it was probably written, along with "Ylla," rather late in the series of Martian stories (probably early 1949). "The Summer Night" develops the central mystery of Ylla—her ability to pick up the thoughts of Earthmen as they approach Mars. Martians gathered for a summer evening of music under the stars are astonished when the singer and even the musicians become the media for fragments of alien music of unknown origin. The harsh, almost barbaric quality of the sound terrifies the assembly and drives the Martians home in panic, where fragments of other strange rhymes surface in children's play and even in dreams. The musical echoes are all traditional Anglo-American songs and rhymes similar to those which Ylla reads from the mind of Nathaniel York. The story forms a natural bridge between "Ylla," where only one very sensitive and very lonely Martian receives the thoughts of Earth's first astronaut, and "The Earth Men," where a larger crew approaches Mars with stronger (and much more confusing) composite memories.

Bradbury also added "The Taxpayer," a true bridge between the second expedition of "The Earth Men" and "The Third Expedition" (a title which evolves in C from "Mars Is Heaven!"), and retained "The Disease" as a bridge between the stories of the Third and Fourth Expeditions. In this way, he provided an introductory bridge or bridging story for each of the four tales of exploration which open the chronicles.

In the final section of the C-Chronology, Bradbury developed the opening "Threat of War on Earth" into a bridge titled "The Luggage Store." The final five stories remain uninterrupted by bridges, but in C "There Will Come

Soft Rains" moves down between "The Long Years" and "The Million-Year Picnic." These three closing stories are now dated 2026, more than twenty years after the war on Earth brought all but a few marooned settlers and explorers home. The revision in chronology accommodates the 20-year time-span required for Doc Hathaway's story in "The Long Years," but the revised timeline creates a new logic problem for "The Million-Year Picnic" by delaying the Thomas family's pre-holocaust departure for Mars by twenty-one years. Bradbury's solution was to reposition "There Will Come Soft Rains" late in the chronology, revealing that the destruction of Earth did not happen all at once, but rather over a period of years leading up to a final atomic cataclysm. The penultimate position of "Soft Rains" explains how families like the Thomases and their neighbors could have survived the earlier war years and managed to leave for Mars just ahead of Earth's final descent into chaos.

The middle of the C-Chronology reveals a total reworking of Bradbury's vision of the settlement of Mars. He dropped three stories entirely—"The Naming of Names," "Sketch: what happened to Negroes?", and "Mr. Edgar Allan Poe Comes to Mars." These deletions indicate that Bradbury was thinking more of the structure of the book as a whole than of individual stories—each deleted story has a basic plot element that puts it at variance with the general progression of the *Chronicles*. The Poe piece presents a new 'first expedition' story that in no way fits into the fabric of the Martian conquest described and bridged so carefully through the first four stories of the text. Both "The Naming of Names" and "Sketch" are philosophically insightful, but they describe destinies for the Earth settlements on Mars that are at variance with the nearly complete vision of failure and redemption as narrated in the final five *Chronicle* stories. Under different titles, all three of these stories would eventually find their way into some of Bradbury's best story collections of later years; but as the *Chronicles* moved closer and closer to completion, it became apparent that these stories would only diffuse the developing unity of the book.

The bridge into the mid-section stories (retitled "The Settlers") continues to serve this major transitional purpose in C. "The Passing Years" bridge almost certainly becomes "The Naming of Names"—it is the only bridge in C that spans years instead of a single month or day. In this bridge Bradbury chronicles the way that, over time, the Earthmen rename and master the Martian terrain. This context, coupled with the bridge's unique date prefix and the fact that Bradbury had removed (and would eventually retitle) the B-Chronology story of that name, argues well for the assumption that Bradbury simply moved the title from story to bridge in the C-Chronology. But other revisions in the mid-section of C are far more significant. These two bridges and the surviving four stories from B—"The Priests," "Way [In the] Middle of the Air," "The Martian," and "Usher II"—are reordered and merged into a larger body of three new stories and six new bridges. The seven stories now in the book's mid-section work with the eight bridges to tell an integrated story of initial settlement, and the waves of settlers that follow. The new stories present, in turn, an early frontier settlement along the lines of the American West ("They All Had Grandfathers"); a Johnny Appleseed figure, determined to plant a forest of trees and shrubs which bring sweet memories of Earth as well as the essential oxygen exchange which the colonists need to survive ("The Green Morning"); and a night meeting between two lone travelers, one a pioneer from Earth, the other a Martian, both trapped for a moment out of time, and both unsure whether the other represents the past or the future of Mars ("The Night Meeting"). These new settlers are followed by the priests ("The Fathers"), the Negro pioneers from the American South ("Way in the Middle of the Air"), the eccentric millionaire ("Usher II"), and the old people ("The Martian") who come in successive waves in the four stories which Bradbury had carried over from both the A- and B-Chronologies. The six new mid-book bridges reinforce the wave-like dynamic of settlement, and the occupational diversity of the settlers. There would be other last minute changes before publication, but in essence the outlined text of the C-Chronology represents the final contents of *The Martian Chronicles*.

The surviving A-, B-, and C-Chronologies point to a fairly rigorous process of revision and expansion by which Bradbury turned these stories into what amounts to a first novel. But by themselves, the three chronologies cannot provide convincing evidence that the final work is anything more than a collection of imaginative stories linked by common subjects and themes. The true nature of the book only becomes apparent through an analysis of Bradbury's actual revisions, and the new materials which he produced specifically for *The Martian Chronicles*.

Story Revisions

Early magazine versions exist for twelve of the eighteen C-Chronology stories.[6] Collations of these texts against those in the first hardcover edition reveal heavy revision which, for some stories, amounts to major rewriting. Much of the revising is structural, providing internal bridges and links between stories. But at least half of the revised passages reveal significant stylistic development as well.

Structural changes often provide clues to the order in which some stories were written. The magazine texts for "Ylla" and "The Summer Night" already show a full development of the Martian culture which the earlier stories of first contact lack.[7] Bradbury added similar descriptions as he revised the earlier tales to form subsequent Earth landings in the *Chronicles*. "The

Earth Men," as transformed into a tale of the Second Expedition, provides good examples. In revision, "The Earth Men" includes descriptions of the colorful masks which symbolize the increasingly illusive nature of Bradbury's fragile Martians:

Magazine text:

The little town was full of people going in and out doors and saying hello to one another. Through windows you could see people eating food and washing dishes. (72)

First edition text:

The little town was full of people drifting in and out of doors saying hello to one another, wearing golden masks and blue masks and crimson masks for pleasant variety, masks with silver tips and bronze eyebrows, masks that smiled or masks that frowned, according to the owner's disposition. (36)

The Earth Men can find no adult interested in their presence, and try to tell their tale to a little Martian girl. In revision, Bradbury has her quickly clap "an expressionless golden mask over her face," and listen to the story "through the slits of her emotionless mask." Themselves masters of illusion, the natives believe that the astronauts are merely deranged Martians who can produce the image of strange weapons, spacesuits, and a ship from the stars. When the Earth Men are locked away in an asylum, they are treated by a Martian psychologist who, in the revised text, wears a mask with three faces.

Until revision, the four stories of initial contact with Mars were not interconnected—each originally stood as a distinct vision of first contact. In revision for the *Chronicles*, Bradbury left "Ylla" largely untouched as a Martian's view of the First Expedition, and added passages to the other stories which placed them in a sequence as the Second, Third, and Fourth Expeditions. But the interweave works even deeper into the book. Bradbury also added two of his protagonists from the concluding stories of the *Chronicles* to Captain John Wilder's crew of the successful Fourth Expedition—Sam Parkhill, the hotdog stand owner of "The Off Season," and Doc Hathaway of "The Long Years." In revising "The Long Years," he provides further linkage by having Doc Hathaway rescued by Captain Wilder himself, who has been on deep space exploration missions during the twenty years of war on Earth. Here, as well as in "The Off Season," Bradbury builds on Wilder's conservationist image by revealing how he was sent out to the space frontier to prevent his interference with the colonial exploitation of Mars.

Other changes accommodate the advance of the chronology into the twenty-first century by altering the birthdates of crew members and the years of the expedition landings. Bradbury is also careful to develop a sense for the physical strain of low oxygen on Mars, a consideration lacking from the earlier versions of the contact stories. And in a very important long addition to "And the Moon Be Still as Bright," Doc Hathaway tells Captain Wilder how his scouting mission across the planet uncovers the pathetic end of the Martian culture—the incredibly ancient race has been suddenly and silently exterminated by the chicken pox carried by the crews of the three earlier expeditions.

These changes are significant in tracing the evolution of independent stories into book chapters, but the stylistic changes are an even stronger indicator of the extent of Bradbury's rewriting. Collation reveals that most stories were heavily revised—some as much as seventy percent. The majority of this revision involves stylistic development of dialogue and the descriptions, images, and suspense elements of the individual stories.

"There Will Come Soft Rains" is perhaps the most heavily revised story in the *Chronicles*. Very little is altered in terms of events—it remains the pathetic and tragic story of the death of an automated house, long after the family it serves has been destroyed in the first flash of an atomic blast. But the descriptions become richer and more powerful in revision, as we can see in the descriptions of the little robot mice that scurry about cleaning the house on its final day:

Magazine text:

Out of warrens in the wall, tiny mechanical mice darted. The rooms were acrawl with the small cleaning animals, all rubber and metal. They sucked up the hidden dust, and popped back in their burrows. (34)

First edition text:

Out of the warrens in the wall, tiny robot mice darted. The rooms were acrawl with the small cleaning animals, all rubber and metal. They thudded against chairs whirling their mustached runners, kneading the rug nap, sucking gently at hidden dust. Then, like mysterious invaders, they popped into their burrows. Their pink, electric eyes faded. The house was clean. (206)

Later in the day, the return of the family dog triggers another descriptive revision:

Magazine text:

Behind it whirred the angry robot mice, angry at having to pick up mud and maple leaves which, carried to the burrows, were dropped down cellar tubes into an incinerator which sat like an evil Baal in a dark corner. (34)

First edition text:

Behind it whirred angry mice, angry at having to pick up mud, angry at inconvenience.
For not a leaf fragment blew under the door but what the wall panels flipped open and the copper scrap rats flashed swiftly out. The offending dust, hair, or paper, seized in miniature steel jaws, was raced back to the burrows. There, down tubes which fed into the cellar, it was dropped into the sighing vent of an incinerator which sat like evil Baal in a dark corner. (207)

The full development of the mice is only one of many animal images in "There Will Come Soft Rains" that come alive through Bradbury's revising hand. He adds chemical snakes of fire retardant foam, and a fire that backs off, "as even an elephant must at the sight of a dead snake." But the most fascinating new passages center on the introduction of an electronic nursery to the story, described in striking detail before the house begins to burn:

Four-thirty.
The nursery walls glowed.
Animals took shape: yellow giraffes, blue lions, pink antelopes, lilac panthers cavorting in crystal substance. The walls were glass. They looked out upon color and fantasy. Hidden films clocked through well-oiled sprockets, and the walls lived. The nursery floor was woven to resemble a crisp, cereal meadow. Over this ran aluminum roaches and iron crickets, and in the hot still air butterflies of delicate red tissue wavered among the sharp aroma of animal spoors! There was the sound like a great matted yellow hive of bees within a dark bellows, the lazy bumble of a purring lion. And there was the patter of okapi feet and the murmur of a fresh jungle rain, like other hoofs, falling upon the

summer-starched grass. Now the walls dissolved into distances of parched weed, mile on mile, and warm endless sky. The animals drew away into thorn brakes and water holes.

It was the children's hour. (208)

Later, as the fire consumes the house, the nursery responds to this final deadly stimulus:

In the nursery the jungle burned. Blue lions roared, purple giraffes bounded off. The panthers ran in circles, changing color, and ten million animals, running before the fire, vanished off toward a distant steaming river. . . . (210)

In these nursery descriptions, Bradbury was developing the controlling image of one of his most often anthologized horror tales, "The Veldt" (originally titled "The World the Children Made," 1950). But here, they add yet another image of animal vitality to Bradbury's descriptions of the doomed house. Similar deep revisions can be found throughout "There Will Come Soft Rains." A side-by-side comparison of the final third of the story reveals just how completely Bradbury rewrote this penultimate story for *The Martian Chronicles*.

Not all of his revisions were expansive. In story after story, collation uncovers many passages of dialogue which are tightened up to great effect in revision for the book. The dialogue passages of "The Third Expedition" ("Mars Is Heaven!") are typical. Captain John Black and his crew find, to their amazement, that they've landed in an exact replica of an early twentieth century midwestern American town, complete with old phonograph recordings, period artwork, and villagers. In one passage, Black and two of his officers question an old lady about the town. A parallel comparison of the pre- and post-revision texts shows how Bradbury deleted forty percent of the passage by eliminating the bewildered echoing lines of the astronauts and the peevish pouting of the old lady—all changes for the better. The serene and motherly old lady of the revised passage surprises the reader—irritability and peevishness were hallmarks of Martian behavior in "Ylla" and "The Earth Men." The tightened dialogue of "The Third Expedition" eliminates this telltale characteristic and allows the Martian woman to set her illusion with much more subtlety—a stratagem which is only appreciated in the harrowing conclusion of the tale.

It is this illusion that carries the story, and Bradbury refines the element of suspense by adding material to Black's gradual realization of the terrifying truth. The town seems to be populated by the dead relatives of his crew members; all the men leave their weapons and rush to meet long lost loved ones. Reunited with his own brother and parents, Black is convinced that Mars is a Heaven of sorts, a place where the dead blissfully re-enact their Earthly routines. But later, as he tries to fall asleep in his childhood home, logical thought returns:

> And this town, so old, from the year 1926, long before *any* of my men were born. From a year when I was six years old and there *were* records of Harry Lauder, and Maxfield Parrish paintings *still* hanging, and bead curtains, and "Beautiful Ohio," and turn-of-the-century architecture. What if the Martians took the memories of a town *exclusively* from *my* mind? They say childhood memories are the clearest. And after they built the town from *my* mind, they populated it with the most-loved people from all the minds of the people on the rocket!
>
> And suppose those two people in the next room, asleep, are not my mother and father at all. But two Martians, incredibly brilliant, with the ability to keep me under this dreaming hypnosis all the time? (64–65)

These memories are Bradbury's, who, like John Black, was born in 1920. Added largely in revision, this passage highlights the deadly subtlety of the Martian illusion. For John Black, this numbing realization precedes his own death by mere seconds.

In just four months, between his return from New York in late June 1949, and the birth of his daughter Susan in early November, Bradbury transformed these stories into chapters of a greater work. But the final sense of completion only came with the writing of new material—the transitional bridges.

The Bridges

Most of the Martian stories were written before Bradbury's June 1949 trip to New York provided the inspiration to fuse these materials into a novel. In fact, all but five of the stories in the C-Chronology preceded the book into print in some form. But the bridges are a different story. Only "Rocket Summer" appears in the A-Chronology, with the note that it is "unfinished." Presumably all eleven bridges—representing a tenth of the total text but more than a third of the C-Chronology titles—were written specifically for the book.

"Rocket Summer," although very brief, sets the mood for the possibilities of rocket travel and the opening of a new frontier. It's still winter on Earth, but the rockets are already changing the world: "The rocket stood in the cold winter morning, making summer with every breath of its mighty exhausts. The rocket made climates, and summer lay for a brief moment upon the land ..." (13). Many of the bridges end in ellipsis, leading the way to "Ylla" and beyond.

In "The Taxpayer," Bradbury first reveals the re-awakened need for frontier freedoms that the rocket brings to many. The anonymous taxpayer expresses this need as dissatisfaction with established civilization in the best tradition of American frontier literature: "To get away from wars and censorship and statism and conscription and government control of this and that, of art and science! You could have Earth! He was offering his good right hand, his heart, his head, for the opportunity to go to Mars!" (47). There are also references to atomic war looming on the horizon, a bridge to later stories which gives a sense of urgency to the settlement of Mars.

After the story of the Fourth Expedition, Mars—for a time—will be Earth's. With "The Settlers," Bradbury begins to document the waves of settlement, continuing through all the bridges in the middle section of the book. In "The Shore," he extends the wave metaphor to echo the American experience: "Mars was a distant shore, and the men spread upon it in waves. Each wave was different, and each wave stronger" (111). Each successive bridge defines one or more waves:

> The first wave carried with it men accustomed to spaces and coldness and being alone, the coyote and cattlemen, ... ("The Shore," 111)

> And what more natural than that, at last, the old people come to Mars, following in the trail left by the loud frontiersmen, the aromatic sophisticates, and the professional travelers and romantic lectures in search of new grist. ("The Old Ones," 149)

But Bradbury's waves of settlers are all American waves. Again, the bridges explain:

> The second men should have traveled from other countries with other accents and other ideas. But the rockets were American and the men were American and it stayed that way, while Europe and Asia and South America and Australia and the islands watched the Roman candles leave them behind. The rest of the world was buried in war or the thoughts of war. ("The Shore," 111)

And the settlers not only were American, but they built American, trying "to beat the strange world into a shape that was familiar to the eye, to bludgeon away all the strangeness" ("The Locusts," 101). They brought in Oregon pine and California redwood to work this transformation, and in time, they succeeded: "It was as if, in many ways, a great Earthquake had shaken loose the roots and cellars of an Iowa town, and then, in an instant, a whirlwind twister of Oz-like proportions had carried the entire town off to Mars to set it down without a bump...." ("Interim," 113). Finally, the old Martian names and places were buried beneath the new frontier history: "Here was the place where Martians killed the first Earth Men, and it was Red Town and had to do with blood. And here where the second expedition was destroyed, and it was named Second Try, and each of the other places where the rocket men had set down their fiery cauldrons to burn the land, the names were left like cinders, ..." ("The Naming of Names," 130).

The bridges chronicle the way that the pioneering imperative populates the new land and imposes a civilized order over the natural order of the Red Planet. The final bridges reach to events back on Earth, and show how the roots of the new life are not yet deep enough to keep the settlers from returning home when the rumors of war become reality.

Bradbury's bridges complete the transformation of the Martian stories into chapters of an integrated greater work. The bridges chronicle the cosmic scope of the group endeavor to fulfill dreams in a new world; the stories chronicle individuals striving to make the dreams come true. Together, the unbroken chronology of bridge and story reveals in very human terms the wonder and deadly perils of a new frontier, full of recurring reminders that there can be no fulfillment on the frontier without sacrifice and loss.[8]

The Publishing Legacy

As one might expect, the dynamic shaping of *The Martian Chronicles* did not end with the C-Chronology. Doubleday's May 1950 first edition contains twenty-five of the twenty-nine titles in C. The final revisions deleted the stories "They All Had Grandfathers" and "The Fathers." "The Disease," planned as a bridge explaining the extinction of the Martians, also disappears, as does "The Wheel." A late addition, a bridge titled "The Watchers," brings the final chapter count to twenty-six, including fifteen stories and eleven bridges.

"The Disease" provided situational irony, but in depicting the death of Ylla's husband by means of the bacteriological legacy of the Earthmen he had slain, Bradbury had sensationalized an otherwise subtle and effective story. The deletion of this bridge improves the impact of "Ylla" and quickens the tempo of the opening stories of first contact. In terms of plot, the deletion was compensated by revisions to the Fourth Expedition's story in the opening pages of "And the Moon Be Still as Bright." Bradbury's addition of Hathaway and his medical report on the death of the Martians eliminates the need for a bridge between the Third and Fourth Expedition stories, and effectively develops the irony of mankind's unintentional genocide.

"The Wheel" initially provided a whimsical but ineffective epilogue to "Way in the Middle of the Air." Here again, deletion of a bridge increases the tempo of the chronicles, this time without the need to add material elsewhere. The logic for a new bridge in the final section of the *Chronicles* is also clear. "The Watchers," with its repeated radio calls from Earth to COME HOME, provides the final motivation for the return exodus of the settlers.

It isn't clear whether deletion of the two stories was an authorial decision, or was prompted by editorial concern over content. The spiritual implications of "The Fathers" might have been considered controversial, but there is little (other than prostitution) to consider controversial in "They All Had Grandfathers." ("The Fathers," much the finer of the two pieces, would appear in the companion story volume, *The Illustrated Man*, a year later.) Whatever the reason, it is likely that the stories were removed at the last minute—surviving references to Father Peregrine of "The Fathers" remain in two bridges, "The Shore" and "The Luggage Store."

The subsequent publishing history of the work is no less complicated, and reveals that Bradbury and his agent, Don Congdon, were able to retain a great deal of marketing flexibility as the book quickly won public acclaim. Even after book publication, Bradbury was able to retitle and even repackage some of the stories for reprint in American and English periodicals. In November 1950, *Esquire* reprinted "The Summer Night," combined with "The Earth Men," as "The Great Hallucination." In February 1951, the English version of *Argosy* reprinted the same conflation as "Danger Wears Three Faces." "Ylla" also appeared in the English *Argosy* under its original magazine title, "I'll Not Look for Wine." Nearly every other story has a magazine reprint history, but the longest trail belongs to "The Third Expedition." *Argosy* of England reprinted it just before book publication as "Circumstantial Evidence." Over the next few years, it appeared in *Esquire* under the original title, "Mars Is Heaven!", in *Coronet* (condensed) as "They Landed on Mars," in England's *Authentic Science Fiction* as "Welcome Brothers," and in England's *Suspense* as "While Earthmen Sleep." Such a recounting doesn't include the many anthology and textbook appearances and even comic book adaptations of the *Chronicle* tales.

Argosy of England eventually published eight of the stories, and this unofficial serial set up a ready-made reading public for English book publication in 1951. The English first edition deleted "Usher II," restored "The Fathers" as "The Fire Balloons," and in a move which probably reflected the altered contents, changed the title of the entire book to *The Silver Locusts* (an image found in "The Locusts" bridge of all versions). Two years later, the Science Fiction Book Club of England published yet a third variant text. This edition added a new story, "The Wilderness," to *The Silver Locusts* text, and restored the original *Martian Chronicles* title to the book. Beginning in 1963, some American editions have established a "complete" text, a fourth variant that includes all of the seventeen stories and eleven bridges that *ever* appeared in *any* edition of the book. Yet a fifth variant text was recently introduced by Doubleday's Fortieth Anniversary Edition, which restores "The Fire Balloons" to the original text, but does not include "The Wilderness." Just to add to the confusion, there are editions of the original *Martian Chronicles* text titled *The Silver Locusts*, and *Silver Locusts* texts titled *The Martian Chronicles* (see Appendix B). Every variant remains in print, in original or paper editions.

But even through the complex weave of the reprint history, it is apparent that *The Martian Chronicles* has never (in any variation) lost its original richness of design or unity of composition. It remains an imaginative exploration of the romance and reality found in any frontier experience, and reminds us that the invasion of a new frontier has a cost for both the displaced and the displacers. But is it a novel, or a collection of stories linked by ideas and adventures? The unique history of the text suggests an answer to this critical question.

The Critical Legacy

Winesburg, Ohio may, in a general sense, be the spark for the creative fire that became *The Martian Chronicles*. Both writers are natural storytellers, capable of capturing moments of life with great emotional impact, and linking these moments with unifying elements of place and character. But Bradbury's debt to Anderson stops here. Anderson, already a novelist, wrote his Winesburg tales in a single creative burst during the autumn of 1915. He wrote them quickly, almost exactly in the order of the finished book, and made very few revisions. In contrast, Bradbury initially wrote his stories as truly independent pieces, over a long period of time, without a sequence in mind or the long lost "Earthport" outline at hand. Ultimately, he did not follow Anderson's design for *Winesburg*; when he did think to unite these pieces, a long and intense process of revision and new writing followed. In terms of process, the textual history of *The Martian Chronicles* more closely parallels that of Faulkner's *Go Down, Moses* than it does *Winesburg, Ohio*. For that project, Faulkner fused ten stories and sketches into a greater whole that centered upon questions of race and man's evolving relationship to the wilderness. The bridging passages added to "The Fire and the Hearth" and "The Bear," along with the new story "Was," complete the chronicles of the McCaslin family established in the other stories. Finally, the original stories and sketches, hastily offered for piece money to periodicals, were care-fully revised and expanded for the final work. Although the new chapters remain distinct pieces of fiction, they are integral parts of a generations-long chronicle which Faulkner eventually came to regard as a novel; in all later printings, he deleted "and Other Stories" from the volume title.[9]

The Martian Chronicles shares this creative pattern. The same kind of transformation from a story collection to a unified fable occurs through the intensive rewriting and reshaping of the independent stories. The result is that the *Chronicles* transcend the classification of "science fiction" that is attributed to its constituent parts. Critics sensed this difference from the start, beginning with Christopher Isherwood, whose early review propelled Bradbury from genre notoriety into the mainstream of American letters. For Isherwood and others, the powerful style and imagination created a Martian setting that, in its totality, became a most compelling American parable.[10]

Are these unifying factors enough to give the *Chronicles* recognition as Bradbury's first novel? Traditionally, critics would demur, and for the same reasons given in classifying *Winesburg, Ohio.* Even *Go Down, Moses* (along with *The Unvanquished*) and *The Red Pony* (not to mention *Tortilla Flat* and *The Pastures of Heaven*) are considered cycles of stories, something between a story collection and a novel. In his introduction to the widely-taught Penguin edition of *Winesburg, Ohio*, Malcolm Cowley suggested that such a cycle has "several unifying elements, including a single background, a prevailing tone, and a central character. These elements can be found in all the cycles, but the best of them also have an underlying plot that is advanced or enriched by each of the stories." This definition works for the *Chronicles* as well—at least, as far as it goes. The background is the decline of an Old World, the prevailing tone is the suspense of exploring a New World, and the central character, Man-kind. The central plot or fable is the chronicle of the frontier experience.

But in Bradbury's case, a very crucial question remains unanswered by the definition: are these in fact the same stories that existed prior to the evolution of the greater work? The answer rests within the textual record. Here the lay-ers of revision, both in the outlines and the stories themselves, show far more internal transformation than most works of this kind. Of the twenty-six first edition titles, fourteen (eleven bridges and three stories) were here first printed. The twelve previously published stories all show substantive revision.[11] In most cases the rewriting involves a third to one-half of the words and punctuation of the text; in some, it involves as much as three-quarters of the material. Of these twelve, only seven appear in the *Chronicles* with their original titles.

What we find then is a new work in which the sum of the original parts does not equal the revised whole. More than half of the composite text is new or rewritten; nineteen of the twenty-six chapter titles are new or rewritten;

and all twenty-six chapter titles are given date prefixes which are, with few exceptions, unique to editions of the *Chronicles*. Clearly, a textual editor in search of the author's final intent for these stories could not look elsewhere—the copy-text for any authoritative edition of the *Chronicles* would have to be based on the first edition, or on pre-publication forms of the text that reflect the author's massive revisions. The previously published story texts do not reflect those revisions, and in most cases don't even reflect the author's intent to write the greater *Chronicles* saga.

The publishing record also demonstrates the coherence of the greater work. Although there are five variant texts to the *Chronicles*, none offers more than a five percent variation in content. This fact is even more remarkable when the entire canon of Martian tales is considered. Despite the existence of at least twenty-one other Martian tales, the many subsequent editions have added only one story ("The Wilderness") which was not in Bradbury's plan for the first edition text. It's also clear that Bradbury felt very strongly that the revised chronicles represented his final intent, even when they stood alone as stories. As Appendix A shows, the various chronicles have been reprinted and collected nearly fifty times, perhaps more widely than any similar work. Anthology and textbook appearances triple this total.[12] Yet with few exceptions early on, only the revised form—the chronicle form, if you will—is ever reprinted.

The evolution of *The Martian Chronicles* makes a strong case for the argument that the textual history of a work can have a crucial impact on its genre classification. From a bibliographical point of view, *The Martian Chronicles*, like *Go Down, Moses*, is more a novel than such "bricolage" cousins as *Winesburg, Ohio* and *The Red Pony*, where pre-existing parts become a new whole without substantial internal transformation. Discourse of the latter kind works within the framework limitations of the existing materials; that is, the author "assembles" rather than "creates" the larger work, building from extant stories which share unifying elements. From the bibliographer's perspective, one may easily see how more ambitious experiments like *The Martian Chronicles* transcend the limitations of pre-existing materials through the revising hand of the author.

In sewing together "some sort of tapestry" with his Martian stories, Bradbury essentially wrote an entirely new book. That book became *The Martian Chronicles*. And that book was his first novel. Once he transformed his stories into chronicles, rewriting them and bridging them together, they were changed forever. They might be pulled out from time to time and republished elsewhere as stories, but together they lock into a work that is more than the "half cousin to a novel" that Walter Bradbury ordered up one June day in New York, a long time ago.

Appendix A

Publishing History of the Individual Chronicles

The complete chronicles appear below in chapter order. Each includes a publishing history, listed chronologically. The histories include periodical reprints, Bradbury story collections, or single story books—that is, the texts over which Bradbury was likely to have exercised some degree of authorial control. Anthology and textbook appearances are not included here.

Title changes also appear in the publication history. Unless a separate title is specifically listed, all the printings of a given story have the title developed by Bradbury for *The Martian Chronicles*. Use or disuse of the date prefix is noted.

"January 1999: Rocket Summer." New bridge passage.

"February 1999: Ylla." Originally published *Maclean's* (Canada) 1 January 1950, as "I'll Not Look for Wine." Revised for *The Martian Chronicles* [May] 1950. Original reprinted *Argosy* (England) July 1950; reprinted as revised *Avon Fantasy Reader #14*, 1950, as "Ylla." Collected as revised *The Vintage Bradbury* (1965), as "Ylla."

"August 1999: The Summer Night," Originally published *The Arkham Sampler* Winter 1949, as "The Spring Night." Revised for *The Martian Chronicles* ([May] 1950). Reprinted *Esquire* November 1950, combined with "The Earth Men," as "The Great Hallucination"; reprinted *Argosy* (England) February 1951, combined with "The Earthmen," as "Danger Wears Three Faces."

"August 1999: The Earth Men." Originally published *Thrilling Wonder Stories* August 1948, as "The Earth Men." Revised for *The Martian Chronicles* [May] 1950. Reprinted *Esquire* November 1950, combined with "The Spring Night," as "The Great Hallucination"; reprinted *Argosy* (England) February 1951, combined with "The Spring Night," as "Danger Wears Three Faces"; reprinted *A Treasury of Great S.F. Stories #1* 1964. Collected, *The Stories of Ray Bradbury* (1980), as "The Earth Men."

"March 2000: The Taxpayer." New bridge passage.

"April 2000: The Third Expedition." Originally published *Planet Stories* Fall 1948, as "Mars Is Heaven!". Reprinted *Argosy* (England) April 1950, as "Circumstantial Evidence." Revised for *The Martian Chronicles* ([May] 1950). Reprinted *Esquire* December. 1950, as "Mars Is Heaven!"; reprinted *Coronet* June 1950, as "They Landed on Mars" (condensed); *Authentic Science Fiction #29* (England) January 1952, as "Welcome Brothers"; *Suspense* (England) November 1958, as "While Earthmen Sleep." Collected as revised, *The Stories of Ray Bradbury* (1980), as "Mars Is Heaven!"

"June 2001:—And the Moon be Still as Bright." Originally published *Thrilling Wonder Stories* June 1948, as " . . . And the Moon Be Still as Bright." Revised for *The Martian Chronicles* [May] 1950.

"August 2001: The Settlers." New bridge passage.

"December 2001: The Green Morning." New story. Reprinted *Read 1* December 1960, as "December 2001: The Green Mountains."

"February 2002: The Locusts." New bridge passage.

"August 2002: Night Meeting." New story. Reprinted *Identity* 1974; reprinted *Weird Worlds #1* 1978, as "Night Meeting." Collected, *The Vintage Bradbury*, as "Night Meeting."

"October 2002: The Shore." New bridge passage.

"The Fire Balloons." Originally published, *The Illustrated Man* (American editions only, [February.] 1951; deleted from all English editions). Reprinted *Imagination* Apr. 1951, as "In This Sign." Added to all English editions of *The Silver Locusts* ([Sep.] 1951) and *The Martian Chronicles* (1953), and some subsequent American editions of *The Martian Chronicles* (beginning 1963). Reprinted *And It Is Divine* December 1975 (abridged).

"February 2003: Interim." New bridge passage.

"April 2003: The Musicians." New bridge passage.

"The Wilderness." Originally published *Today* 6 April 1952. Rewritten and reprinted *Magazine of Fantasy and Science Fiction* November 1952. Collected, *The Golden Apples of the Sun*, ([March] 1953). Added to English editions of *The Martian Chronicles*, 1953. Reprinted *Everybody's Digest* September 1953, as "Honeymoon on Mars." Collected, *The Stories of Ray Bradbury* (1980), *Collected Stories 1* (1990).

"June 2003: Way in the Middle of the Air." New story. Reprinted *Other Worlds July* 1950, as "Way in the Middle of the Air"; reprinted *Duke* August 1957, as "The Day the Negroes Left Earth."

"2004–2005: The Naming of Names." New bridge passage.

"April 2005: Usher II." Originally published *Thrilling Wonder Stories* April 1950, as "Carnival of Madness." Revised for *The Martian Chronicles* ([May] 1950). Reprinted *Argosy* (England) Nov. 1950, as "The Second House of Usher"; reprinted *Esquire* Nov. 1951, as "The Immortality of Horror." Deleted from *The Silver Locusts* (1951) and English editions of *The Martian Chronicles* (1953). Added to English editions of *The Illustrated Man* (1952), as "Usher II."

"August 2005: The Old Ones." New bridge passage.

"September 2005: The Martian." Originally published *Super Science Stories* November 1949, as "Impossible." Revised for *The Martian Chronicles*, ([May] 1950).

"November 2005: The Luggage Store." New bridge passage.

"November 2005: The Off Season." Originally published *Thrilling Wonder Stories* December 1948, as "The Off Season." Revised for *The Martian Chronicles* ([May] 1950). Collected, *The Stories of Ray Bradbury* (1980).

"November 2005: The Watchers." New Bridge passage.

"December 2005: The Silent Towns." Originally published *Charm* March 1949, as "The Silent Towns." Rewritten for *The Martian Chronicles* ([May] 1950). Collected, *The Stories of Ray Bradbury* (1980), as "The Silent Towns."

"April 2026: The Long Years." Originally published *Maclean's* (Canada) 15 September 1948, as "The Long Years." Reprinted *Argosy* (England) March 1949; reprinted *Planet Stories* and *Planet Stories* (Canada) Spring 1949. Revised for *The Martian Chronicles* ([May] 1950). Reprinted *American Science Fiction* #19 (Australia) [1953], as "Dwellers in Silence."

"August 2026: There Will Come Soft Rains." Originally published *Collier's* 6 May 1950, as "There Will Come Soft Rains." Revised for *The Martian Chronicles* ([May] 1950). Reprinted *Argosy* (England) August 1950, *The New York Post* 13 March 1955, *Scholastic Scope* 5 April 1971, without title prefix. Collected, *The Vintage Bradbury* (1965), *The Stories of Ray Bradbury* (1980), and *There Will Come Soft Rains* (1989), without title prefix.

"October 2026: The Million-Year Picnic." Originally published *Planet Stories* Summer 1946, as "The Million-Year Picnic." Reprinted *Argosy* (England) February 1950, as "The Long Weekend." Revised for *The Martian Chronicles* [May] 1950. Reprinted *Tops in Science Fiction* Spring 1953, *Tops in Science Fiction #1* (England) 1954, without title prefix. Collected, *S Is for Space* (1966), *The Stories of Ray Bradbury* (1980), and *Classic Stories 2* (1990), as "The Million-Year Picnic."

Appendix B

Publishing History of *The Martian Chronicles*

All variants include the eleven bridges that Bradbury wrote for the first edition text. Thus Variants 1 and 2 have 26 total titles, Variants 3 and 5 have 27, and Variant 4 has 28. Editions through 1990 are listed by content variation.

Variant 1: Original Text, with 15 Stories:

The Martian Chronicles. Garden City, NY: Doubleday, [May] 1950. First edition.
———. NY: Bantam Books, [1951]. First American paperback edition. Adds prefatory quotations by Bradbury.
———. Garden City, NY: Doubleday, [1952]. Reprinting of first American edition for the Science Fiction Book Club.
———. Garden City, NY and Toronto: Doubleday, 1958. New edition with a two-page prefatory note by Clifton Fadiman.
The Silver Locusts. London: Transworld Publishers, 1963. The original 1950 American *Martian Chronicles* text, with the 1958 prefatory note by Clifton Fadiman.
The Martian Chronicles. Garden City, NY: [March] 1978. Reprinted for the Science Fiction Book Club.

Variant 2: English *Silver Locusts* Text, with 15 Stories:

The Silver Locusts. London: Rupert Hart-Davis, [September] 1951. English first edition. Deletes "Usher II" and adds "November 2002: The Fire Balloons."
———. London: Corgi, 1956. First English paperback edition.
The Martian Chronicles. London and NY: Granada, 1979. Paperback. First printing of *The Silver Locusts* text under *The Martian Chronicles* title. Includes a cover scene from the NBC TV mini-series.
———. London and NY: Granada, [1980]. Hardback printing of *The Silver Locusts* text under *The Martian Chronicles* title.

Variant 3: English *Martian Chronicles* Text, with 16 Stories:

———. [London]: The Science Fiction Book Club, [1953]. Adds "May 2003: The Wilderness" to *The Silver Locusts* text.

Variant 4: The Complete Text, with 17 Stories:

The Martian Chronicles. NY: Time, Inc., 1963. Paperback. Contains the original Doubleday text plus "The Fire Balloons" and "The Wilderness."
———. Garden City, NY: Doubleday, 1973. Hardcover. Includes illustrations from the 1971 Italian edition and a profile and bibliography by William F. Nolan.
———. Avon, CT: The Limited Editions Club, 1974. Illustrated by Joseph Mugnaini. Adds a nine-page introduction by Martin Gardner.
———. Avon, CT: Heritage Club, 1976. Illustrated by Joseph Mugnaini.
———. NY: Bantam Books, 1979. Illustrated (b&w) by Ian Miller.

Variant 5: The "Restored" Original Text, with 16 Stories:

The Martian Chronicles. NY: Doubleday, 1990. Fortieth Anniversary edition. Restores "November 2002: The Fire Balloons" to the original text.

Appendix C

Unchronicled Martian Stories

These Martian tales never appeared in *The Martian Chronicles*. They are listed in order of first publication; unpublished manuscripts, listed alphabetically, conclude the listing.

Published Stories:

"The Piper" (as Ron Reynolds). *Futuria Fantasia* No. 4 [September 1940].

"The Piper" (revised). *Thrilling Wonder Stories* February 1943.

"The Visitor." *Startling Stories* November 1948. Collected in *The Illustrated Man* (1951).

"I, Mars." *Super Science Stories* April 1949. Collected in *I Sing the Body Electric* (1969), *The Stories of Ray Bradbury* (1980), as "Night Call, Collect."

"The One Who Waits." *The Arkham Sampler* Summer 1949. Collected in *The Machineries of Joy* (1964).

"The Lonely One." *Startling Stories* July 1949.

"The Naming of Names." *Thrilling Wonder Stories* August 1949. Appears in the A- and B-Chronologies of *The Martian Chronicles*; deleted from the C-Chronology. Collected in *A Medicine for Melancholy* (1959).

"Holiday." *The Arkham Sampler* Autumn 1949.

"The Mad Wizards of Mars." *Maclean's* (Canada) 15 September 1949. Possibly corresponds to "The October Man" in the A-Chronology of *The Martian Chronicles*; appears in the B-Chronology as "Mr. Edgar Allan Poe Comes to Mars"; deleted from the C-Chronology. Collected in *The Illustrated Man* (1951), as "The Exiles."

"Payment in Full." *Thrilling Wonder Stories* February 1950.

"Death Wish." *Planet Stories* Fall 1950. Collected in *Long After Midnight* (1976), as "The Blue Bottle."

"The Other Foot." *New Story* March 1951. Appears in the B-Chronology of *The Martian Chronicles* as "Sketch: what happened to Negroes?"; deleted from the C-Chronology. Collected in *The Illustrated Man* (1951) as "The Other Foot."

"The Strawberry Window." *Star Science Fiction Stories* 3 (NY: Ballantine, 1954). Collected in *A Medicine for Melancholy* (1959).

"The Lost City of Mars." *Playboy* January 1967. Collected in *I Sing the Body Electric* (1969).

"The Messiah." *Welcome Aboard* (Great Britain) Spring 1971. Collected in *Long After Midnight* (1976). Adapted (by other writers) for the NBC teleplay of *The Martian Chronicles* (1979).

"The Aqueduct." Privately printed as *The Aqueduct*. Glendale, CA: Roy Squire Press, 1979. Collected in *The Stories of Ray Bradbury* (1980).

"The Love Affair." Privately printed as *Love Affair*. Northridge, CA: Lord John Press, 1982. Appears in the A-Chronology of *The Martian Chronicles*; deleted from the B-Chronology. Collected in *The Toynbee Convector*, 1988.

Unpublished Stories, Bridges, and Fragments:

Copies or originals of these typescripts are located in William F. Nolan's Bradbury Collection at Bowling Green State University, or in private collections.

"Christmas on Mars." TS., 6-page story. According to William F. Nolan, the typescript was sold to *Esquire* for a holiday issue, probably in the early 1950's, but never went to press. Probably never intended for *The Martian Chronicles.*

"The Disease." TS., 4-page "bridge" section with title page (pulled from printer's copy). Identified in the A-, B-, and C-Chronologies, but deleted from the first edition prior to publication.

"Fly Away Home." TS., 15-page story with title page dated March 3rd, 1952. Probably never intended for *The Martian Chronicles.*

"Martian Bulwark." TS., 19 pages. Dates from 1942–44, and includes a cover page from Julius Schwartz, Bradbury's first agent.

"The Martian Ghosts." TS., two versions, totalling 6 pages.

"They All Had Grandfathers." TS., 13 pages with title page (pulled from printer's copy). Appears in all three *Martian Chronicles* planning chronologies, but deleted prior to publication.

"The Wheel." TS., 1-page "bridge" section with chronology title page (pulled from printer's copy). Identified in the C-Chronology, but deleted from the first edition prior to publication.

Three untitled single-page story fragments and two "bridge" sections titled "Thistle-Down and Fire" (1 page) and "Fire and the Stars" (2 pages). According to William F. Nolan, these fragments and bridges were originally intended for *The Martian Chronicles*, but were never completed.

Notes

1. Ray Bradbury, "The Long Road to Mars," foreword to *The Martian Chronicles* (NY: Doubleday, 1990), pp. viii–ix. Written for the Fortieth Anniversary Edition. Further references to the foreword are noted parenthetically in the text as *MC* 40.

2. The relevant portion of Professor Mogen's 1980 interview with Bradbury appears in Mogen's *Ray Bradbury* (Boston: G. K. Hall, 1986), p. 84. In this interview Bradbury relates a more detailed version of the *Winesburg* connection, and identifies Henry Kuttner as the writer who first introduced him to Anderson's novel.

3. Nolan, William F., *The Ray Bradbury Companion* (Detroit: Gale, 1975), p. 43. This work remains the primary published source of accurate biographical and bibliographical information on Ray Bradbury. Mr. Nolan's experiences as a science fiction writer, editor, and long-time friend of Ray Bradbury provided the basic materials for this study. I am deeply grateful to Bill Nolan and to Professor Donn A. Albright of the Pratt Art Institute, whose long friendship with Bradbury and first-hand knowledge of his work were indispensable in solving many publishing mysteries of *The Martian Chronicles*. I am also indebted to Donn Albright and to Mr. Jim Welsh of Bethesda, Maryland for providing materials from their forthcoming comprehensive bibliography of Bradbury's work.

4. Moskowitz, Sam, introduction to the original version of "The Piper," reprinted in *Futures to Infinity*, ed. Sam Moskowitz (NY: Pyramid, 1970), pp. 181–82.

6. The complete publication history for each of the *Chronicles* chapters is located in Appendix A; book publication history of *The Martian Chronicles* appears in Appendix B. Page numbers for the magazine and first edition passages quoted in this article appear parenthetically in the text.

7. In his preface to a reprint of "Ylla" in August Derleth's *The Outer Reaches* (NY: Pellegrini & Cudahy, 1951), Bradbury describes how he drafted the story seven times before initial publication in *Maclean's* 1 January 1950 issue. Only Bill Nolan's copy of the final typescript stage survives, but this acknowledged process of revision reveals how "Ylla" stands as the transitional project between the earlier three stories of first contact and the revised form of these stories as they finally appear in *The Martian Chronicles*.

8. The major discussions of the frontier themes in *The Martian Chronicles* and other Bradbury fiction include David Mogen, *Ray Bradbury*, pp. 63–93, and his two contributions to the Science Fiction Westerns series, *Wilderness Visions* and *New Frontiers, Old Horizons* (San Bernardino, CA: Borgo Press, 1981 and 1987). Other significant studies precede Mogen, and include: Wayne Johnson, *Ray Bradbury* (NY: Ungar, 1980), pp. 112–19; Edward Gallagher, "The Thematic Structure of *The Martian Chronicles*, in *Ray Bradbury*, ed. Martin Greenberg and Joseph Olander (NY: Taplinger, 1980), pp. 55–82; and Gary Wolfe, "The Frontier Myth in Ray Bradbury," also in Greenberg and Olander's *Ray Bradbury*, pp. 33–54.

9. The principal examination of Faulkner's process of revision in *Go Down, Moses* remains Joanne Creighton's *William Faulkner's Craft of Revision* (Detroit: Wayne State University Press, 1977), pp. 85–148. Relevant bibliographical studies include James B. Meriwether's "The Short Fiction of William Faulkner: A Bibliography," in *Proof* 1 (1971): pp. 293–329, and Joseph Blotner's endnotes to *Uncollected Stories of William Faulkner*, ed. Joseph Blotner (NY: Random House, 1979). Of the many published checklists of collections, the most useful is Meriwether's *The Literary Career of William Faulkner: A Bibliographical Study* (Princeton, NJ: Princeton University Library, 1961; reissued University of South Carolina Press, 1971).

10. Isherwood's ground-breaking review appeared in *Tomorrow* (October 1950), pp. 56–58.

11. As one might expect, the revisions to "I'll Not Look for Wine" ["Ylla"], "Carnival of Madness" ["Usher II"] and "Impossible!" ["The Martian"] are the lightest—these three stories were published in periodicals after Bradbury completed revisions for book publication in the fall of 1949, and show considerable effects of this revising process in the magazine versions. Nevertheless, each appears in *The Martian Chronicles* with a new title and several hundred words of revised or new text.

12. Research by Donn Albright and Jim Welsh for their forthcoming Bradbury bibliography *October's Friend* reveals a total of 144 anthology and textbook reprints of *Martian Chronicle* chapters through 1992—including 47 different textbook reprints of "There Will Come Soft Rains."

JACQUELINE FOERTSCH

The Bomb Next Door:
Four Postwar Alterapocalyptics

... there is no more space for war.

—Baudrillard[1]

The widely discussed *postapocalyptic*[2] has come to include novels, plays, and films which depict a world having sustained, immediately prior or centuries earlier, worldwide nuclear conflagration. These texts may be characterized by the presence of an arid and ruined landscape, few and radically altered survivors, and an atavistic, kill-or-be-killed code among them which structures and directs the plot. In popular fictions (e.g. the *Mad Maxes* starring Mel Gibson) they are overlain with the trappings and hardware of science fiction, yet there are more sophisticated examples that rely less on space-age toys and weaponry and more on examining the internal and interpersonal experiences of these postapocalyptic survivors as well—Russell Hoban's *Riddley Walker* (1979),[3] Raymond Briggs' *When the Wind Blows* (1982), and Lynne Littman's *Testament* (1983) to name a few provocative examples. In the more thoughtful of these works, the postapocalyptic makes a powerful antinuclear statement through head-on collision with and a sprawling land on the other side of what, thanks to works like these, will hopefully never happen—global holocaust. By depicting postnuclear worlds so horrific and unrecognizable as to give the most war-loving among us nightmares, these

From *Genre* 30, no. 4 (Winter 1997): 333–58. © 1998 by the University of Oklahoma.

texts attempt to head off the disaster they depict through the very telling of their stories.

Yet the easily recognizable features and cultural popularity of this genre have come to obscure the equally important *alterapocalyptic*, a body of texts related to issues of nuclear destruction and the position of the bomb in society which, while not neglected as individual works, are rarely considered as a group in this manner. Recent feminist texts such as Paul Auster's *In the Country of Last Things* and Margaret Atwood's *The Handmaid's Tale* as well as canonical postwar novels such as Ray Bradbury's *Fahrenheit 451* and George Orwell's *1984* belong not only to the broad category of "dystopia" they are often assumed under but to the far more incisive subgenre of apocalyptic literature which highlights their relevance to the cold war and our current nuclear age.[4] I refer to "the position of the bomb" above in order to highlight the movement which marks the distinction between post- and alterapocalyptic texts: the temporal direction suggested by the *post* which positions us in the bomb's destructive wake slides into a spatial designation, the *alter*, the bomb is copresent in a still-recognizable universe but curtained menacingly offstage, enabling totalitarian powers to maintain an oppressive society.

In contrast to its more radical counterpart, then, the alterapocalyptic describes a world which has averted universal catastrophe but at great price. Human life has been spared, but the threat that this situation could be reversed at any time haunts and controls the affected society. The state apparati are largely ideological instead of repressive; results of limited nuclear and traditional warfare are showcased only occasionally in demonstrations against an unknowable enemy, while the social avenues of control such as work, family, home life, and personal relationships are policed to the nanometer. Discussing *1984* (though his remarks are widely applicable here), Murray N. Rothbard describes a "perpetual but peripheral cold war" which "as pursued by the three superpowers of *Nineteen Eighty-Four* was key to their successful imposition of a totalitarian regime upon their subjects" (5). As far as this threat is understood, then, as a specifically nuclear one, these novels speak just as effectively, however indirectly, as do the postapocalyptics against the hypernationalism of the cold war and nuclear proliferation in any era.

* * *

It has been argued by prominent theorists that language in a postapocalyptic text (indeed, in a postapocalyptic universe) cannot stand the force of nuclear devastation and explodes, is vaporized into senseless oblivion. "Reality," says Derrida, "let's say the encompassing institution of the nuclear age, is constructed by the fable [of nuclear war, as yet only imagined]" (23) and therefore not only resembles literature (itself "fabulously textual," without external referent) but is literature—part of the vast archive of rhetoric and opinion ("doxa") that constitutes textuality from ancient literary forms to modern-day nuclear diplomacy. In a reversal that would be total and itself irreversible, this archive of all language forms would be destroyed at the moment of realization of the nuclear "fable"; "[t]hat is why deconstruction [post-referentiality]," adds Derrida, "at least what is being advanced today in its name, belongs to the nuclear age. And to the age of literature" (27). Also, in his study of nuclear literature, Peter Schwenger notes that words explode "in spite of themselves"—in imitation/anticipation of the bomb (xvi), and Derrick De Kerckhove has identified the fragmentizing capabilities of nuclear bombs as only a modern-day descendent of the "atomized" Greek alphabet (73).

Language in the alterapocalyptic is likewise susceptible to weakness and obliteration, although in an opposite way: whereas Derrida's postnuclear language explodes and disappears, that of the alterapocalyptic is heaped up and over-burdened with so much multiple-meaning it becomes paralyzed and impotent. Language in this genre suffers a bloating and an inertia, a hyper-metaphoricity which, like cancerous cells out of control, quickly chokes off the original organism. Thus a "yes" or "no" or a surreptitious glance bears so many vectors of implication it is impossible to interpret. We have moved, thus, from a Derridian lexicon to one developed by another French postmodernist, Jean Baudrillard, who describes more than once the condition of postmodernity in markedly similar terms: "Tentacular, protuberant, excrescent, hypertelic: this is the fate of inertia in a saturated world. To deny its own end through hyper-finality—is this not also the process of cancer?" (*Fatal Strategies* 13). Also,

> [w]e are living in a society of excrescence, meaning that which incessantly develops without being measurable against its own objectives. The boil is growing out of control, recklessly at cross purposes with itself, its impacts multiplying as the causes disintegrate. That is leading to enormous congestion of the systems, to their deregulation through hypertely, through an excess of functionality, through virtual satiation." ("The Anorexic Ruins" 29)

The illness-laden terminology by which Baudrillard critiques "systems"—not only of nuclear stockpiling but more generally of "communication, information, production, destruction" (*Fatal* 12)—bears significance for all discussions of nuclear conflict as well as for my specific investigation of the alterapocalyptic: while the nuclear "moment" may begin as the fiery explosion that resembles traditional warfare, the bulk of damage done is in its aftermath, through its longer-term, much more insidious illness-effects—cancers and radiation sickness leading to death, lifelong debilitating symptoms, psychological and emotional devastation.[5] In the alterapocalyptic universe, illness has not been averted merely because nuclear catastrophe has, as the strain of living in its never-waning shadow only sends its symptoms "underground"—resurfacing seemingly without cause in the tic, the outbreak, the paranoia and madness. In the ailing social states of these texts, protagonists struggle to break through this inertia and hypertrophy to "meaning" but remain for the most part trapped in language.

I have, of course, violated several Derridian parameters in formulating the preceding sentence as I have. Not only have I posited a prize resembling "truth" beyond the law (and the lie) that is language, I have equated this trap with heinous political dictatorship (instead of the much more acceptable, even comforting trap of, say, human consciousness), thus suggesting that a move past language is both as possible and as desirable as is freedom. As ultimately unreachable (even nonexistent) as this outer zone may be—in these novelistic worlds or in our own—the alternative vision I locate in the texts provides nevertheless a provocative challenge to the prevailing standard—to the linguistic game-playing ever insisted upon by Derrida (though perhaps more damagingly by text-analyzing Derridians in an ever-lengthening line behind him), even when the stakes are enormously high. While he speaks out frequently and effectively against social injustice, the harm done by capitalism, and even nuclear weapons, Derrida's unrelenting assault on the "metaphysics" of meaning makes it impossible to valorize, even understand, the opposition to political falsehood undertaken by the novelists investigated here: even the overthrow of the "apocalyptic tone" in philosophy must come, says Derrida, from the "apocalyptic tone" itself (Carpenter 129).

So, for example, in typical deconstructive fashion, Joseph Andriano congratulates Atwood's Offred (*The Handmaid's Tale*) for "frequently pun[ning words] to assure their multiplicity of meaning. An anarchy of words, as on a Scrabble board, is infinitely preferable to a rigidly inscribed monolithic text" (91–2). Elsewhere, he notes that "the system" has "a crack in the tablet that assures the ultimate crumbling of Gilead" while Magali Cornier Michael celebrates the "gaps" in Offred's world that assure her escape. But should we really promote such playfulness in readings of political oppression and resistance? Why even worry about the fate of Offred, or societies like hers under authoritarian rule, when the tenets of deconstruction assure us that no evil is sustainable, that slavery is freedom after all?

In a countering argument Patrick D. Murphy has identified "the didactic signals of [dystopia authors'] chosen genre" and distinguished the sublimated response—produced by "dream literature" (Joanna Russ's term) which "lead[s] simply to a cathartic reduction of anxiety" and "enables escapism or reinforces smug assumptions"—from the cognitive response—produced by fiction which "encourages discomforting reading and social action through implicitly or explicitly commenting on the reader's contemporary predicament." Quoting Darko Suvin, Murphy notes that this "'significant utopia'" is formally closed but "'thematically open: its pointings reflect back on the reader's "topia"'" (26). Closure—narrative, philosophic, but also here the closed off world of total totalitarianism—is, of course, anathema to the savvy postmodernist within us, yet shall we delight in the havoc-wrecking properties of "doublethink" (deconstruction in its earliest incarnation) when it has been much more accurately defined as "the Party's ultimate goal of thought, control" (Macklin 176)?

Perhaps Baudrillard's grimmer outlook—his pessimistic estimation of the "yuppies" in charge of the present and his mournful longing after the "hard generation" which saved then lost the past—provides most appropriately here the ethical countermeasure to Derrida's aesthetics of postmodernity. Almost as frequently as does Fredric Jameson, Baudrillard implores us to remember and regret the loss of history, yet while Jameson seeks to add history back into a postmodern culture he more or less thoroughly enjoys, Baudrillard will have none of the present, decries it all, and disdains those settled into complacence, laxity, and "soft ideology." Certainly Baudrillard is a consummate postmodernist, allied with Derrida and other deconstructionists in many respects; he is of course (in)famous for arguing that the Gulf War never took place, and has defined even "human rights, dissidence, antiracism, the antinuclear movement, and the environment" as the new "gentle ideologies ... for an agreeable generation—the children of crisis who are acquainted with neither hard ideologies nor radical philosophies" ("Anorexic" 43). Yet even before he has finished witnessing this collapse of old ideals into the arms of their enemy, Baudrillard launches an indictment against this younger generation, challenging the deconstruction of opposites (here present and past) which constitutes the Derridian perspective. The combination identifiable in Baudrillard's writing, of classic postmodernism as aggravated and animated by the vestiges of still-kicking Marxist revolutionary philosophy, reminds readers forcefully that language ("ideology"), while it is our home, is simultaneously a trap—structure as weighted down by stricture—which, I contend, the alterapocalyptic invites us most urgently to attempt to move from beneath.

* * *

Indeed the characters of these novels are trapped in many respects. The alterapocalyptic, denied the temporal trajectory promised in the *post*apocalyptic, can move neither into the past nor into the future to escape its fate. As Baudrillard himself has asked, "By what miracle could we go back in time to head off [history's] disappearance?";[6] and Jonathan Schell has noted that to return to the prenuclear state would entail no less than a rewriting of history, a disarming of matter itself and our nondisposable understanding of its properties. Likewise the alterapocalyptic cannot, indeed dare not, go too far into the future to set the scene of disaster it depicts, lest it touch off the nuclear catastrophe its narrative has already depicted as realizable at any second and thus dissolve its very status as an alterapocalyptic. Also the "alterapoc" hangs back from a far-in-the-future designation so as to maintain its relevance to modern readers. Murphy has pointed out that "hugging close to the shore of present time" enables dystopian authors to "enforce a cognitive function and didactic purpose" in their fiction (27), and several readers[7] of the novels under consideration here have pointed to these narratives' positioning in the near-future or even in the "exaggerated" present as a source of their power and meaning.

In their emphasis on the "presentness" of these novels, the notion of a copresent, alternative universe emerges, again emphasizing the lateral (spatial) dynamic in play.[8] Thus these narratives are temporally constrained but spatially various: in addition to their being alternatives to our world, they contain within them alternative worlds of their own—mysterious and alluring off-stages which act as both unspeakable menace and avenue of escape. While these novels, then, do not look *backward* or *forward*, their characters can crane their necks to the *right* and *left*—sensing themselves in foreign and hostile territory and always on the lookout for an entry point into its opposite, as well as perceiving the world (as they have indeed been forced to perceive it) as controlled by strict oppositions of right and left, repressive and progressive political convictions which tear their worlds apart.

I said above that the off-stage in these texts is both a threat to what security their characters possess and a tantalizing avenue of escape which in turn would threaten to topple the oppressive regimes which strive to close off such avenues; if not deny their very existence. In the off-stage the repressive forces maintain the thinly veiled bomb, often referred to as "war" or "the enemy," but understood by all as the only form of destruction yet unleashed on a global scale—nuclear destruction. Yet as was the case during the actual cold war, this frightening outer territory is often falsely depicted so, in an effort to keep citizens trapped in a prevailing ideology instead of cognizant of another world similar to their own if not markedly superior. Thus these terrifying outer worlds, when finally penetrated, are often discovered to be liberating, revolutionary spaces where bands of insurrectionists are already gathering force. Even when the outer worlds are relatively bleak and disorganized, the very occupation of them is an act of resistance against the repressive forces which would posit a singular world—not an duality or, more likely, an aggregate of varying positions, but a single-minded, all-encompassing monolith, opposition to which equals extinction.

To the degree that the forces in these novels are capable of closing off competing versions of their worlds, successfully depicting the bomb as the only alternative out there, they are equally able to manipulate and encumber language in a way that traps and discourages their inhabitants even more thoroughly. In four novels which significantly represent the alterapocalyptic, I will examine the role of this "off-stage," as it houses and showcases the nuclear threat as well as reveals an avenue of escape which will mean either liberation or undoing for these novels' inhabitants and the ever-weakening language which sustains them. I move here not in chronological order of publication but from the most open and hopeful among these texts to the darkest, most despairing, dystopic and "tongue-tied"; the further along this scale a text finds itself, the more effective is its depiction of the nightmare that is total totalitarianism and the more memorable and arresting the offstage to the alterapocalyptic space—as both astonishing horror and ungraspable dream.

Paul Auster's *In the Country of Last Things* (1987) is the least controlled of the alterapocalyptics in these several respects: the outside world is theoretically accessible and, more importantly, a recent and inspiring memory;[9] the language of a less repressive time has been at least partially preserved; and the disorder defining the characters' lives, though dangerous and desperate, is largely unmonitored, resembling the circumstances of Orwell's unencumbered "proles."[10] Indeed, both escape and meaning can be had in this country *for a price*. Here money (or whatever bizarre commodity does its work on a given day) is retained from a stabler if more mercenary time, and the fact that it still has value not only within its nation of origin but in other, less fearsome places—i.e., is still *in communication with* the outside world—allows us the early insight that the boundaries of this country of last things are penetrable and thus dissolvable.

The "outside" in this novel enjoys a surprisingly vital existence, with actual characters who exist and remain there and with several of the characters trapped "in country" having former identities in this other place as well. Indeed, the very title of the novel reminds us that this place, hellish as it may be, is still only a "country," not a "world," leaving places within reach of the imagination and memory which are not this one. Anna Blume was at one time resident of this outer world who has now come to the country of last things in search of her brother, a reporter on assignment in this terrifying place but disappeared for over a year. Anna recalls scenes from her life in

which she talks to her brother's editor and is given a picture of her brother to
carry with her. While no one recognizes the man in the photo once she comes
to the strange new land, the fact that she is able to carry such *hard evidence*,
such a one-to-one correlation between a signifier and a signified, signals that
while we have entered a nightmarish world, we have perhaps not come so far
from home after all.

However, Auster's readers soon learn that just because it is easy to enter
such a country does not mean that leaving it will be equally effortless. Anna
suggests in the futile letter home to her brother's editor which constitutes
the entire narrative that this place has a fearful tendency to suck you in, that
the mounds of garbage and debris she walks over daily offer numerous possibilities to trip, disable, and trap her there where she's fallen permanently.[11]
The landscape writhes with such ambushes, as there is nothing left but garbage—all valuable possessions such as decent shelter and nutritious food having disappeared long ago—and the gangs of thugs that struggle for control
over this or that rubbish mound. As Anna and the other scavengers, with
whose "industry" she finally has good success, struggle through the piles of
junk looking for things to sell, Anna realizes that it is not only things she is
desperately trying to retrieve but the meanings that were once attached to
them as well:

> How can you talk to someone about airplanes, for example, if that
> person doesn't know what an airplane is? It is a slow but ineluctable
> process of erasure.... Entire categories of objects disappear—
> flowerpots for example, or cigarette filters, or rubber bands—and
> for a time you will be able to recognize those words, even if you
> cannot recall what they mean. But then, little by little, the words
> become only sounds, a random collection of glottals and fricatives,
> a storm of whirling phonemes, and finally the whole thing just
> collapses into gibberish. The word "flowerpot" will make no more
> sense to you than the word "splandigo." (89)

As these words disappear, those remaining become over-burdened and slug-
gish, tumorous with extra meanings they cannot support, and soon fail. Anna
cannot communicate with anyone her ideas for escape, and she ultimately
has "to give up the idea of going home" (89). The gaps these disappeared
words create cut off communication and leave "each person . . . speaking his
own private language" (89)—a condition of total separation and irrelevance
to each other, here a condition of illness and death for a society.

Interestingly the monetary unit for which this various junk is sold is the
"glot," reinforcing the notion of a unit of currency that is also a unit of speech

or meaning. It is in fact meaning that these denizens hoard and trade and hope will last them through the winter or, in Anna's case, until the border of another land, as we will see below. Thus while the reference to a "country" in the novel's title offers the comfort of an identifiable, thus ultimately traversable boundary, it is countered a good bit by this notion of "last things," of a place which sucks up matter as does a black hole, infinitely increasing its space and density until no escape is ever possible. Indeed, Anna's brother, lost somewhere in this very same country, with his clever sister armed with photos and information about him in pursuit, may as well have wandered into the wilds of another planet for all the good a search for him will accomplish.

As her ties to that original outer world grow more and more tenuous, Anna stumbles upon two other "withouts" in the course of the novel which lead her into significant and healing love relationships. These withouts are actually "withins," secret and somehow fortified enclaves of people like herself which foster acts of resistance, however minimal, and support and sustain those who find their way there. The first is a library of scholars which she quite inadvertently flees into during a food riot. The main reason these men give for their not being harmed is that, aside from their all being Jews, they are all great thinkers and writers and the philistinic society around them has not deemed them a large enough threat to contend with. That distinctions such as this not only still exist but actually count for something in this world of utter chaos and violence may seem a bit farfetched but at least reminds us once again that there is an outer world which still communicates with, i.e., controls the rules of, the doomed and forsaken territory.

After a period of relative happiness in the library, Anna is injured during an escape from evil authorities and blacks out. When she comes to, she finds she has been rescued and offered refuge by her second, even more fortuitous "without," Woburn house. The place is a hospice for the injured and starving who make their way to its doors, operating on a revolving lottery system which is intricate but readily observed by the otherwise clamoring throngs outside. Yet this refuge, too, is only temporary, as the house suffers its inevitable collapse at the hands of looters and suspicious authorities. At novel's end, a party of escapees makes its way to the border on the authority of some falsely obtained travelling papers. Anna prays in her letter home that they will still be worth their writing when they arrive at the crossing, yet we can hope that so long as there is still such a thing as value in this country something will be able to be traded for the travellers' freedom. Interestingly, the territory they have lit out for bears a striking resemblance to the very "labor camps" which are used as threats by the authorities—"a place west of the city" [where] ... life ... [may be] better than it is in the city" (32). All we know of these camps is that hard work is involved, but then there is no doubt hard work in store for the escapees in whatever land they happen into. Yet as open as the future may be to them, there is at this point no going back. Anna never meets up with her brother, and no mention is made by novel's end of returning to "you," the brother's editor, [to whom the entire letter/novel is addressed and] who remains in Anna's country of origin.[12]

The "outside" of Ray Bradbury's *Fahrenheit 451* (1953) is also "within"— within language itself and the books which are sought out and torched to ashes by "firemen" serving a censoring and repressive government for the avenues of escape they offer. While the chaos of Auster's novel affords its characters a measure of freedom that allows for their ultimate escape, Bradbury's world is over-ordered and deadly silent. There is no conversation or honest expression of emotion, only the mindless babble of pre-fab entertainment to fill in the devastatingly quiet background.

Late in the novel the protagonist, Montag, tells the old scientist, Faber, "I could feel it [a revolutionary urge] for a long time, I was saving it up, I went around doing one thing and feeling another. It was all there. It's a wonder it didn't show on me, like fat" (116). At this moment Montag realizes that the double life one must assume in order to survive under this book-burning regime results in a doubling of all meaning, a "fattiness" or tumorous overgrowth of experience itself that is actually visible on the body,[13] and that it is not the growth itself but its very visibility which marks the revolutionary as "symptomatic" and exposes him to the wrath of the authorities. Thus words in this nightmarish society are steadily removed from circulation, an act which reconstitutes them as social ill and the casual, demonstrative use of them as deranged and disruptive, punishable by death.

In an effort to maintain social health as it is now defined, the residents of this society keep quiet. They stay at home or in small, benign, blithering groups, policing each others' speech through eavesdropping and more sophisticated surveillance methods afforded by new technology. Montag's wife Mildred is our chief representative of this silenced population,[14] opening her mouth only to expound the most trite of clichés—that is, to say nothing at all. She describes a new interactive television script she is about to read during the course of a daytime drama acted out on the three walls of their living room which is actually an enormous two-way TV:

> "Here for instance, the man says, 'What do you think of this whole idea, Helen?' And he looks at me sitting center stage, see? And I say, I say—" She paused and ran her finger under a line on the script. "'I think that's fine!' And then they go on with the play until he says, 'Do you agree to that, Helen?' and I say, 'I sure do!' Isn't that fun, Guy?"

[Montag] stood in the hall looking at her.
"It's sure fun," she said. (18)

Mildred's words, while giddy and effusive, are meaningless and thus nonexistent—exactly as the regime which controls her leisure time (and in fact she
has no other kind) would have it. In contrast Montag's words are seldom but
pregnant with the meaning they seek to hide but eventually cannot. Even
his silences, the look he gives his wife in the above scene, for example, are
so swelled with suppressed meaning they eventually explode, revealing his
disloyalty to the book-burners who control him and marking him for demo-
lition by these forces.

I would add that the "off-stage" in this novel works in ways remarkably
similar to those I have outlined above. From a radio that "hums somewhere"
the threat of "war" that "'may be declared any hour'" (30) keeps the population
distracted from making war on its own repressive government. Near the end
of the novel Faber describes "walking camps" down by the tracks where scholars and thinkers meet but with which Montag can only connect after what is
in fact a pseudonuclear conflagration.[15] As in Auster's novel, while they pay
a great price, the survivors of Bradbury's harsh and repressive world eventually find each other and go on together. They relieve themselves of the words
they store within their minds (that last sanctuary which, says Bradbury, can
never be violated)—of their pent-up, piling-up significance by sharing them
with each other.[16] The knowledge contained by these men flows out, easing
the embolic state that threatened each of them, and the words they memorize
and store in their brains are thus restored to their true weight, their true significance, stabilizing the pressure nonexistence was forcing on them.

Once again, as with Auster's novel, the "without" or off-stage not only
exists but is eventually reached, ensuring a relatively upbeat outcome for the
novelistic characters who reach this place. In Margaret Atwood's *The Handmaid's Tale* (1986), the off-stage is both maddeningly present and ultimately
unreachable, initially threatens the omnipotence of Offred's suffocating universe but ultimately offers her no refuge. Early in the novel a group of Japanese
tourists penetrates, quite easily we must assume, this repressive, strictly stratified Republic of Gilead which has entrapped Offred and women like her—
who have retained their fertility in the wake of "ecological devastation"[17]—in
its menacing, debilitating clutches. The pernicious den mother Aunt Lydia
warns that "The Republic of Gilead ... knows no bounds. It is within you"
(31), and yet these "westernized" strangers in short skirts, open-toed shoes, and
pink toenail polish parade themselves before the constricted handmaids, caus-
ing, one might think, a surge of frustration, envy, and murmurings of mutiny
among the women who glimpse the conditions of the outside world.[18]

But the society Atwood depicts is so confining that Offred and her companion Ofglen cannot even admit to having seen these outrages, cannot acknowledge they are capable of seeing on penalty of severe punishment. The uniform they wear includes a large white headdress that makes looking up burdensome and acts as a blinder for all peripheral views, ensuring that the handmaids' vision is limited and downward-directed. Likewise, they cannot admit to wanting to be seen, as one of the tourists asks to take their picture, and the interpreter accompanying them, widely understood to also be a government spy, asks if they would mind this too much. Like the loaded words which clog the arteries of Bradbury's universe, this simple question is really a trap. Offred knows that the official doctrine equates being looked at with sexual penetration (which is supposed to be equally distasteful to these "chaste" women) and so declines the tourists' request. The spies in Gilead are called "The Eyes," whose main job, ironically, is to make sure the handmaids themselves cannot see or ever be seen.

In Bradbury's novel doubled language and the treachery and repression it attended were countered to some degree by the "truth" Montag was to find in the language of the classics that could be burned to ash but never truly forgotten. In Gilead, no such countervailing force is present, and both the actuality and deception contained in words shine forth in equal measure with each utterance, leaving Offred powerless and alone in her revolutionary thoughts for much of the story. She is allowed to walk with another handmaid during the course of her daily errands, but this, like the interpreter's question, is another test. In an early scene Offred and Ofglen exchange the usual, required pleasantries, and Offred tries to read in her partner's gaze and intonation, in fibers of meaning so tiny even the Eyes cannot spy it, a spark of rebellion:

> During these walks she has never said anything that was not strictly orthodox, but then, neither have I. She may be a real believer, a Handmaid in more than name. I can't take the risk.
> "The war is going well, I hear," she says.
> "Praise be," I reply.
> "We've been sent good weather."
> "Which I receive with joy."
> . . . Sometimes I wish she would just shut up and let me walk in peace. But I'm ravenous for news, any kind of news; even if it's false news, it must mean something. (26)

By novel's end our understanding of "false news" must include every utterance in the novel: the reports of war Offred hears on TV, her clandestine meetings with Nick and then finally Ofglen; even her own reportage is impossible to gauge for honesty and accountability. Is there a resistance movement, an "us" which Ofglen invites Offred to join, or should Offred be wary when it "occurs to [her] that [Ofglen] may be a spy, a plant, set to trap [her]" (218)? Does it matter that "they only show us victories, never defeats" (106) on the TV news when the helicopters could be props, the prisoners of war actors? What does it mean when Nick, at novel's end, delivers her over to rescuers (who could just as easily be torturers) by using her real name when, if he were part of the spy network, even that kind of ultra-secret information could easily be uncovered? What is to be our response when, in the middle of Offred's reconstruction of a romantic liaison with Nick, she interrupts the narrative to warn us, "I made that up. It didn't happen that way. Here is what happened" (338)? Does her fantasizing ultimately undermine her project, weaken her ability to record and thus survive the horrors of her imprisonment and exploitation, or is this entire narrative, maybe even these so-called horrors, nothing but fantasy—the ravings of madwoman which scholars of such literature may many centuries later find intriguing but ultimately mystifying?

At one point in the story Offred is brought by her Commander to a house of prostitution for a night of costumed kinkiness where Offred's loved and lost friend Moira serendipitously works as a "Jezebel." As does Anna Blume in her inner sancta, Offred finds in this whorehouse-*cum*-liberation front the comforts and freedoms of an earlier time and draws deeply from Moira's wide-reaching and empowering wealth of information. She learns of her own mother's banishment to the Colonies, again, as in Auster's novel, a set-up of forced labor camps on the outskirts of the central zone, again described here (but not really depicted) as a fate worse than death. She hears the story of Moira's harrowing, almost successful escape from Gilead on the Underground Femaleroad and her capture and relegation to this place which, while having its benefits (not the cigarettes so much as the freedom to sit and smoke them), has finally drained the life force from her. She is indifferent and careless in the telling of her story, and after their brief encounter Offred can only hope for her well-being, as "[she] never saw her again" (325).

While neither this venue of relative freedom nor the "black van" Offred surrenders to at novel's end are revealed as sources of survival for the women, what little hope we may have for Offred's future lies in the structure of the novel's final sentence. Offred is lead away from her Commander's house by two guards whom, Nick says, are really conveyors of refugees for the Mayday Underground, and Offred, with no other choice than to follow and hope "step[s] up, into the darkness within; or else the light" (378). These references to her final journey being a "step up" that is ultimately "light" rather than "dark" tip the scales of our uncertainly, at least to a tiny degree, in favor of an optimistic reading of this story's outcome. Whatever hope we glean from this formulation, however, is irrevocably undercut by the "Historical Notes" which immediately follow the novel proper, a provocative epilogue which Atwood has set up as a "critical apparatus"—a lecture delivered by an inept and patronizing male scholar to a conference of like-minded scavengers of Offred's life and other artifacts from the now-defunct Republic of Gilead. The "off-stage" constructed here is the final frontier, the last word a narrator like Offred or a novelist like Atwood (any narrator or any novelist, that is) is powerless to defend herself against or, in many cases, even hear.

Here this other-world to the territory Offred works so hard, has maybe even given her life, to map out is revealed as ignorant of, mostly indifferent to, Offred's story, destroying her chance for textual survival. While the speaker and his collaborator are mostly receivers of the lopsided history-as-usual that has come down to them, the gaps they cannot fill in the story cause them impatience with Offred's very effort, and she is ultimately almost erased from her own story: there is, we learn, a wealth of information as to who the possible "Commander" was—a central figure in traditional histories yet in Offred's story only a menacing shadow. There is also, according to these "scholars," a little more information about "Luke" (Offred's husband before the revolution) and "Nick," especially the Mayday Underground and Eyes, male-run organizations in both of which Nick took part. Yet there is finally nothing definite to be said of Offred, not even her name, centrally not her fate, and she herself is blamed for the scanty factual information surrounding herself: ". . . many gaps remain. Some of them could have been filled by our anonymous author, had she had a different turn of mind. She could have told us much about the workings of the Gileadean empire, had she had the instincts of a reporter or spy" (392).

Thus Offred's emotional, sensual, intensely personal worldview is rejected by these hyperrational "reporters" for the enormous lack it represents in the fulfilling of their needs. They occupy a world so far off-stage from that of Offred's that communication between the two is, we come to understand, all but impossible. Unfortunately, it is this other territory which is before us now, at novel's end, and which remains to remap the Republic of Gilead along its new rulers' own conventional, equally repressive lines. The magnitude of Offred's loss and tragedy is elided in "Professor Pieixoto's" barrage of speculations as to her outcome and in her romanticization in his last remarks as "Eurydice," mythic and alluring in her mute transience. Unlike the other-worlds of Auster's and Bradbury's novels, this territory offers Atwood's protagonist no entrance and thus no escape, secures for only her oppressors a point of refuge and the silencing last word that attends such a position.

Likewise George Orwell's *1984* (1949), which was fairly obviously a model for Atwood's own project,[19] holds out a place of refuge only to snatch it cruelly away from the novel's protagonists at the end of their story, leaving them finally stranded and doomed. As a founding example of the alterapocalyptic novel, it has in many ways been unequalled since,[20] and the nightmarish society Orwell depicts is the most repressive of all those discussed here, its language most overburdened and paralyzed by false meaning. In the "critical apparatus" Orwell included at the end of his novel,[21] the intricacies and absurdities of "Newspeak" must be charted out, as no natural familiarity with "Oldspeak" (standard English) would suffice in understanding it. While in Auster's "country," words disappear, in Bradbury's small town the classics are sent up in flames, and in Offred's Gilead even shop signs are merely pictorial, so high a crime is reading, in Oceania, the disappearance of all of these— words, stories, and history itself—is the dreaded ritual preparing for and succeeding upon the disappearance of the people whose lives these words shaped and documented. Always a disappeared "story" (word, news article, novel, or life) is revealed to have posed a threat to the reigning political structure; thus, according to Orwell's Appendix, a word like "free" maintains its "free from" implications but must sacrifice those elicited by "free to" to the notion of "service"; in Newspeak "to serve" is also "to be free." The signifier "service" (really subservience) is now not only suited in its original meaning but saddled with its opposite as well, and one of the ultimate goals of Newspeak, implies the unnamed linguist of the Appendix, is to halve all of language in just this respect, doubling thus disabling meaning: "Newspeak was designed not to extend but to *diminish* the range of thought, and this purpose was indirectly assisted by cutting the choice of words down to a minimum" (247).

Each of three vocabularies works in a similar way, eliminating certain concepts through the grafting of them onto words with opposite meanings or hybrid words that are simply nonsense. The "A" vocabulary consists of the bulk of everyday speech, but the "debulking" process will eventually eliminate most root words, leaving just a few nouns or verbs and many repetitive and complicated suffixes and prefixes to drag them down. The fewer verbs available, the less agency or exercise a society enjoys; the fewer nouns and adjectives, the narrower the field of vision (recall Offred's huge blinders). In the "B" and "C" vocabularies political language and scientific jargon, respectively, hypertrophy and explode; the longer and more multi-purpose a term the less meaning it has, and the less harm it can do: "doubleplusgood duckspeaker." It is this meltdown of language into phantasmagoric hybrids that has sealed the fame of Orwell's novel. "Doublespeak" has had implications in political theory ever since, and Orwell's protagonist Winston Smith commits the "thoughtcrime" which the rest of the novel and all future definitions of "the Orwellian" are about.

It is indeed a private, unspoken wish for a "space" (an off-stage) to call his own which constitutes Winston's fateful "thoughtcrime." The buying of a diary (this open space) to actually act upon this wish is a secondary and much less serious gesture; although it could be used as evidence against him, the nervous tics and premature aging produced by the lies he lives under (recall Montag's "fat") will undo him eventually anyway: "He thought of a man whom he had passed in the street. . . . They were a few meters apart when the left side of the man's face was suddenly contorted by a sort of spasm . . . : it was only a twitch, a quiver, rapid as the clicking of a camera. . . . He remembered thinking at the time: That poor devil is done for" (56). Stashing himself into an alcove in his cramped room, the one place unreachable by the roving eye of the telescreen, Winston scribbles into the blank pages of his diary the horrors of his censored life in an effort to communicate with the future. Although this "off-stage" is certainly temporally situated, it is brought into immediate proximity, as if it were a neighboring, more neighborly country, by Winston's address to it: "*To the future or to the past, to a time when thought is free, when men are different from one another and do not live alone . . . : From the age of uniformity, from the age of solitude, from the age of Big Brother . . . —greetings*" (26–7). As did the "scholars" of Offred's story, Winston addresses this other time as a "second present," as a situation with as much immediacy and significance to him as his actual present and with which he will communicate without the use of mediums or seances, only his own abilities to express himself.

Soon other "off-stages" usurp the power and attraction these withouts, "the future" and his diary, initially hold for him: the wooded love nest he shares with Julia, the seedy bedroom in a proletarian section of the city they eventually find, the thrilling inner escape offered by Goldstein's "Book" which Winston pores over and gathers the strength necessary for revolution from. But like the ever shifting battle lines that position Oceania against Eastasia one week, Eurasia the next, like the ominous and ultimately horrendous tortures waiting in "Room 101"—all these other secret territories are eventually revealed as government weapons, elaborate traps set for the likes of Winston and Julia, both of whom are captured and sentenced. Winston had taken a chance reading the surreptitious glances of Julia as welcoming instead of threatening but longs to succeed once more in reading the equally cryptic yet promising O'Brien. It is this communication that Winston forces and ultimately misinterprets which results in the pair's downfall.

While it is the horrors of Room 101 which seal Winston's capitulation to the powers of Big Brother, it is his understanding that no counterforce exists, that all rooms he enters from here on will be rooms 101, that broaches this capitulation in the first place and starts him irrevocably on the path to self-destruction. His revulsion by the revolting rat torture, his betrayal of Julia—these horrors have finally released him at novel's end, and he is left with only utter, drunken hopelessness—the perception of a world without end, that is, without edges, that has driven him completely over his own brink, without hope of return:

> Winston, sitting in a blissful dream, paid no attention as his glass was filled up. He was back in the Ministry of Love, with everything forgiven, his soul white as snow. He was in the public dock, confessing everything, implicating everybody. . . .
> . . . O cruel, needless misunderstanding! O stubborn, self-willed exile from the loving breast! Two gin-scented tears trickled down the side of his nose. But it was all right. . . . He had won victory over himself. He loved Big Brother. (245)

In the pub or at the Ministry, drunk or doomed, crying tears of redemption or madness—all places and all states of mind fuse into one, as all language congeals into a suffocating and fatal[22] mass. While Bradbury's hero is largely liberated by novel's end and Auster's and Atwood's stories offer at least a shred of hope for their protagonists' escape, no such possibility exists for Winston. Were he liberated by the armies of Eastasia the next hour, the sanity necessary to claim that freedom has been sealed off and bombed to oblivion.

* * *

I argued above the Baudrillard helps us to understand language as both structure and stricture and would concede here that Derrida (and for that matter, Foucault) does not oppose Baudrillard on this point but instead shares his understanding of language as both home *and* prison—collapsing these opposites into each other in classic Derridian/Foucauldian fashion: we are trapped most thoroughly in our most private space; freedom (the tiniest measure of it) comes only from realizing this situation. Yet Derrida and Foucault describe the enormity of linguistic structure ("there is nothing outside the text"/"the system of power") and attribute to this our ability to live, resignedly or in gleeful ignorance, within its cozy confines, while the writing of Baudrillard suggests that our imprisonment, while boundless, also surrounds and suffocates us; we are both alive within and buried beneath the structure of language, and this sense of being buried alive certainly permeates the alterapocalyptic as I have defined it throughout. Its restrictive space suggests to us that consciousness under a repressive regime is zombie-like, a condition of the walking dead.

In the ultimately downward trajectory characterizing Baudrillard's scheme of things, and in progressively alarming fashion, Auster, Bradbury, Atwood, and Orwell depict worlds getting roomier all the time—as airplanes, flowerpots, books, news, the past, friends, and lovers disappear one by one— that nevertheless make space for only an ever-amassing nothingness, pressing down upon and paralyzing whatever and whoever remains. While there is probably still enough "stuff" occupying the spaces of Auster and Bradbury to enable optimistic conclusions, those of Atwood and especially Orwell are barren and bereft—of hidden treasures, last paths of escape, even but most importantly co-conspirators and the presence of mind to recognize them; the relentless opening up of the societies they describe will shortly close off life or freedom (if there is a difference) completely and permanently. Yet despite the bleakness of all four of these alterapocalyptic visions, none posit nuclear holocaust as an acceptable alternative; on the contrary, the bomb—the destructive force it harbors and wields as threat—is blamed as strongly for these wretched states as it is for those depicted in postapocalyptic narratives. Explicit references to an all-powerful authoritarian regime in Orwell's and Bradbury's cold war narratives and graphic depictions of a ruined natural universe in Auster's and Atwood's more recent novels keep the spectre of the bomb and its political and environmental implications clearly in the reader's mind. An understanding of the many seminal texts which have always supported the antinuclear statement made by these postapocalyptic narratives, but send their message laterally instead of head-on, insidiously instead of instantaneously, only increases the strength of that voice and the effort toward global preservation it mobilizes.

NOTES

1. *Fatal Strategies* 14.

2. See for instance Peter Schwenger's *Letter Bomb: Nuclear Theory and the Exploding Word*; the Winter, 1984 special issue of Diacritics on "Nuclear Criticism" (especially essays by De Kerckhove, Ferguson, and MacCannell); William Chaloupka's *Knowing Nukes: The Politics and Culture of the Atom*; Richard Dellamora's *Postmodern Apocalypse: Theory and Cultural Practice at the End*; and articles by Morrissey and Scheick.

3. While I recognize the minute strains of this novel which mysteriously found their way into *Mad Max: Beyond Thunderdome*, the loosest of "adaptations" of Hoban's work, I find the two texts so otherwise unrelated that I do not consider the film a textual relative of this novel, but instead separate and even oppose them in this instance.

4. The novels under consideration here were selected for the fullness of the example they provide. Often the alterapocalyptic is a subgeneric strain in postwar texts, so that we may recognize not only alterapocalyptic narrative but also the alterapocalyptic in narratives as well. Examples include Arthur Koestler's *Darkness at Noon*, Anthony Burgess's *A Clockwork Orange*, and Samuel Becket's *Endgame*.

Likewise, Vietnam War film and literature, whose historical *raison d'être* was itself a conscripted, miserably failed alternative to nuclear war, demonstrate elements of the alterapocalyptic.

5. In a book-length project related to the ideas presented here, *Enemies Within: The Cold War and AIDS Crisis as Plagues of Postmodernism* (forthcoming), I elaborate on this illness phenomenon in the immediate postnuclear period find and this shift from violence to illness to mirror the shift from modernism to postmodernism that simultaneously occurred. Yet my term "plague" refers not to the biological crises (polio, global warming, emerging viruses and most significantly the bomb and AIDS) threatening this period but to the violence and hostility which initiated them and marked suspected carriers (e.g. "reds" and gays) for persecution and in some cases worsened their suffering.

6. I appreciate also Baudrillard's definition of a "temporal bomb": "Where it explodes, everything is suddenly blown into the past; and the greater the bomb's capacity, the further into the past they go" ("Anorexic" 34). See also David Seed who has linked similar theories of Baudrillard's to Bradbury's *Fahrenheit 451* in a remarkable reading of Montag's wife Mildred's "disappearing mouth" (231–2).

7. For Auster's novel, see Howard 92–3, McCaffery and Gregory 18, Washburn 63, Woods; for Bradbury's novel, see Seed 225 and 240, Johnson 84 and 86, and Touponce 79–80; for Atwood's novel, see Michael 138; for Orwell's novel, see Howe 321, Rose 89, and Rothbard.

8. Joseph Andriano notes that Atwood's "Gilead constructs [a] horizontal text" (90) and Rothbard points out that even though Orwell set his novel almost 40 years in the future, the nearness of his vision to his own time is embodied in the title itself: the year 1984 is just lateral "transposition" of the last two numbers of the year in which the book was written (9).

9. Comparing the potential for resistance in *1984* and *The Handmaid's Tale*, Ruud Teeuwen points out that "Remembrance is a much vaguer presence in *Nineteen Eighty-Four*. Oceania has been in place for decades at the time we join Winston's life in it, and memories of a prerevolutionary life have, for the most part, lost the intensity of the personal. Gilead exists for just three years. . . . In *The Handmaid's Tale* memories are still suffused with detail. Where despair is a dull presence in Winston's life, it is an acute pain in Offred's" (117). Adding the idea that memory is tied to resistance, that totalitarian authority cannot be acquired "without a transitional phase of rigorous repression of the memories, desires, and idiosyncracies of old, original contexts" (118), Teeuwen widens this discussion to apply nicely to the situation of Auster's novel as well.

10. More than one Orwell critic has indeed pointed to just this segment of Orwell's vision as a surprisingly wide hole in the net, which a true big-brotherian regime would never allow. See Rahv 315 and Deutscher 338. In defense of my positioning of *1984* at the end of this study, as the most dystopian (thus most alterapocalyptic) of the four texts examined here, I would point out that while Orwell, who felt revolution would come from the most gifted among the proletarian class, includes proles in his vision, they offer no escape for Winston and Julia—recall that the room over Mr. Charrington's shop is a trap—and no permanent alleviation of the difficulties shaping their lives.

11. I am surprised by several readers of this novel who have seen in its landscape thinly veiled representations of modern-day New York. Tim Woods uses the analogies of Charles Reznikoff, whose poetry "is engaged with the 'strange and

transitory beauties of the urban landscape' [actually a quote from Auster's own work, *The Art of Hunger* (39)]" (109) and of Michel de Certeau who writes of "'walkers, *Wandersmänner*, whose bodies follow the cursives and strokes of an urban "text" they write without reading'" (deCerteau 124; Woods 111). Likewise, Gerald Howard has found the garbage and housing crises of modern-day New York to be recast in the novel only "to their grim conclusions" (93). In fact the landscape of Auster's novel is anything but "beautiful," its scrabbling thieves and urchins enacting anything but the lithe and easy strokes and cursives of writing in their clumsy and stunted forays for garbage. This unforgettable layering of an urban "reality" with a fetid stew that could just as likely fill the valleys of hell is one of the novel's chief strengths as dystopic vision.

12. Dennis Barone has argued that even this sphere is successfully reentered, if not by Anna herself at least by the letter she writes: "We know that [Anna's message does get through] because the novel is actually told in a third-person narration. Someone has received Anna's story-as-letter, had read it, and, in turn, is now telling Anna's story to us. This is a story of triumph, not of disintegration" (8). Other readers of this novel, meanwhile, are less optimistic. Katharine Washburn calls Anna's letter (the entire narrative) "a document cast into the void, mailed to some sort of dead letter zone at the end of the world" (62) and Sven Birkets insists that, "If I'm right about the gated city and what it represents, these words are the last Anna will ever write" (68).

13. Again, Baudrillard's terminology is relevant here, as "obesity"—of communication systems, of signification, even of American bodies—is not only symptom but also cause of our enslavement to these systems and is for him synonymous with "obscenity."

14. While depicted in the narrative as a most willing consumer of the diet of inanity and inertia fed her by her society, Montag's wife Mildred has been described by Donald Watt as a victim suffering physical symptoms due to socially-induced repression, just as is Montag himself. Following her suicide attempt with sleeping pills, and the authorities' cold and mechanical stomach-pumping treatment, says Watt,

> [t]he implication is clear: Mildred is no special case. The poisonous darkness within her has become endemic to their way of life. The darkness suggests all the unimagined psychic bile that builds up in people, to embitter them, alienate them from one another, snuff out any inner light on their mode of existing. (201)

15. This scene is demonstrative of the *preapocalyptic*, a small, especially problematic strand of thought within mixed-apocalyptic (containing elements of pre, post, or alter) texts which genuinely *looks forward to* and longs for the bomb and all its "cleansing" devastation, as life in its current form has become intolerable. Erich Fromm, who has commented on *1984* and other dystopiae in postmodern literature discovers a mechanized dystopia in the text of existence itself in the '50s and '60s—a "technological nightmare" that had turned people into zombies and made the darkest alternative to "boring aliveness" seem attractive. In *The Revolution of Hope* (1968) Fromm argues that "The rate of our automobile accidents and preparation for thermonuclear war are a testimony to this readiness to gamble with death" (43). For a related discussion see Watt 212–3.

16. In my forthcoming *Enemies Within* (cited above, n5), I develop the homo-erotic implications of Bradbury's all-male community in this scene of orgasmic unburdening, as well as those of Orwell's "love triangle" as occupied by Julia, Winston, and O'Brien.

17. This phrase is Patrick D. Murphy's, employed during his description of Offred's universe as suffering "the aftermath of nuclear war and women's oppression." In the novel itself, Offred puns the biblical "balm in Gilead" as "bomb in Gilead" (218), again reinforcing the implied nuclear pre-history and co-history of the narrative.

18. In spite of what I will argue to be the novel's ultimately bleak ending, it is enormous gaps like these in Gilead's supposedly water-tight system of control which fosters optimistic readings such as that of Lucy M. Freibert, who declares that "Offred promises to come off a winner" and that the novel "offer[s] women a mea-sure of hope," even though she curiously posits only moments later that "The system brooks no resistance or dissent" (281). Thus Freibert insists on an impossibly dif-ficult challenge to overcome which our superheroine Offred successfully overcomes anyway. Above I have noted Andriano's and Michael's equally overenthusiastic assessments of Offred's many powers.

19. Atwood's *Handmaid's Tale* experiments with the distinctly feminist notion of a dystopia by including many elements from her male predecessors', thus "control-ling for" the surrounding circumstances of their respective stories and letting only "the feminine" within her new version shake out. The various inhabitants of Gilead are strictly stratified and marked along these strata with colored uniforms, much the way Huxley's alphas, betas, gammas, etc., were in *Brave New World* (1931), and the reproductive function of women is taken over in both texts (though in different respects) by an intervening government authority. As with Orwell's Oceania, Gil-ead is a place of severe deprivation, unlimited and unwitting encounters with spies, and technological excellence in home observation/invasion methods. Atwood's all-seeing "eye" over her bed corresponds to Orwell's telescreen. The armoire in which she reads the revolutionary note equates with the desk in which Winston hides his journal and the alcove where he makes his entries. We might argue that Winston's journal itself is Offred's entire narrative, a variation on the earlier theme which sug-gests that in the feminist dystopia the personal, hidden voice must be allowed to take over from the distancing third person Orwell used.

20. Remarks from Laurence M. Porter are helpful to me in underlining this point:

> In most such [apocalyptic] works, an element of hope subsists, because the hero differentiates himself from the surrounding chaos through (physical or mental) escape (Vonnegut), resistance (Camus), or both (Grass). . . . Thomas Mann's composer is engulfed, but leaves a legacy of genius. Orwell's mediocre hero, in contrast, is engulfed and leaves nothing. (62)

In the midst of his study of Ray Bradbury, Wayne L. Johnson makes a similar point, with strong relevance to the genre-based discussion underway here as well: "Pessimists about the future of mankind have not always envisioned atomic extermination. An uncomfortable survival under a worldwide totalitarian state has also been suggested as a grim possibility. George Orwell's *1984* represents the hub of such writing . . ." (83).

I argue above that "cracks" in "the system," while read by some as essential to the postmodern vision of even totalitarian systems, are in fact detractions from the political statement which are dystopia's mission. In my estimation, Orwell's vision is the most seamless of these; while his world holds many cracks, none is truly an escape but only a deeper-dug grave in the mud of big-brotherian control.

21. Readers of Atwood scholarship are familiar with the debate, entered into by almost everyone who publishes commentary on *The Handmaid's Tale*, as to the meaning of the "Historical Notes" appended to it. Similarly, discussion as to the meaning of Orwell's "Appendix" has centered around whether it represents some sort of liberation, if not for Winston himself, at least for the seemingly doomed world of Oceania. Larry W. Caldwell has argued that the novel's grim ending is of only "apparent finality," since in the Appendix "a voice from 'outside' the narrative, evoking a world altogether distinct from Winston's" reassures the reader that Big Brother did not in fact have the last word. Richard K. Sanderson points out, however, that the moving final scene of the novel proper and not the dry technicality of the Appendix is what readers remember as the "ending" of *1984* and that, even when considering the Appendix as the novel's official last word, the fluent doublespeak understood and demonstrated by its author makes him or her seem anything but a reliable harbinger of a post–Big Brother age. Using the same terminology as does Caldwell, although with the result of the opposite conclusion, Sanderson argues, "By trying to reconcile the novel and the Appendix, we experience for ourselves—'outside' the novel as it were—what it might be like to inhabit a world in which the authenticity . . . of all documents is in doubt" (594). Thus while the "Historical Notes" of Atwood's text have the effect of closing off the Gileadean empire (in addition to Offred's role as storyteller), the Appendix to Orwell's has the opposite effect—of opening out the Orwellian nightmare described previous to it, to include and engulf us all.

22. Berel Lang describes in "*1984*: Newspeak, Technology, and the Death of Language" "death" as the "meeting point for all varieties and sources of information— a common and simplified language into which they can be translated" (167–8) that restricts the horizontality of language, finally suffocating the life depending on it.

Works Cited

Andriano, Joseph. "*The Handmaid's Tale* as Scrabble Game." *Essays on Canadian Writing*. 48 (1992–1993): 89–96.

Atwood, Margaret. *The Handmaid's Tale*. New York: Fawcett Crest, 1985.

Auster, Paul. *In the Country of Last Things*. New York: Penguin Books, 1987.

———. "Interview." Larry McCaffery and Sinda Gregory. *Contemporary Literature*. 33.1 (1992): 1–23.

Barone, Dennis. "Introduction: Paul Auster and the Postmodern Novel." *Beyond the Red Notebook: Essays on Paul Auster*. Ed. Dennis Barone. Philadelphia: U of Pennsylvania P, 1995. 1–26.

Baudrillard, Jean. "The Anorexic Ruins." *Looking Back on the End of the World*. Eds. Dietmar Kampter and Christoph Wulf. Trans. David Antal. New York: Semiotext(e), 1989. 29–45.

———. *Fatal Strategies*. Trans. Philip Beitchman and W.G.J. Niesluchowski. New York: Semiotext(e), 1983.

Birkets, Sven. "Fiction, Reality, and In the Country of Last Things." *The Review of Contemporary Fiction.* 14.1 (1994): 66–9.

Bradbury, Ray. *Fahrenheit 451.* 1953; New York: Ballantine Books, 1973.

Caldwell, Larry W. "Wells, Orwell, and Atwood: (EPI)Logic and Eu/Utopia." *Extrapolation.* 33.4 (1992): 333–45.

Carpenter, Mary Wilson. "Representing Apocalypse: Sexual Politics and the Violence of Revelation." *Postmodern Apocalypse: Theory and Cultural Practice at the End.* Ed. Richard Dellamora. Philadelphia, U of Pennsylvania P, 1995. 107–35.

Chaloupka, William. *Knowing Nukes: The Politics and Culture of the Atom.* Minneapolis: U of Minnesota P, 1992.

De Kerckhove, Derrick. "On Nuclear Communication." *Diacritics* 14.2 (1984): 72–81.

Dellamora, Richard. *Postmodern Apocalypse: Theory and Cultural Practice at the End.* Philadelphia: University of Pennsylvania Press, 1995.

Derrida, Jacques. "No Apocalypse, Not Now: (full speed ahead, seven missiles, seven missives)." *Diacritics.* 14.2 (1984): 20–31.

———. "Of an Apocalyptic Tone Recently Adopted in Philosophy." Trans. John P. Leavey, Jr. *Oxford Literary Review.* 6.2 (1984): 3–37.

Deutscher, Isaac. "The Mysticism of Cruelty." *Nineteen Eighty-Four: Text, Sources, Criticism.* 2nd ed. Ed. Irving Howe. New York, Harcourt, Brace, Jovanovich, 1982. 332–43.

Ferguson, Frances. "The Nuclear Sublime." *Diacritics* 14.2 (1984): 4–10.

Freibert, Lucy M. "Control and Creativity: The Politics of Risk in Margaret Atwood's *The Handmaid's Tale.*" *Critical Essays on Margaret Atwood.* Ed. Judith McCombs. New York: G.K. Hall & Company, 1988. 280–291.

Fromm, Erich. *The Revolution of Hope: Towards a Humanized Technology.* New York: Harper and Row, 1968.

Howard, Gerald. "Publishing Paul Auster." *The Review of Contemporary Fiction.* 14.1 (1994): 92–95.

Howe, Irving. "*1984*: History as Nightmare." *Nineteen Eighty-Four: Text, Sources, Criticism.* 2nd ed. Ed. Irving Howe. New York, Harcourt, Brace, Jovanovich, 1982. 320–32.

Huxley, Aldous. *Brave New World.* 1932. New York: Perennial Library, 1969.

Johnson, Wayne L. *Ray Bradbury.* New York: Frederick Ungar Publishing Company, 1980.

Lang, Berel. "*1984*: Newspeak, Technology, and the Death of Language." *Soundings.* 72.1 (1989): 165–77.

MacCannell, Dean. "Baltimore in the Morning . . . After: On the Forms of Post-Nuclear Leadership." *Diacritics* 14.2 (1984): 33–46.

Macklin, Ruth. "Modifying Behavior, Thought, and Feeling: Can Big Brother Control from Within?" *Reflections on America, 1984: An Orwell Symposium.* Ed. Robert Mulvihill. Athens and London: U of Georgia P, 1986. 159–78.

Michael, Magali Cornier. *Feminism and the Postmodern Impulse: Post–World War II Fiction.* New York: State UP of New York, 1996.

Morrissey, Thomas J. "Armageddon from Huxley to Hoban." *Extrapolation.* 25.3 (1984): 197–213.

Murphy, Patrick J. "Reducing the Dystopian Distance: Pseudo-Documentary Framing in Near–Future Fiction." *Science Fiction Studies.* 17.1 (1990): 25–40.

Orwell, George. *1984.* New York: Harcourt, Brace, Jovanovich, 1949.

Porter, Laurence M. "Psychomachia versus Socialism in *Nineteen Eighty-Four.*" *The Revised Orwell.* Ed. Jonathan Rose. East Lansing: Michigan State UP, 1982. 61–74.

Rahv, Philip. "The Unfuture of Utopia." *Nineteen Eighty–Four: Text, Sources, Criticism:* 2nd ed. Ed. Irving Howe. New York, Harcourt, Brace, Jovanovich, 1982. 310–16.

Rose, Jonathan. "Eric Blair's School Days." *The Revised Orwell.* Ed. Jonathan Rose. East Lansing: Michigan State UP, 1982. 75–96.

Rothbard, Murray N. "George Orwell and the Cold War: A Reconsideration." *Reflections on America, 1984: An Orwell Symposium.* Ed. Robert Mulvihill. Athens and London: U of Georgia P, 1986. 5–14.

Sanderson, Richard K. "The Two Narrators and Happy Ending of *Nineteen Eighty-Four.*" *Modern Fiction Studies.* 34.4 (1988): 587–95.

Scheik, William J. "Romantic Tradition in Recent Post-Nuclear Holocaust Fiction." *English Romanticism and Modern Fiction.* Ed. Allan Chavkin. New York: AMS, 1993. 163–91.

———. "Continuative and Ethical Predictions: The Post-Nuclear Holocaust Novel of the 1980s." *North Dakota Quarterly.* 56.2 (1988): 61–82.

Schell, Jonathan. *The Fate of the Earth.* New York: Knopf, 1982.

Schwenger, Peter. *Letter Bomb: Nuclear Holocaust and the Exploding Word.* Baltimore: Johns Hopkins UP, 1992.

Seed, David. "The Flight from the Good Life: *Fahrenheit 451* in the Context of Postwar American Dystopias."

Teeuwen, Ruud. "Distopia's Point of No Return: A Team-Taught Utopia Class." *Teaching Atwood's* The Handmaid's Tale *and Other Works.* Eds. Sharon R. Wilson, Thomas B. Friedman, and Shannon Hengen. New York: Modern Language Association of America, 1996. 114–21.

Touponce, William F. *Ray Bradbury and the Poetics of Reverie: Fantasy, Science Fiction, and the Reader.* Ann Arbor: UMI Research Press, 1984.

Vonnegut, Kurt. *Player Piano.* 1952. New York: Avon Books, 1967.

Washburn, Katharine. "A Book at the End of the World: Paul Auster's *In the Country of Last Things.*" *The Review of Contemporary Fiction.* 14.1 (1994): 62–5.

Watt, Donald. "Burning Bright: '*Fahrenheit 451*' as Symbolic Dystopia." *Ray Bradbury.* Eds. Martin Harry Greenberg and Joseph D. Olander. New York: Taplinger Publishing Company, 1980.

Woods, Tim. "'Looking for Signs in the Air': Urban Space and the Postmodern in *In The Country of Last Things.*" *Beyond the Red Notebook: Essays on Paul Auster.* Ed. Dennis Barone. Philadelphia: U of Pennsylvania P, 1995. 107–128.

WALTER J. MUCHER

Being Martian: Spatiotemporal Self in Ray Bradbury's The Martian Chronicles

> ... the ego constitutes itself for itself, so to speak, in the unity of a [hi]story.
>
> —Edmund Husserl

During the Late Modern,[1] the question of identity has been more of a psychological program than a physical one. It has questioned the realm of the Absolute and its transcendental nature as adjudicated by the ideas of Time and Space proposed by Early Modern thinkers such as Rene Descartes and Sir Isaac Newton. Early empirical scholars, such as John Locke and David Hume, questioned the process by which all sentient beings acquire knowledge of the external. Others, like Immanuel Kant, proposed the idea of truth on an *a priori* reality known by humans given its all-encompassing design. What is somewhat clear is that for the Late Modern, identity is, in some manner, a mental construct of those experienced spaces and those experienced times brought into review post-experientially by the mind (Henri Bergson, William James and Edmund Husserl). And, in such a review of experienced moments (i.e. the mental combination of particular experiences of Time and Space), there is an expected end, the phenomenological construction of an identity to be brought to fulfillment, not by nature, but by choice. Still, one must somewhat contend that the program might be p/re-written, as Edmund Husserl notes in *The Phenomenology of*

From *Extrapolation* 43, no. 2 (Summer 2002), 171–87. © 2002 by the University of Texas at Brownsville and Texas Southmost College.

Internal Time-Consciousness [*PITC*] and that the conscious individual follows course until finally reaching the telos of his self.

In this spirit Ray Bradbury's *The Martian Chronicles* (1958) can be understood as the historical reading made by the protagonists as they re-create a "diary" of their lives and loves in their quest for Mars. It reflects the Late Modern's incursion into a psychological and phenomenological humanism in which, in their search for a new self, the protagonists re-create a world of multiple readings which re-trace their exploits, moving forward while continuously looking back over their own experiential shoulders. Bradbury's overall structure posits each story as an entry of a universal consciousness, which retains the memory of a world gone by as well as the prophecy of a world to be.[2] His narrative represents the temporality of Martianness, that is, in a Lacanian sense, it represents the space in which Martianness may be attainable, for it opposes a "thing," the "Martian self," as "one that has not yet been made a symbol ... [but] has the potential of becoming one" (Lacan 46). Furthermore, as David Carr may declare, one could conclude that in Bradbury's *The Martian Chronicles*, "to be a human individual is to instantiate a special sort of relationship to time" (94). This is because the diary-like narrative reminds us that "at the bottom it is, to be sure, to be always 'located' in an ever changing now, and thus to be subjected, like everything else, to temporal sequences" (Carr 94). Key to this is that Bradbury's protagonists do not just "undergo or endure or suffer this sequence as it comes, one thing at a time" (Carr 94). But, in fact, what is central to my discussion is that the protagonists, eventually, will come to realize that "Whatever else it is, to exist as a person is to experience and to act" (Carr 95).

This idea of spacetime incurred during the period of the Late Modern is reflected especially in Edmund Husserl's phenomenological proposal that knowledge of our world is determined by our psychic interpretation of the experienced world. Husserl would come to see time as an inner sense of ordering and understanding the world as given in first impressions. For Husserl, time structures the constituting synthesis of perceiving the phenomena, itself a step toward re-establishing a crucial link between Being and Time. As such, being is defined, by all accounts, as the end result of a subjective act of self-definition, one located in space by its differentiating time sequence. This means that the subject of the Late Modern is determined by the very act of reading its own history, which, eventually, is imposed upon the events in question by the protagonist/reader him-, her-, and/or it-self. "History," according to Claude Lévi-Strauss, "has replaced mythology and fulfills the same function" (43). With it, historic narratives ensure and maintain the proper relation between man's past, present and future within space, a space which, in its narrative, temporally contains the "unity of life." As Helga Nowotny notes, the

Late Modern "was rather a question of defining time and space anew for the greatest possible—and for the first time democratic—variety of perspectives and points of views, of positions and subjective experiences" (20). And, in that experience, of life itself.

The creation of a self during the period of the Late Modern, a period that could well be defined as an industrially and early technologically centered age, required total dominion of the ego over spacetime. Preluding Jean-François Lyotard's work, *The Postmodern Condition*, Lewis Mumford defines this preoccupation of the Late Modern as an empowerment over spacetime:

> The new bourgeoisie, in counting house and shop, reduced life to a careful, uninterrupted routine: so long for business: so long for dinner: so long for pleasure—all carefully measured out, as methodical as the sexual intercourse in Tristam Shandy's father, which coincided, symbolically, with the monthly winding of the clock. Timed payments: timed contracts: timed work: timed meals: from this period on nothing was quite free from the stamp of the calendar or the clock. Waste of time . . . one of the heinous sins. (34)

As Mumford notes, for the bourgeoisie experiential spacetime had to be useful. Like Jules Verne's Phinneas Phogg (*Around the World in Eighty Days*), man began to set their lives to the beat of a watch's second hand. Between 1880 and 1918 "technological, artistic and scientific achievements . . . converged to break down the well-rehearsed spatial and temporal structures of social perception and transform them into a broad experiential field . . ." (Nowotny 19). The Late Modern deemed it necessary to exteriorize and reify the internal wants and needs of the self by rewriting its history, and with it the way man interacts with his and/or her historical self.

Husserl's phenomenological concept of "internal time-consciousness" represents the essence of this historical spacetime. "The idea of an 'event,'" writes David Carr, "is already that of something that takes time, has temporal thickness, beginning and end; and events are experienced as the phases and elements of other larger-scale events and processes" (Carr 24). As Carr notes, it is in his Cartesian Meditations that Edmund Husserl proposes "that the ego 'constitutes itself for itself, so to speak, in the unity of a *Geschichte*'; or, as one could say, in one possible translation of *Geschichte*, the unity of a *life*" (74; my emphasis). Furthermore, "The idea of a purely phenomenological psychology," writes Husserl, "does not have just the function . . . of reforming empirical psychology. For deeply rooted reasons, it can also serve as a preliminary step for laying open the essence of a transcendental phenomenology" ("Phenomenology" 27). Husserl's claim against empiricism lies in redirecting his inquiry toward the intentionality of the world, as understood by Descartes. Husserl reminds us that for Descartes the world presents itself as existing "for us, [it] exists only as the presentational content of our presentations" ("Phenomenology" 27). As such, the world exists because we exist.

Husserlian time-consciousness basically argues against the precariousness and uncertainty with which the sequence of events were described by empirical psychologism of the sixteenth and seventeenth century, such as that of John Locke and David Hume:

> When we speak of the analysis of time-consciousness, of the temporal character of objects of perception, memory, and expectation, it may seem, to be sure, as if we assume the Objective flow of time. What we accept, however, is not the existence of a world-time, the existence of a concrete duration, and the like, but time and duration appearing as such. (*PITC* 23)

Husserl points to the false assumption of Locke that our perceptions are the impressions upon our minds of a real, static and absolute world, which lies outside of ourselves. Empiricists such as Locke and Hume, according to Husserl, had argued for this "Objective flow of time" which confidently expresses the "concrete" world as given by the repetitive sensory perceptions of causal events from the external world. But for Husserl, this time perception is truly the intentional perception of our internal senses. "To be sure," adds Husserl, "we also assume an existing time; this, however, is not the time of the world of experience but the *immanent time* of the flow of consciousness" (Husserl 23). In a word, all consciousness is, eventually, the content or object (*noema*) of the consciousness of something. And for Husserl this something was our own perceptive act, and not an original perception in itself. "Thus," Joan Stambaugh remarks in her introduction to Martin Heidegger's *On Time and Being*, "there is no such thing as a worldless subject (exemplified by Descartes' *res cogitans*), nor is there a world in any meaningful, phenomenological sense of that word without human being" (viii). That is, a world independent of our own conscious act of perceiving and describing what we perceive.

Husserl lays claim to two creative principles of perception which make up the perception of the now: that is (1) retention, or the just-pastness of an event, and (2) protention, that is, the just-future of an event. Husserl's celebrity consists in describing how retention and protention differ from recollection and expectation of the future respectively.[3]

Consider Husserl's example of the hearing of a sequence of tones, that is, "we hear a melody . . . we perceive it. . . . While the first tone is sounding, the second comes, then the third, and so on. Must we not say that when the second tone sounds I hear *it*, but I no longer hear the first, and so on?" (*PITC* 43) For Husserl, though, this act is not so simple. For though it is true that the particular tone expires as the next arises to take its place, its objective reality is still maintained due to primary memory, and to the expectation of its successor (*PITC* 43).

Perception of a melody demands, first, that there be present a "primal impression" which constitutes the tonal now, that is, the immediately sound-ing tone of the melody. Secondly, there is at the same time as the perceived tone, an existing peripheral tonal experience active in the constituted con-scious act of perceived tonal now. This "fresh" or "primary memory" which holds near to the perceiving now the just-past tone in consciousness is known as retention. As such "when the tonal now, the primal impression, passes over into retention, this retention is itself again a now, an actual existent. While it itself is an actual (but not an actual sound), it is the retention of a sound that has been" (*PITC* 50).

Retention constitutes the living horizon of the now; I have in it a con-sciousness of the "just past." But what is originally constituted thereby—per-haps in the retaining of the tone just heard—is only the shoving back of the now-phase or the completed constituted duration, which in this complete-ness is no longer being constituted and no longer perceived. (*PITC* 66)

Finally there is the expectation, or protention expressed by the tonal now as it opens into receiving its tonal successor in the melody. With it a new tonal now is poised, pushing the "present" tonal now back into the no-longer (that is, the just-pastness) of the tone. Husserl referred to it as pro-jected phantas:

> ... every act of memory contains intentions of expectation whose fulfillment leads to the present. Every primordially constitutive process is animated by protentions which voidly [*leer*] constitute and intercept [*auffangen*] what is coming, as such, in order to bring it to fulfillment. (*PITC* 76)

The foreground is nothing without the background; the appearing side is nothing without the non-appearing. It is the same with regard to the unity of time-consciousness—the duration reproduced is the foreground; the clas-sifying intentions make us aware of a background, a temporal background. (*PITC* 78)

Furthermore, Husserl states that an "expectational intuition is an inverted memorial intuition, for the now-intentions do not go 'before' the process but follow after it" (*PITC* 79). Thus, the perception of the totality of the melody depends on the capacity to consciously pre-perceive the following tonal now as a protentive constitutive reality of the "present" tonal now and of retentive tonal now.

This sequence of tonal experiences constitutes "modes" or a "continuous flux" of sequential now-points:

> Every temporal being "appears" in one or another continually changing mode of running-off, and the "object in the mode of running-off" is in this change always something other, even though we still say that the Object and every point of its time and this time itself are one and the same. (*PITC* 47)

For Husserl, spatiotemporal being, as David Carr notes, follows this relation between retention and protention by which they are taken together to make up what may be referred to as a "field of occurrence," that is, where the present may stand out from amidst its surroundings (23).

But it would be wrong to say that retention and protention are just empty forms of experience. They are not to be considered as mere crucibles to be filled by recollections or dreams, as empiricists might claim. It is impossible to conceive an act which is devoid of a past or of a future, that is, of retention and protention.

David Carr correctly translates this relational act between retention, protention and the primal now to mean that "to be conscious temporally is to 'constitute' these phenomena from an ever changing now-perspective through our protentive-retentive grasp" (Carr 95). But it is clear that this "constitution," as Carr proposes, is still just a cognitive act reminiscent of the empirical perceptive acts Husserl himself condemns. "As these notions are understood by Husserl," writes Carr, "without past and future there can be no present and thus no experience at all" (Carr 29). It is evident that Husserl, and Carr, believe in a world ruled by sequential spacetime: that is, by causal events. Husserl's perceptive act presupposes that the world is a sequential given, such as in a film strip or a musical score, where each event is followed eventually and necessarily by its following successor: for example, as in a movie where each film cell is followed by its succeeding film cell, or in a musical score where each tone is followed by its successor, all in a pre-scribed order. As such, Husserl's phenomenological spacetime maintains league with the transcendentalism of Newton, the rationalism of Descartes and empiricism of Locke and Hume. Its only difference lies in treating and establishing the perceptive act of consciousness as an active constitutive event itself.

Bradbury's narrative in *The Martian Chronicles*, on the other hand, questions not these theories, but, rather, questions the Late Modern's influence upon the self's social journey of hope into the future, especially as it parallels the colonizing and expansionism of the Americas, and the socio-ethnic problems in said act by an industrial and post-industrial community which had no regards for the other. This is compounded by the need to re-invent a self-identity that could be harmonious to these new possibilities, a shucking of the old in search for a new and improved self (such as that represented by Nietzsche's superman in *Also Sprach Zarathustra* and the nihilistic process exposed in *Der Wille zur Macht*).

Three moments in *The Martian Chronicles* are focal to the phenomenological reading of spacetime that I propose, and that may even hint at the cyclical self-reflective nature expressed by a Late Modern conceptualization of spacetime. They are: 1) "February 1999: Ylla," "August 1999: The Summer Night," "August 1999: The Earth Men," and "April 2000: The Third Expedition"; 2) "August 2002: Night Meeting"; and 3) "October 2026: The Million-Year Picnic." These moments are focal in understanding my argument that, as laid out by the Late Modern, man's re-collection of spacetime is retentive/protentive, rather than presentive. Spacetime is still a collection of Aristotelian "now-moments." But, instead of being recognized at its surfacing, they are reflexively construed as conscious remembrances of the "just-past." What is more, the game of self-identity played out by Bradbury is one pertaining to the future as the horizon of the expected. As I stated before, the text, a diary-like narrative, basically asks who or what is the Martian. It is only in retrospect, by reaching the last entry of the chronicle, that one can see how the solution to this problem follows Husserl's concept of time-consciousness. As Husserl contends about the perception of time-consciousness, the solution was always there, in the horizon, like a melody, waiting to be played out fully before providing the answer. Like a musical score, diaries or chronicles contain all the scores ready to be played.[4]

In *The Martian Chronicles*, each entry in the colony's diary leads, ultimately, to revealing the historical score of Martian identity, as it becomes obvious once one reaches "The Million-Year Picnic." It is by realizing each entry, and by recollecting such entries from the perspective of their succeeding entries, that the full value of Bradbury's narrative is realized. Each entry is a date in a calendar, as each musical note is a tone in a musical score, or each cell is a scene in a film; they all follow a prescribed sequence which, in retrospect, reveals a given whole.

In "February 1999: Ylla" Mr. K's implicit hatred toward the arrival of the first Earth expedition to Mars is fueled by his fear of loss of identity, as a (Modern) male and as a Martian. The Earthmen bring with them a decentering lust—in the form of the industrial and technological marvels of the Late Modern—as witnessed by Mr. K's wife's dreams (3–4, 8). But this un-eventful arrival is of a double nature, for it occurs only in the wantonness of Mrs. K's dreams. In reality, the objectified knowledge of this arrival is covered and denied by Mr. K's murder of the Earth crew. Mr. K's actions are fueled by a need to safeguard himself and the Martians from losing their idyllic—Victorian—identities as Martians. After all, his wife was lusting for foreigners that, by all accounts, contradicted Martian (Modern) norms, and especially his own self.

But the damage had already been done. The Martians had been infected telepathically by the overriding intentions of the Earthmen's self. The Martians found themselves singing rhymes in languages they did not know ("August 1999: The Summer Night" 15). The premonition, or, rather, the fulfillment of the end is given early, when the Martian women wake-up with screaming fear.

> [Martian women] "Something terrible will happen in the morning."
> [Martian husbands] "Nothing can happen, all is well with us."
> [Martian women] A hysterical sobbing, "It is coming nearer and nearer and nearer!" ("August 1999: The Summer Night" 16)

This dialogue between the Martian women and their husbands forms the essence for what Margaret Lee Zoreta identifies as the "monologic attitude toward alterity," that is, "the obliteration of the other" (57). Zoreta identifies this attitude as standing against Bakhtin's concept of the dialogic, that is, as Zoreta states, as

> a polyphonic coexistence of "understanding as the transformation of the other's into 'one's own/another's'" (57)

This imperialistic attitude against the other fuels the fear of not only the Martians, as noted above by the cry of the Martian women, but also the fear of the Earthlings of not succeeding in their quest for Mars.

As the narrative of the next two expeditions reveals, the Martians, in an act of preserving their sanity and, eventually, their identity, decide to eliminate the threat to their identities by eliminating the expeditions. In particular, the second expedition, "August 1999: The Earth Men," deals with the psychic stability of the Martian self. Arriving in a world wracked by mass psychosis, the Earthmen are shuffled from one Martian to another, to end locked-up in a mental institution. In the same manner that Mrs. K suffered from the maddening illusiveness of her dreams, the Martian population has been infected with an unexplainable telepathic psychosis of an other which threatens their society: Martians now believe that they are Earthlings (25).

Their only recourse is to eradicate the source of such deviations from the established societal norm.

> Yes. You know, such cases as yours need special 'curing'. The people in that hall are simpler forms. But once you've gone this far, I must point out, with primary, secondary, auditory, olfactory, and labial hallucinations, as well as tactile and optical fantasies, it is pretty bad business. We have to resort to euthanasia. ("The Earth Men" 27–28)

Reality is a construction of primary and secondary sensory perceptions that the human mind orders into a working reality. Thus the description made by the Martian psychologist, Mr. Xxx, of the psychosis suffered by the Martians can be defined simply as cognitive experience. The experiential act is basically the collective sum of what British empiricists, such as Locke and Hume, have described as "primary, secondary, auditory, olfactory, labial, tactile and optical" perceptions. The Martian psychologist could have been reading either Locke or Hume, for he describes the mental faculty of forming the real, as British empiricists in the seventeenth and eighteenth century proposed. But, in this case, these perceptions are the perceptions of an other's reality, and, at that, one menacing to the stability of Martian reality. For a people who have found a sounder form of living, these intruding multiple sensorial acts merely complicate the Martians' definition of being. Not because they are real, but because they are somebody else's "real." The Late Modern, somewhat founded on these empirical tenets, embodies the same definition for reality as that offered by the Martian psychologist. But the Industrial Modern, represented by the Earth expeditions, endangers the continuance of these simple tenets of Martian living. Eventually, the Martian psychologist falls victim to the same insanity of which he accused the Earthlings. And as indicated, his only recourse is to eradicate the source of his infection by killing himself. It is here that the consequence of the industrial world merges with the surfacing of the new dangers of the global world as reflected in the last chapter of *The Martian Chronicles*: "The Million-Year Picnic."

In "April 2000: The Third Expedition" Bradbury extends this idea of an identity based on memory and imagination, and plays upon a sense of telepathy and hypnosis as a constitutive act between experiential subjects, and not merely as an individual act. As Captain John Black tries restlessly to sleep he wonders how a Martian city can be so similar to an Earth town.

> Suppose all these houses aren't real at all, this bed not real, but only figments of my own imagination, given substance by

telepathy and hypnosis through the Martians, thought Captain
John Black.
    What if the Martians took the memories of a town exclusively
from my mind? ("The Third Expedition" 46)

Reminiscent of Descartes' argument of an evil genie, introduced in his
First Meditations, Captain Black questions the reality that surround him as
an illusion created for his benefit, in his, and his crew's, minds. But, after the
Earthmen are killed by the population, the Martians still hold Earth forms,
and as their masks melt, one must question: what is the reality that Bradbury
wanted the reader to see (47–48)? For the psychosis seems to have greater
hold on the Martians this time around. No longer is the Martian's psychosis
a mere psychosis, as in the second expedition where the Earthmen were a
mental sickness, now it is a physical virus that eats away at the physical as well
as the mental self of the Martians.
    It is the last chapter of *The Martian Chronicles*, "October 2026: The Mil-
lion-Year Picnic,"[5] which offers to the reader the open closure of being by
retrospectively questioning, as well as answering, the beginning of the ordeals
on Mars as well as the end of the true lunacy on Earth. It also reflects back
to the fears expressed by the Martian women in "The Summer Night." The
story deals with a family that goes to Mars for a picnic. But it will reveal itself
as the last hope for the race, for Earth, in its narrow mind, has destroyed
itself. Faced with the horrors of the past, the father's last act is one of defiance
against what he had held as true: he burns copies of texts which once defined
the human race and the individual self.

> I'm burning a way of life, just like that way of life is being burned
> clean of Earth right now.... Science ran too far ahead of us
> quickly, and the people got lost in a mechanical wilderness, like
> children making over pretty things, gadgets, helicopters, rockets;
> emphasizing the wrong items, emphasizing machines instead of
> how to run the machines. (179–180)

Fire is the purifying element of creation. But left to the incapable hands
of man, it becomes a dangerous toy. For such reasons one remembers a shoot-
ing star, the first conscious viewing of electricity at work, or the simple act of
viewing a movie. When the father destroys all links to the past he is burning
all that was burned before him: "All the laws and beliefs of Earth were burnt
into small hot ashes which soon would be carried off in a wind" (180). The
father is looking back one last time, looking up at the remembrance of what
is, and must be, lost for his family to continue. It is that spirit of annihilation

and re-birth that he takes a last wistful glance toward the Earth, an intense search "for Earthian logic, common sense, good government, peace, and responsibility" (173). All the virtues of the Modern. But the father knew that in its enthusiasm to be heralded as the great hope of a technological driven society, the world sent itself aflame in nuclear smoke.

Bradbury's last piece is in fact his first piece. Written well before all the other stories included, or not, in *The Martian Chronicles*, it becomes the motivating telos of the collection. The narrative's theme seems to become clear: to establish the identity of the true Martians. Until now the narrative had demonstrated the "colonizing" process that identity suffers by denying, to break its links with the past, in this case its identification with Earth/Old World. But "The Million-Year Picnic" attempts to break with the past, as the father burns the last physical links with the Old World (i.e. the rocket they came in and the documents). Here "Earth," writes Gary K. Wolfe, "has become less a planet in his mind than a way of life to be rejected" (47). In a Heraclitean move the father takes his family down one of the Martian canals. When asked by his son, Robert, how far down the river they have to go, the father answers "a million years" (172). Time and space are brought together in their being on the river. It is not enough just physically to go down the river, but they must also denude themselves of their "past."

This transposition of time over space reflects how one must deal with their "new" identity. A total annihilation of their past self is demanded for them to carry on, as Nietzsche would expect. To establish the new self, all ties to the past must be broken.

The truth is that neither the past nor the futures are unlinked, as it would seem. For the opened ending of "The Million-Year Picnic" is not only a view forward toward a new Martian self, but it is also a retrospect of the Martian past. A million years is to travel back to the Martian beginning and to the apocalyptic dreams of the Martian women in "The Summer Night." Foreseeing the end of the Martian civilization, the women had unknowingly foreseen the coming of the Earthlings, and the end of their civilization. What Ylla had lustingly foreseen in her waking dreams earlier, in those strange forms and sound, had become the feared nightmares and psychotic experiences of a dying Mars. A waking dream, as the oracles would call it, for it foretold the end of the old civilization and the beginning of the new.

In a similar fashion, the father of "The Million-Year Picnic" foresees the coming of his Earthlings, the family with which he expects to repopulate Mars. "Now we're alone. We and a handful of others who'll land in a few days. Enough to start over" (180). But these Earthlings would not be the menace that Mr. K and the Martian women dreaded. Bradbury comes full circle by linking this last hope with Ylla's vision of the Earthmen's first coming.

Interestingly, the end of the Martian race becomes the subliminal catalyst that foresees the end of the Human race.

In the "Night Meeting" ("August 2002"), Tomás Gomez meets with a Martian, Muhe Ca. This piece is central to this idea of joining ends, for it ties together the nature of time and space played out in the chronicle. It is the meeting of past and future, somewhat similarly to Husserl's meeting of the horizons in the present. But just whose past and whose future are we talking about? For both characters are as real to each as they are phantoms to the other. Like Husserl's time-consciousness of music, each character is the other character's next tone. Each one reflects the just pastness of the other's reality. And each has a future horizon, to which they can lay claim, as the becoming of the other's past: "Tomás put out his hand. The Martian did likewise in imitation. Their hands did not touch; they melted through each other" (86). Not only do their physical bodies melt through each other's, but their identities as well. Concrete opposition within givens establishes identity, and at this point all empirical givens have melted away with their hands.

Past and present do not meet. Rather, they melt into a present without really touching each other. What is cannot come into contact with what is not. In theory, the meeting of matter and anti-matter produces the annihilation of all. And in a sense, the present can be seen as this annihilation, for it loses all sense of past and all sense of future. As Spender had discovered earlier, it just is:

> The Martians discovered the secret of life among animals. The animal does not question life. It lives. Its very reason for living is life; it enjoys and relishes life ("June 2001:—And the Moon be Still as Bright" 66).

Spender's sympathy toward Martian life is echoed by the old man to whom Tomás had spoken at the gas station before meeting up with the Martian Muhe Ca.

> You know what Mars is? It's like a thing I got for Christmas seventy years ago—don't know if you ever had one—they called them kaleidoscopes, bits of crystal and cloth beads and pretty junk. You held it up to the sunlight and looked in through it, and it took your breath away. All the patterns! Well, that's Mars. Enjoy it. Don't ask it to be nothing else but what it is. ("Night Meeting" 79)

And what "it" [Mars] is, is the simplicity of being. The multiple colorings of the self as one attempts to describe the soul through its own body.

The Martians had supposedly understood the kaleidoscope effect of life. But Earthmen had opted for the complications of explaining away, and, eventually, of controlling the real through science and technology. As such, it is not the Martian who is the Other, as Earth would have us believe. Rather, it is the intruding Earthness, which shows its otherness previously concealed by its imperialistic superiority.

Simplicity in being, as the Martians discovered, seems to be what the human identity lacks. In the need to reflect and create an identity, the truth of the human being denies its own simple and uncomplicated self. Spender understands the totemic representations of "primitive" people. In adopting the image of animals, the spirit is free to commune and enact its primal being. But more than that, Spender's act, as sympathetic identification with the Martian, reflects the secret of phenomenological spacetime, that is, it is not simple. Rather, phenomenological spacetime avoids the simplicity of just being by continuously emphasizing the relation between past and future, or just-past and just-future.

Tomás and Muhe, Earthling and Martian, are the two poles of this identity dyad. Each represents the other's reality by projecting its negation unto the other. But this reality is not to be taken as an objective reality. Rather it proposes a subjective power, which establishes each other's experienced reality. Descartes would have described it as a divine power. But Bradbury's protagonists follow empiricist modes and, as such, mirroring somewhat Husserl's phenomenological act of perceiving, they establish a less divine source for their perceptions.

Realities, then, are memories projected into our conscious being. As Captain Black had earlier predicted in "The Third Expedition," the Martians had tapped into the unconscious chamber of memories creating, thus, "the ability to keep me under this dreaming hypnosis all of the time" (46). These memories are what sustain our very own self, for they are the contents of past as well as future being, as Tomás and Muhe would come to argue later. And Time will somehow be key to this being:

> [Muhe Ca] "This can only mean one thing. It has to do with Time. Yes. You are a figment of the Past!"
> "No, you are from the Past," said the Earth Man, having had time to think of it now.
> "You are so *certain*. How can you prove who is from the Past, who from the Future? What year is it?" ("Night Meeting" 85)

Not surprisingly, neither wants to be the past of the other, so they accuse each other of being his past. The fear of not being translates into each one's desire to be the other's future. Existentially, it is easier to be the other's future, rather than his past, for without this illusion of futurity, they would no longer find a reason in living. And resorting to dates offers no solution for each has his own arbitrary way of keeping time. "The result of the meeting," according to Edward J. Gallagher, "is a distinct feeling of simultaneous reality, mutual fate, and mutual (spiritual) communion" (68). Intentions aside, whether figments of our past or figments of our future, the present is the meeting place of all our hallucinations, both those that we expect, as well as those that invade and contradict our every sense of reason.

> "The task of projecting your psychotic image into the mind of another via telepathy and keeping the hallucinations from becoming sensually weaker is almost impossible." ("The Earth Men" 29)

But it is done. The Earth Men's perceptive act, reminiscent of Husserl's cognitive act as I described earlier, is a continuous hallucinatory act. And the narrator, as a psychotic genius, is responsible for infecting us with the virus of imagination. To tell a story is to make one feel the story, the place, and the time. These acts illustrate phenomenological spacetime. Sensory hallucinations are the basis for our known selves. Who we are and who we pretend to be are just figments of a long movie script. In the narrative act, these hallucinations are transferred, transformed and eventually adapted into our very own being. The world that surrounds us is a conscious confection of our interpreted world. Who or what surrounds us become definitions of our comprehension. And as such, they form part of the sound stage and supporting cast which help narrate our self.

As I stated above, "The Million-Year Picnic" ends with an open closure. In their plight to escape the savage destruction of Earth, the father promises his boys that he will show them Martians. What the boys do not expect is how familiar those Martians will seem to them.

> They reached the canal. It was long and straight and cool and wet and reflective in the night.
>
> "I've always wanted to see a Martian," said Michael. "Where are they, Dad? You promised."
>
> "There they are," Dad said, and he shifted Michael on his shoulder and pointed straight down.
>
> The Martians were there. Timothy began to shiver.
>
> The Martians were there—in the canal—reflected in the water. Timothy and Michael and Robert and Mom and Dad.

The Martians stared back up at them for a long, long silent time from the rippling water.... ("The Million-Year Picnic" 181)

This is the Father's startling revelation to his children in "The Million-Year Picnic" which marks a new phase, by accentuating the father's assertion that they are the Martians, both by choice and by accident. This "desire" which, from a beginning, is represented as a desire to impose Earthness upon Mars, has now been transformed into a desired fulfillment of abandoning one identity for another. Similar to Lacan's description of the three mirror phases of an infant's self-cognization, the Earth family now look upon the waters of the Martian canal to reveal a new diverted reality: the Martianness in all of us. Looking back at "—And the Moon be Still as Bright" we can identify the first mirror phase of self awareness when Spender's neurotic identification with the sought "Other" (the Martians) leads towards the desired fulfillment of being safe expressed in the Earthmen's desire mimed by the "blankness" of the Earth (Martian) town of "The Third Expedition." This desire becomes a mimicked reality in its second mirror phase as the first Earth colony battles its fears fulfilling their desires upon the shape shifting form of the "last" Martian in "The Martian." As Brenda K. Marshall notes in *Teaching the Postmodern*, "The subject's identity is the image of itself that the subject forms by identifying with other's perceptions of it" (93). This opened form shifts its site of being as it runs from center to center (the different desires of the people of the town, as projected upon the Martian's chameleonic form) until, in its final act of decentering, it becomes all and none of the sites, breaking its veil and washing away any recognizable form from the sight of the colonists. A new reality is now a must, for the colonists desired safeguards, their constructed realities, now are shattered pieces of their othering mirror.

"The Million-Year Picnic" tries to pick up the pieces without recreating it. It is the third mirror phase of self-cognization, when the infant sees itself as the self that sees its reflection. The family, seeing their reflecting forms on the waters of the traversed canal, passes from desiring the "Other" towards an understanding of its own "Otherness." It is this new Martian identity that allows the family to be present with it/self.

The transcourse of time and the change of space have led these remnant beings to re-establish their self-identity. They had a choice, and, in retrospect, their choices were forced upon them. Yet the question of spacetime brings out the reality of how the chronicle brings to light the creation of the self, as did Greece and the religious books in the Middle Ages. The epic as well as the religious story trace, in their own ways, the beginnings of a people and of a society. In the same way, they explicate the process by which the individual self, as well as the collective self, is molded. Santayana once said that those who did not learn from their histories were condemned to repeat it. As the future is open, yet restrictively expected by a past that "prophecizes" its coming into fulfillment, so the identity of the self is openly desired, yet somewhat preconditioned by the body's alterity.

The future follows a text to its "conclusion," temporally, since it recycles itself, as Bradbury seems to allude by leaving the ending suspended by an ellipsis (181). "One key to the story ["The Million-Year Picnic"] is the children. Mars will be given to the children who are still capable of wonder …" as we are foretold earlier by the old man in "Night Meeting" (181). Optimistically, through the father's eyes Bradbury sees a hope for a better future. As in Genesis, Mars is the new land of the twenty-first century Adam and Eve, who with their sons await the daughters from Nod, as well as the birth of their future sister. Such children are not continuations of the Old Order, or so Bradbury seems to hope. As Heraclitus once stated, "Time is a child playing a game of draughts; the kingship is in the hands of a child" (in Freeman frg. 52). In this manner, these "new Martians" could be the inheritors of a new playground free of any legacy. Like the kaleidoscope, the dead cities light up the children's faces with the splendor of the new unknown.

Bradbury's narrative represents the temporality of Martianness, that is, it represents the space in which Martianness may be attainable for it opposes the Martian self to a "thing as one that has not yet been made a symbol, … [but] has the potential of becoming one" (Lacan "Desire" 46). In this sense, the desire demonstrated by Spender to be a Martian, and the desire of the boys to see a Martian are themselves two opposing desires of the fulfillment of the Martian. This "presence" in the desire, or the desired, is outside time. "The fantasy of perversion (of Martianness) is namable. It is in space. It suspends an essential relationship. It is not atemporal but rather outside time" (Lacan "Desire" 17). Furthermore, this desire "creates the space of discourse, the possibility of dialogue … and in so doing engenders (or represents) the space of temporality" (Schleifer 880). But, as hopeful as this project sounds, these children are not yet the children of the postmodern, and even less the children of Nietzsche. For Bradbury hides them from that important transition through which the self has to reveal itself: to face the future, as Heidegger would probably say, in one's death. This transition is the transitional relationship between the individual and death expressed as an "in-between" that operates as a spatiotemporal constitutive of the self. And that is theme for another Time and another Space.

NOTES

1. For the sake of argument in this essay I identify the Early Modern as that period between the 1500s and 1850s and the Late Modern as that period between the 1850s and the late 1960s.

2. Look especially in such stories as "The Summer Night," "The Meeting" and "The Million-Year Picnic."

3. Husserl lays claim to two creative principles of perception which make up the perception of the now: that is (1) retention, or the just-pastness of an event, and (2) protention, that is, the just-future of an event. For Husserl the distinction between recollection and retention is one of proximity to the event (the same applies to the distinction between expectation of the future and protention). Recollection of the past is to remember an act or an event that is no longer occurring; but retention is maintaining "present" the just-pastness of the act in relation to its successive act. Of import is that contrary to empiricists, Husserl proposes continuity in the succession of perceptive acts. Consciousness of the present (the perceptive act) presupposes the consciousness of its "comet trail of retentions," that is, of the trail it leaves behind. In the same way, protentional act differs from expectation of the future in that the expectation of the future is one's intentionality towards some far future act or event (one plans for it, dreads its coming, or looks forward to its becoming), while protention is the implicitly anticipated immediate future envisioned as the horizon of the present. Protention, then, is the conscious knowledge that an act occurs only to be replaced by its succeeding act. In this manner, human time-consciousness is understood as "past-retention-event-protention-future."

4. Bradbury wrote another possible ending which could be seen as complementary yet oppositional to this one. See "Dark They Were, and Golden Eyed." First published as "Naming the Names" in *Thrilling Wonder Stories* (August 1949). In this story the transformation of the family into Martians is due to the environment, and not by choice.

5. In *Jacques Lacan* Anika Lemaire explains: During the [first] mirror phase of the child's development it "recognizes" itself as distinct from the outside world. The term "mirror phase" refers to the awareness of the subject of itself as separate from the mother, for example . . . [it is] an identification with an imaginary (because imagined) . . . autonomous self. [Second phase] the child recognizes him/herself as separate in the mirror phase, but at this phase also identifies him/herself with equal-age peers, reimagining these peers as they replicate the image he/she has seen in the mirror "of the human form" (91).

WORKS CITED

Bradbury, Ray. *The Martian Chronicles*. Garden City, NY: Doubleday, 1958.

Carr, David. *Time, Narrative, and History*. (1986) Studies in Phenomenology and Existential Philosophy. Bloomington and Indianapolis: Indiana UP, 1991.

Freeman, Kathleen. *Ancilla to the Pre-Socratic Philosophers*. Boston: Harvard University Press, 1983.

Gallagher, Edward J. "The Thematic Structure of *The Martian Chronicles*." In Greenberg and Olander 55–82.

Greenberg, Martin Harry, and Joseph D. Olander. "Ray Bradbury." *Writers of the 21st Century*. Edinburgh: Paul Harris Publishing, 1980.

Grudin, Robert. *Time and the Art of Living.* New York: Ticknor and Fields, 1982.

Guffey, George R. "The Unconscious, Fantasy, and 'Science Fiction': Transformations in Bradbury's *Martian Chronicles* and Lem's *Solaris.*" In Slusser, *Bridges of Fantasy* 142–159.

Heidegger, Martin. *On Time and Being.* (1969). Trans. by Joan Stambaugh. NY: Harper Torchbooks [Harper and Row], 1972.

Husserl, Edmund. *Husserl: Shorter Works.* Peter McCormick and Frederick Elliston, editors. Foreword by Walter Biemel. Notre Dame, Indiana: University of Notre Dame Press; Great Britain: The Harvester Press, 1981. 18–35.

———. *The Phenomenology of Internal Time-Consciousness.* [*PITC*] Edited by Martin Heidegger. Trans. James Churchill. Bloomington, IN: Indiana University Press, 1973.

Johnson, Wayne L. *Ray Bradbury.* New York: Frederick Ungar, 1980.

Lacan, Jacques. "Desire and the Interpretation of Desire in *Hamlet.*" Trans. James Hulbert. *Yale French Studies,* 55/56 (1977).

Lemaire, Anika. *Jacques Lacan.* Trans. David Macy. Boston: Routledge & Keegan Paul, 1977.

Lévi-Strauss, Claude. *Myth and Meaning.* New York: Schocken Books, 1979.

Marshall, Brenda K. *Teaching the Postmodern: Fiction and Theory.* New York/London: Routledge, 1992.

Mogen, David. *Ray Bradbury.* Twayne's United States Authors Series, 504. Boston: Twayne, 1986.

Mumford, Lewis. *Technics and Civilization.* Quoted in Jean-François Lyotard, *The Postmodern Condition.* Trans. G. Bennington and B. Massumi. Minneapolis: University of Minnesota Press, 1984.

Nowotny, Helga. *Time: The Modern and Postmodern Experience.* Trans. Neville Plaice. Cambridge: Polity Press, 1994.

Schleifer, Ronald. "The Space and Dialogue of Desire. Lacan, Greimas and Narrative Temporality." *Modern Language Notes,* Vol. 98 no. 5 (Dec 1983): 871–890.

Slusser, George E., et. al. *Bridges of Fantasy: Alternatives.* Carbondale: Southern Illinois University Press, 1992.

Wolfe, Gary K. "The Frontier Myth in Ray Bradbury." In Greenberg 33–54.

Zoreta, Margaret Lee. "Bakhtin, Blobels and Philip Dick." *Journal of Popular Culture.* Vol. 28.3 (Winter 1994): 55–61.

Chronology

1920	Born August 22 in Waukegan, Illinois, the third son of Leonard Spaulding Bradbury, an electrical lineman, and Esther Marie Moberg Bradbury, a native-born Swede. His twin brothers had been born in 1916; one died in 1918.
1926	Sister Elizabeth is born; family moves to Tucson, Arizona, in the fall.
1927	Elizabeth dies of pneumonia; family returns to Waukegan in May.
1932	Father laid off from job as telephone lineman; family moves back to Tucson.
1933	Family moves back to Waukegan.
1934	Seeking employment, father moves family to Los Angeles.
1938	Graduates from Los Angeles High School; first short story, "Hollerbochen's Dilemma," published in *Imagination!*
1939	Sells newspapers on Los Angeles street corner.
1942	Begins earning $20 a week writing short stories and decides to quit selling newspapers to write full time.

1947	Marries Marguerite McClure. Publishes *Dark Carnival*. "Homecoming" wins O. Henry Award and is published in *Prize Stories of 1947*.
1948	"Powerhouse" wins O. Henry Award.
1949	First daughter born.
1950	*The Martian Chronicles* published.
1951	*The Illustrated Man* published. Second daughter born.
1953	*The Golden Apples of the Sun* and *Fahrenheit 451* published.
1954	Receives National Institute of Arts and Letters award for contribution to American literature.
1955	*Switch on the Night*, a children's book, published. *The October Country* published. Third daughter born.
1957	*Dandelion Wine* published.
1958	Fourth daughter born.
1959	*A Medicine for Melancholy* published.
1961	*The Ghoul Keepers* published.
1962	*Something Wicked This Way Comes, The Small Assassin,* and *R Is for Rocket* are published.
1963	Publishes first collection of drama, *The Anthem Sprinters and Other Antics. Icarus Montgolfier Wright* nominated for Academy Award for best short film.
1964	*The Machineries of Joy* published. *American Journey*, his film history of the nation opens at the New York World's Fair; produces *The World of Ray Bradbury* in Los Angeles.
1965	*The Vintage Bradbury* published.
1966	Francois Truffaut's movie *Fahrenheit 451* released. *Twice Twenty-two, Tomorrow Midnight,* and *S Is for Space* are published.
1969	Film version of *The Illustrated Man* released. *I Sing the Body Electric!* published.
1972	*The Wonderful Ice Cream Suit and Other Plays* and *The Halloween Tree* published.
1973	*When Elephants Last in the Dooryard Bloomed*, Bradbury's first collection of poetry, published.

1975   *Pillar of Fire and Other Plays* and *Selected Stories* published.

1976   *Long After Midnight* published.

1977   *Where Robot Mice and Robot Men Run Round in Robot Towns*, a collection of poetry, published. Receives World Fantasy Award for lifetime achievement. Wins four Los Angeles Drama Critics Circle awards for play version of *The Martian Chronicles*.

1979   *This Attic Where the Meadow Greens* published.

1980   *The Stories of Ray Bradbury* and *The Last Circus and The Electrocution* published.

1981   *The Haunted Computer and the Android Pope*, a collection of poetry, published.

1982   *The Complete Poems of Ray Bradbury* and *The Love Affair* published.

1983   *Dinosaur Tales* published.

1984   Film version of *Something Wicked This Way Comes*, screenplay by Bradbury, released. Collection of early mystery stories, *A Memory of Murder*, published.

1985   *Death Is a Lonely Business* published. Receives Body of Work Award from PEN.

1987   *Death Has Lost Its Charm For Me*, poems, published, as well as *Fever Dream*.

1988   *The Toynbee Convector*, a collection of stories, published.

1989   *The Climate of Palettes* published.

1990   *The Day It Rained Forever*, a musical, published; also publishes *A Graveyard for Lunatics: Another Tale of Two Cities*.

1991   *Yestermorrow: Obvious Answers to Impossible Futures*, a book of essays, published.

1992   *Green Shadows, White Whale*, a novel, published.

1996   *Quicker Than the Eye*, a collection of stories, published.

1997   *Driving Blind*, a collection of stories, published. Also publishes *With Cat for Comforter* and *Dogs Think That Every Day Is Christmas*.

1998   *Ahmed and the Oblivion Machines* published.

1999	Inducted into the Science Fiction and Fantasy Hall of Fame at the University of Kansas Center for the Study of Science Fiction.
2000	Receives medal for "Distinguished Contribution to American Letters" from National Book Foundation.
2001	*Ray Bradbury: Collected Short Stories* and *From the Dust Returned* published.
2002	*One More for the Road* published.
2003	*Bradbury Stories* and *Let's All Kill Constance!* published. Wife dies.
2004	Awarded the National Medal of Arts by President George W. Bush and First Lady Laura Bush. *The Cat's Pajamas* published.
2005	*Bradbury Speaks* published.
2006	*Farewell Summer* published.
2007	*Now and Forever* published. Receives special citation for distinguished career from The Pulitzer Board.
2008	*Summer Morning, Summer Night* published.
2009	*We'll Always Have Paris: Stories* published.

Contributors

HAROLD BLOOM is Sterling Professor of the Humanities at Yale University. He is the author of 30 books, including *Shelley's Mythmaking*, *The Visionary Company*, *Blake's Apocalypse*, *Yeats*, *A Map of Misreading*, *Kabbalah and Criticism*, *Agon: Toward a Theory of Revisionism*, *The American Religion*, *The Western Canon*, and *Omens of Millennium: The Gnosis of Angels, Dreams, and Resurrection*. *The Anxiety of Influence* sets forth Professor Bloom's provocative theory of the literary relationships between the great writers and their predecessors. His most recent books include *Shakespeare: The Invention of the Human*, a 1998 National Book Award finalist, *How to Read and Why*, *Genius: A Mosaic of One Hundred Exemplary Creative Minds*, *Hamlet: Poem Unlimited*, *Where Shall Wisdom Be Found?*, and *Jesus and Yahweh: The Names Divine*. In 1999, Professor Bloom received the prestigious American Academy of Arts and Letters Gold Medal for Criticism. He has also received the International Prize of Catalonia, the Alfonso Reyes Prize of Mexico, and the Hans Christian Andersen Bicentennial Prize of Denmark.

WAYNE L. JOHNSON, aside from authoring a book on Ray Bradbury, has contributed to *Critical Encounters: Writers and Themes in Science Fiction* and to numerous journals. He also is the author of *Summer Reading Program Fun*.

LAHNA DISKIN is professor emerita of The College of New Jersey. She is the author of books on Theodore Sturgeon and coeditor of *Possibilities: A Collection of Short Stories* and *Portfolio: A Collection of Short Stories*.

ROBERT PLANK, now deceased, taught the psychology of literature at Case Western Reserve. He authored *George Orwell's Guide Through Hell: A*

219

Psychological Study of 1984 and *The Emotional Significance of Imaginary Beings: A Study of the Interaction Between Psychopathology, Literature, and Reality in the Modern World.*

GEORGE R. GUFFEY is professor emeritus in the English department at the University of California, Los Angeles. His work includes *Bridges to Science Fiction* and volumes in a series of the works of John Dryden, all of which he coedited.

WILLIAM F. TOUPONCE is a professor of English at Indiana University–Purdue University Indianapolis, where he also is director of the graduate certificate program in editing and director of The Center for Ray Bradbury Studies. He is the editor of *The New Ray Bradbury Review*, general editor of *The Collected Stories of Ray Bradbury*, and editor of *Moby Dick: A Screenplay by Ray Bradbury* and the author of other titles as well.

BEN P. INDICK has written many plays and essays. Among his work is *A Gentleman from Providence Pens a Letter.*

SUSAN SPENCER is a professor in the English department at the University of Central Oklahoma. She is a coauthor of *The Eighteenth-Century Novel.*

JONATHAN ELLER is a professor of English and an adjunct professor of American studies at Indiana University–Purdue University Indianapolis, where he also is a cofounder of The Center for Ray Bradbury Studies. He has written introductions to new editions of several of Bradbury's books and is textual editor of two books of the works of Charles S. Peirce. Eller also has been published in several journals.

JACQUELINE FOERTSCH is an assistant professor at the University of North Texas. She is the author of *Bracing Accounts: The Literature and Culture of Polio in Postwar America, Enemies Within: The Cold War and the AIDS Crisis in Literature, Film, and Culture*, and other titles.

WALTER MUCHER has been an adjunct professor of humanities at the University of Puerto Rico and has published on religion and literature, Greek tragedy, and science fiction.

Bibliography

Aggelis, Steven L., ed. *Conversations with Ray Bradbury.* Jackson: University Press of Mississippi, 2004.

Angelotti, Michael. "Afraid of the Dark: Censorship, Ray Bradbury, and *The Martian Chronicles.*" In *Censored Books, II: Critical Viewpoints, 1985–2000*, edited by Nicholas J. Karolides, pp. 296–304. Lanham, Md.: Scarecrow, 2002.

Bailey, K. V. "Mars is a district of Sheffield." *Foundation* 68 (Autumn 1996): 81–86.

Baxter, Stephen. "Martian Chronicles: Narratives of Mars in Science and SF." *Foundation* 68 (Autumn 1996): 5–16.

Bledig, Joan D. "Of Burroughs . . . and Bradbury." *Burroughs Bulletin* (67) 2006, 28–33.

Bleiler, Richard, ed. *Supernatural Fiction Writers: Contemporary Fantasy and Horror.* New York: Scribner's, 2003.

Bloom, Harold, ed. *Ray Bradbury's* Fahrenheit 451. New York: Chelsea House, 2008.

Bluestone, George. "Three Seasons with *Fahrenheit 451.*" *Sacred Heart University Review* 6, nos. 1–2 (Fall–Spring 1985–1986), 3–19.

Bradbury, Ray. *Zen in the Art of Writing.* Santa Barbara, Calif.: Joshua Odell Editions, 1994.

Burleson, Donald R. "Connings: Bradbury/Oates." *Studies in Weird Fiction* 11 (1992): 24–29.

Connor, George E. "Spelunking with Ray Bradbury: The Allegory of the Cave in *Fahrenheit 451.*" *Extrapolation* 45, no. 4 (Winter 2004): 408–18.

de Koster, Katie, ed. *Readings on* Fahrenheit 451. San Diego: Greenhaven, 2000.

221

Federici, Corrado, and Esther Raventós-Pons, ed. *Literary Texts and the Arts: Inter-disciplinary Perspectives*. New York; Frankfurt: Lang, 2003.

Guffey, George R. "*Fahrenheit 451* and the 'Cubby-Hole Editors' of Ballantine Books." In *Coordinates: Placing Science Fiction and Fantasy*, edited by George E. Slusser, Eric S. Rabkin, and Robert Scholes, 99–106. Carbondale: Southern Illinois University Press, 1983.

Harlow, Morgan. "Martian Legacy: Ray Bradbury's *The Martian Chronicles*." *War, Literature, and the Arts* 17, nos. 1–2 (2005): 311–14.

Hoskinson, Kevin. "*The Martian Chronicles* and *Fahrenheit 451*: Ray Bradbury's Cold War Novels." *Extrapolation* 36, no. 4 (Winter 1995), 345–59.

Huntington, John. *The Logic of Fantasy: H. G. Wells and Science Fiction*. New York: Columbia University Press, 1982.

Kagle, Steven E. "Homage to Melville: Ray Bradbury and the Nineteenth-Century American Romance." In *The Celebration of the Fantastic: Selected Papers from the Tenth Anniversary International Conference on the Fantastic in the Arts*, edited by Donald E. Morse, Marshall B. Tymn, and Csilla Bertha, 279–89. Westport, Conn.: Greenwood, 1992.

Laino, Guido. "Nature as an Alternative Space for Rebellion in Ray Bradbury's *Fahrenheit 451*." In *Literary Landscapes, Landscape in Literature*, edited by Michele Bottalico, Maria Teresa Chialant, and Eleonora Rao, 152–64. Rome, Italy: Carocci, 2007.

Logsdon, Loren. "Ray Bradbury's 'The Kilimanjaro Device': The Need to Correct the Errors of Time." *Midwestern Miscellany* 20 (1992): 28–39.

McGiveron, Rafeeq O. "Bradbury's *Fahrenheit 451*." *Explicator* 54, no. 3 (Spring 1996): 177–80.

———. "'Do You Know the Legend of Hercules and Antaeus?' The Wilderness in Ray Bradbury's *Fahrenheit 451*." *Extrapolation* 38, no. 2 (Summer 1997), 102–9.

———. "'To Build a Mirror Factory': The Mirror and Self-Examination in Ray Bradbury's *Fahrenheit 451*." *Critique* 39, no. 3 (Spring 1998): 282–87.

———. "What 'Carried the Trick'? Mass Exploitation and the Decline of Thought in Ray Bradbury's *Fahrenheit 451*." *Extrapolation* 37, no. 3 (Fall 1996): 245–56.

Miller, Calvin. "Ray Bradbury: Hope in a Doubtful Age." In *Reality and Vision*, edited by Philip Yancey, 92–101. Dallas: Word, 1990.

Mogen, David. *Ray Bradbury*. Boston: Twayne, 1986.

Otten, Charlotte F., and Gary D. Schmidt, ed. *The Voice of the Narrator in Children's Literature: Insights from Writers and Critics*. New York; London: Greenwood Press, 1989.

Patrouch, Joe. "Symbolic Settings in Science Fiction: H. G. Wells, Ray Bradbury, and Harlan Ellison." *Journal of the Fantastic in the Arts* 1, no. 3 (1988): 37–45.

Person, James E., Jr. "'That Always Autumn Town': *Winesburg, Ohio* and the Fiction of Ray Bradbury." *Winesburg Eagle* 22, no. 2 (1997): 1–4.

Pfeiffer, John R. "Ray Bradbury's Bernard Shaw." *Shaw* 17 (1997): 119–31.

Pollin, Burton; "Poe and Ray Bradbury: A Persistent Influence and Interest." *Edgar Allan Poe Review* 6, no. 2 (Fall 2005): 31–38.

Reid, Robin Anne. *Ray Bradbury: A Critical Companion*. Westport, Conn.: Greenwood, 2000.

Rønnov-Jessen, Peter. "World Classics and Nursery Rhymes: Emblems of Resistance in Ray Bradbury's *Fahrenheit 451* and George Orwell's *1984*." In *George Orwell and* 1984, edited by Michael Skovmand, 59–72. Aarhus, Denmark: Seklos, Department of English, University of Aarhus, 1984.

Seed, David. "The Flight from the Good Life: *Fahrenheit 451* in the Context of Postwar American Dystopias." *Journal of American Studies* 28, no. 2 (August 1994), 225–40.

Stockwell, Peter. "Language, Knowledge, and the Stylistics of Science Fiction." In *Subjectivity and Literature from the Romantics to the Present Day*, edited by Philip Shaw and Peter Stockwell, 101–12. London: Pinter, 1991.

Szczerbicka, Anna. "The Child Motif in the Short Stories of R. Bradbury." In *Studies in Fantastic Fiction*, edited by Andrzej Zgorzelski, 31–74. Gdansk: Uniwersytet Gdánski, 1988.

Teicher, Morton I. "Ray Bradbury and Thomas Wolfe: Fantasy and the Fantastic." *The Thomas Wolfe Review* 12, no. 2 (Fall 1988): 17–19.

Tibbetts, John C. "The Illustrating Man: The Screenplays of Ray Bradbury." *Creative Screenwriting* 6, no. 1 (January–February 1999): 45–54.

Touponce, William F. "The Existential Fabulous: A Reading of Ray Bradbury's 'The Golden Apples of the Sun.'" *Mosaic* 13, nos. 3/4 (1980): 203–18.

———. "Laughter and Freedom in Ray Bradbury's *Something Wicked This Way Comes*." *Children's Literature Association Quarterly* 13, no. 1 (Spring 1988): 17–21.

———. *Ray Bradbury*. San Bernardino, Calif.: Borgo Press, 1989.

———. "Some Aspects of Surrealism in the Work of Ray Bradbury." *Extrapolation* 25 (1984): 228–38.

Trout, Paul A. "*Fahrenheit 451*: The Temperature at Which Critics Chill." *Cresset* 57, no. 1 (1993): 6–10.

Valis, Noel M. "*The Martian Chronicles* and Jorge Luis Borges." *Extrapolation* 20 (1979): 50–59.

Weller, Sam. *The Bradbury Chronicles: The Life of Ray Bradbury*. New York: William Morrow, 2005.

Whalen, Tom. "The Consequences of Passivity: Re-Evaluating Truffaut's *Fahrenheit 451*." *Literature/Film Quarterly* 35, no. 3 (2007): 181–90.

Whitehall, Geoffrey. "The Problem of the 'World and Beyond': Encountering 'the Other' in Science Fiction." In *To Seek Out New Worlds: Science Fiction and World Politics*, edited by Jutta Weldes. New York: Palgrave Macmillan, 2003.

Whitehead, David. "The Sci-Fi Tales of Ray Bradbury." *Book and Magazine Collector* 92 (1991): 26–35.

Wilmeth, Thomas L. "The Flowers That Will Not Close: Wolfe, Bradbury, and the Power of Description." *Thomas Wolfe Review* 19, no. 2 (1995): 9–12.

Wood, Diane S. "Bradbury and Atwood: Exile as Rational Decision." In *The Literature of Emigration and Exile*, edited by James Whitlark and Wendell Aycock, 131–42. Lubbock: Texas Tech University Press, 1992.

Zipes, Jack. "Mass Degradation of Humanity and Massive Contradictions in Bradbury's Vision of America in *Fahrenheit 451*." In *No Place Else: Explorations in Utopian and Dystopian Fiction*, edited by Eric S. Rabkin, Martin H. Greenberg, and Joseph D. Olander, 182–98. Carbondale: Southern Illinois University Press, 1983.

Acknowledgments

Wayne L. Johnson, "Medicines for Melancholy." From *Ray Bradbury.* © 1980 by Frederick Ungar Publishing Co. Inc.

Lahna Diskin, "Bradbury on Children." From *Ray Bradbury*, Taplinger Publishing, edited by Martin Harry Greenberg and Joseph D. Olander. © 1980 by Martin Harry Greenberg and Joseph D. Olander.

Robert Plank, "The Expedition to the Planet of Paranoia." From *Extrapolation* 22, no. 2 (Summer 1981): 171–85. Copyright © 1981 by the Kent State University Press. Reprinted with permission.

George R. Guffey, "The Unconscious, Fantasy, and Science Fiction: Transformations in Bradbury's *Martian Chronicles* and Lem's *Solaris*." From *Bridges to Fantasy*, edited by George E. Slusser, Eric S. Rabkin, and Robert Scholes. © 1982 by the Board of Trustees of Southern Illinois University.

William F. Touponce, "Reverie and the Marvelous." From *Ray Bradbury and the Poetics of Reverie: Fantasy, Science Fiction, and the Reader.* UMI Research Press. © 1984, 1981 by William Ferdinand Touponce.

Ben P. Indick, "Stage Plays." From *Ray Bradbury: Dramatist.* Published, in 1989, by the Borgo Press, San Bernadino, CA. © 1977, 1989 by Ben P. Indick.

Susan Spenser, "The Post-Apocalyptic Library: Oral and Literate Culture in *Fahrenheit 451* and *A Canticle for Leibowitz*." From *Extrapolation* 32, no. 4

(Winter 1991): 331–42. © 1991 by the Kent State University Press. Reprinted with permission.

Jonathan Eller, "The Body Eclectic: Sources of Ray Bradbury's *The Marian Chronicles*." From *The University of Mississippi Studies in English*, New Series 11–12 (1993–1995): 376–410. © 1995 by the University of Mississippi.

Jacqueline Foertsch, "The Bomb Next Door: Four Postwar Alterapocalyptics." From *Genre* 30, no. 4 (Winter 1997): 333–58. © 1998 by the University of Oklahoma.

Walter J. Mucher, "Being Marian: Spatiotemporal Self in Ray Bradbury's *The Martian Chronicles*." From *Extrapolation* 43, no. 2 (Summer 2002), 171–87. © 2002 by the University of Texas at Brownsville and Texas Southmost College.

Every effort has been made to contact the owners of copyrighted material and secure copyright permission. Articles appearing in this volume generally appear much as they did in their original publication with few or no editorial changes. In some cases, foreign language text has been removed from the original essay. Those interested in locating the original source will find the information cited above.

Index

Characters in literary works are indexed by first name (if any), followed by the name of the work in parentheses